LATIN READING COURSE

Part Two

LATIN READING COURSE

Part Two

by
J. A. HARRISON, M.A.
Senior Classics Master
The Methodist College, Belfast

LONDON
G. BELL AND SONS LTD
1976

First Published 1971
Reprinted 1973, 1974, 1976

ISBN 0 7135 1636 4

Printed in Great Britain by
The Camelot Press Ltd, Southampton

Preface

Since the publication in 1961 of *Latine Legamus* there have been many requests that this reading material should be expanded into a Course leading to the reading of the Latin authors unadulterated. This is an attempt to meet that demand. Parts One and Two form a three-year course for a class with four 40-minute lessons a week which does both translation and composition. A class with five periods a week which omits the English-Latin should complete both parts in two years.

This Course is a compromise, it is hoped a happy compromise. It is intended for those teachers who endorse the importance of acquiring reading skill as soon as possible but who are not entirely convinced of the efficacy of recent experiments in language teaching. It is 'progressive' in that English-Latin is an optional, not an integral part of it; it is 'traditional' in that standard grammatical terms are used and no attempt is made to re-create the conditions under which one learned one's native language. The main emphasis throughout is on learning to read and on enjoying reading Latin.

Explanations are given at some length. These are intended for the maturer pupil who should be able to work through the course with little assistance from the teacher. They also serve as guides to the teacher in explaining new material to young beginners who will require much help, especially in the first three months.

Other features of the Course are the Introductions where pupils are told something of the history and civilisation of the people whose language they are learning, the full range of vocabularies and the maps where all place names mentioned in the stories are shown.

I should like to thank my colleagues in the Classical department who, after an experimental year's use of the material, made many valuable suggestions, and especially Mr. T. W. Mulryne who wrote most of the material in the Introduction. My co-author in *Latine Legamus*, the late Mr. S. J. Wilson, was prevented by illness from contributing to this Course but he at once gave permission for his contributions to *Latine Legamus* to be used in this larger work.

I have made frequent use of the *Oxford Classical Dictionary* and Carcopino's *Daily Life in Ancient Rome*, books which are essential to any classical library.   J. A. H.

Acknowledgments

Illustrations on the pages numbered are acknowledged as follows:
Ny Carlsberg Museum, Copenhagen, p. 10; Mansell Collection, pp. 10, 27, 30, 31, 40, 56, 60, 69, 70, 82–3; Landesmuseum, Trier, p. 18; Fototeca Unione, p. 26; Dr. I. D. Margary, p. 29; Dr. J. K. S. Joseph, p. 33; Illustrated London News, p. 35; Deutsches Archäologisches Institut, Athens, p. 50; Press Association, p. 53; British Museum, p. 60; Feature-Pix, p. 74; Italian Institute, p. 76; Bibliothèque Nationale, pp. 81, 84; Museo Vaticano, Rome, p. 107; Crown Copyright Reserved (Ministry of the Environment), p. 113.

Acknowledgments are also due to the Loeb Classical Library (Harvard University Press: Heinemann Ltd.) for permission to reproduce the passages quoted on pp. 2, 4, 8, 9, 12, 13 and 15; to Columbia University Press for pp. 3, 5, 6 and 12, from *Roman Civilisation*, by N. Lewis and M. Reinhold; to Penguin Books Ltd. for p. 11, from Plutarch's *Fall of the Roman Republic*, tr. Rex Warner; and to the Clarendon Press, Oxford, for p. 20, from *Everyday Life in Rome in the Time of Caesar and Cicero*, by H. A. Treble and K. M. King.

Contents

ST. PAUL'S JOURNEY TO ROME
(in ten parts)

CAESAR'S INVASIONS OF BRITAIN
(in ten parts)

Introduction

THE STORY OF ROME

4 The Second Century B.C.: Expansion

In the Introduction to the first part of this Course the story was told how Rome developed from her beginnings as an insignificant Italian town into the strongest city in the whole of Italy and how the great wars against Carthage took place. Rome's final victory in that struggle meant that she was the strongest state not only in Italy, but also in the whole Mediterranean world; whether her leaders really wanted it or not, she rapidly began to acquire an Empire. How this happened must now be told, and if you look up the places we shall mention on a map, you will see just how far the Roman Empire spread.

Rome was engaged in fighting in three main areas: the East (especially Macedonia and Greece), the West (especially Spain), and once more in North Africa (Carthage). These wars did not take place one after the other; rather they overlapped, but we shall deal with each of the areas in turn.

(i) The Macedonian Wars

Philip, king of Macedon, had promised to help Hannibal in his attack on Rome, but he had not been able to do so. But the Romans did not forget Philip's promise and, when Hannibal had been defeated, they turned their attention East. Philip had as an ally the king of Syria called Antiochus III. This combination looked so powerful that it might in the end threaten Rome itself, but at first the Roman people were very reluctant to start a new war. This was very natural since the struggle against Hannibal had been so long and hard. Eventually however, in 200 B.C., war was declared. The war started slowly but in 198 a general called T. Quinctius Flamininus was appointed. In 197 the decisive battle was fought at Cynoscephalae in Thessaly and Philip was defeated. The Romans, however, did not treat Philip very harshly. At the Isthmian Games near Corinth in 196 Flamininus declared that all the Greeks should be free. Plutarch, a Greek who much later wrote a biography of Flamininus, describes the scene in the following way:

'A great throng of people were sitting in the stadium and watching the athletic contests . . . the trumpet signalled a general silence and the herald made proclamation that the Roman Senate and Titus Quinctius Flamininus, proconsular general, having conquered king Philip and the Macedonians, restored the Greeks to freedom, without garrison and to the enjoyment of their ancient laws. At first the proclamation was by no means generally heard . . . and people called out to have it made again; but when silence had been restored, and the herald, in tones that reached the ears of all, had recited the proclamation, a shout of joy arose, so incredibly loud that it reached the sea. The whole audience rose to their feet, and no heed was paid to the athletes, but all were eager to spring forward and greet and hail the saviour and champion of Greece. And that which is often said of the volume and power of the human voice was then apparent to the eye. For ravens which chanced to be flying overhead fell down into the stadium. The cause of this was the rupture of the air; for when the voice is borne aloft loud and strong, the air is rent asunder by it and will not support flying creatures.'

Whether you believe the last part of Plutarch's story or not, the Greeks were certainly overjoyed at the pronouncement. However, it was not long before there was further trouble.

Some Greeks had joined the Romans against Philip but were annoyed at Flamininus' settlement because they had hoped to profit greatly from the war. These and other Greeks who became restless, soon made an alliance with Antiochus III of Syria. Hannibal, the famous Carthaginian general, was also with Antiochus, who had given him refuge after the defeat of Carthage. Antiochus was planning to advance into Europe and despite a warning from Rome he occupied Thrace and entered Greece. His allies, however, did not give him the help he expected and in 191 he was defeated at Thermopylae in Greece, and in the following year at Magnesia in Asia Minor. The commander in this second battle was another Scipio, a brother of the great Scipio Africanus who had finally defeated the Carthaginians. Antiochus was treated severely and died soon after. The Greeks who had helped him, or at least had promised help, were punished and lost the privileges which Flamininus had conferred on them.

Philip of Macedon had not joined with Antiochus in this second war, and there was no further fighting before Philip died in 179. He was succeeded by his son Perseus, although the Romans had wanted another of Philip's sons to be king. Soon enough there was trouble. Some of Perseus' enemies complained to Rome and she declared war.

For three years the fighting on both sides was half-hearted but in 168, at Pydna, Perseus was defeated by L. Aemilius Paullus. Roman troops plundered many towns, although the towns had surrendered. Perseus himself was brought to Rome and in the triumphal procession he was led in chains in front of Paullus who was seated in his magnificent triumphal chariot. Many Greeks who had sided with Perseus were punished, but Rome was still not willing to rule directly the territory he had held. It was only after another Macedonian war—the fourth—in 149–8 that Rome made Macedonia a province. The final chapter of the whole series came in 146 when in Greece itself there was a revolt. The Roman commander was L. Mummius and the city of Corinth was at the centre of the revolt. This is how Pausanias, a Greek of the second century A.D., describes the last event of the war:

'As soon as night fell, the Achaeans who had escaped to Corinth after the battle fled from the city, and most of the Corinthians fled with them. At first, although the gates were open, Mummius hesitated to enter Corinth, suspecting that some ambush had been laid within the walls. But on the third day after the battle he proceeded to storm Corinth and set it on fire. The majority of those found in it were put to the sword by the Romans, but the women and children Mummius sold into slavery. . . . The most admired votive offerings and works of art were carried off by Mummius. . . . In all the cities that had made war against Rome Mummius demolished the walls and disarmed the inhabitants.'

Rome was now in control of the Eastern Mediterranean, just as her victory over Carthage had given her control in the West. With the defeat of Antiochus she had subdued Syria; Egypt was in reality under her control, and now Macedon and all the rest of Greece had been forced to submit.

(ii) Wars in the West

The defeat of Carthage in the great Punic Wars had given Rome control of Spain, in which were established two provinces. The Spaniards resented Roman control, and it was not long before unrest broke out into open revolt (196 B.C.). The first revolt was very swiftly put down but there was no lasting peace. Another Roman victory was won in 191 B.C. by L. Aemilius Paullus but not until 179 did T. Sempronius Gracchus manage to bring about anything like stability and co-operation, by using more conciliatory measures than the other Roman generals.

This lasted until 153 when war broke out again and went on for twenty years. The Spaniards had some success early in the campaign, but by 150 they had been forced to submit to the Roman generals Licinius Lucullus and Sulpicius Galba. However, any chance of an early end to the fighting was spoiled by the following incident which is recorded by Appian in his *Roman History*:

'When Lucullus discovered that the Lusitanians were making incursions in his neighbourhood he sent out his best lieutenants and slew about 4,000 of the enemy. He killed about 1,500 others while they were crossing the straits near Gades. The remainder took refuge on a hill, and he drew a line of circumvallation around it and captured an immense number of them. Then he invaded Lusitania and gradually devastated it. Galba did the same thing on the other side. When some of their ambassadors came to him desiring to renew the very treaty which they had made and then transgressed, he received them favourably and made a truce and even pretended to sympathise with them because they had been compelled by poverty to rob, make war and break treaties. "For," he said, "poorness of soil and penury force you to do these things. But I will give my poor friends good land, and settle them in fertile country in three divisions."

'Beguiled by these promises they left their own habitations and came together at the place appointed by Galba. He divided them into three parts and, showing to each division a certain plain, he commanded them to remain in this open country until he should come and assign them their places. When he came to the first division he told them as friends to lay down their arms. When they had done so, he surrounded them with a ditch and sent in soldiers with swords who slew them all while they lamented and invoked the names of the gods and the pledges which they had received. In like manner he hastened to the second and third divisions and destroyed them while they were still ignorant of the fate of the first. Thus he avenged treachery with treachery, imitating barbarians in a way unworthy of a Roman.'

People in Rome itself were shocked by this incident but Galba suffered no harm. The Spaniards were now all the more eager to resist the Romans and they were led by Viriathus, who had escaped the slaughter. They carried on a kind of guerrilla war against the Roman troops, and both sides had some successes. At one stage it was agreed that the part of Spain called Lusitania should be governed by its inhabitants in freedom, but this treaty also was broken and fighting continued. Other Spaniards joined the Lusitanians, and resistance to Rome was concentrated in the city of Numantia. It was not until the year 133 that Numantia was taken by another Scipio, this time called 'Aemilianus'. The city was burned to the ground and the leaders brought to Rome. Spain no longer gave Rome any trouble, but the fight had been long and bitter.

(iii) The End of Carthage

Ever since the end of the war with Hannibal Carthage had been unable to make war without the approval of Rome. She had some niggling quarrels with neighbouring states, and Rome intervened. A deputation was sent from Rome, led by M. Porcius Cato. He discovered that Carthage was in fact in quite a prosperous condition and he was determined that Carthage should somehow be removed for ever. Plutarch describes Cato's return to Rome and then adds this:

'Moreover, they say that, shaking his toga, Cato purposely let drop in the Senate some African figs. And then, as they admired their size and beauty, he said that the country that produced them was only three days' sail from Rome. And he was even more violent on this point, so that whenever he declared his opinion in the Senate on any matter whatsoever he added the following, "And I also think that Carthage must be destroyed".'

The Latin words for this are *delenda est Carthago*, and Cato and others who thought like him said it so often that they finally had their wish. In the year 146, the same year as that in which Corinth was destroyed, Scipio Aemilianus captured Carthage. The result is described by Cassius Dio in this way:

'Scipio sent to the Senate the following message: "Carthage is taken. What are your orders now?" When these words had been read, they took counsel as to what should be done. Cato expressed the opinion that they ought to raze the city and blot out the Carthaginians. Thereupon the Senate became involved in a great dispute and contention. . . . As a result of the discussion all became unanimous in favour of destroying Carthage, since they felt sure that its inhabitants would never remain entirely at peace. The whole city was therefore utterly blotted out of existence, and it was decreed that for any person to settle upon its site should be an accursed act. The majority of the men captured were thrown into prison and there perished, and some few were sold. But the very foremost men together with the hostages . . . spent the rest of their lives in different parts of Italy in honourable confinement.'

5 The Roman Revolution

(i) *From the Gracchi to Sulla*

As we have seen, the century after the Punic Wars was one of great expansion for Rome; the next century, while the Empire continued to expand, was one in which the Roman constitution, as described in the Introduction to Part One of this Course, came under intense pressure and finally had to be completely remodelled. This period is often called 'The Roman Revolution'. The noble families whose members had traditionally been able to control the government at Rome found increasingly that others wanted to challenge their right to rule, and were often prepared to use quite extreme methods to gain their ends. The nobles were not slow to reply with equal measures, and so there was frequent disorder and street fighting.

This change in Rome is often traced back to two brothers who had the name 'Gracchus' (see LXVII)—we have already mentioned their famous father, the general. The elder brother Tiberius held the office of tribune in 133 B.C. At this time Rome was facing something of an economic crisis, which Tiberius thought could best be solved by granting to Roman citizens plots of state land which they could then farm. By introducing this Tiberius ran up against some very powerful nobles (though he himself belonged to a noble family and was supported by other nobles). He wanted to become tribune for a second year to continue his work, but his opponents considered this to be illegal. When the elections came along, there was considerable disorder. Appian describes the result in this way:

'The Senate assembled at the temple of Fides. After reaching such decision as they did reach, they marched up to the Capitol, Cornelius Scipio Nasica leading the way. When he arrived at the temple and advanced against the partisans of Gracchus, they yielded out of regard for so distinguished a citizen and because they observed the senators following with him. The latter, wresting the clubs out of the hands of the Gracchans, and breaking up benches and other furniture that had been brought for the use of the assembly, began beating them, pursued them, and drove them over a precipice. In the tumult many of the Gracchans perished, and Gracchus himself, vainly circling round the temple, was slain at the door close to the statues of the kings. All the bodies were thrown by night into the Tiber.'

Ten years later in 123 the second Gracchus, Gaius by name, was tribune. He had not forgotten what had happened to his brother, and brought forward again the same sort of proposals. But he went much further. He passed a law which allowed poor Roman citizens to buy grain at a greatly reduced price; he introduced measures which strengthened the position of that class of Romans called *equites*, who were second in rank in the state only to senators: he no doubt hoped that they would help to provide a strong opposition to the traditional government. Most controversial of all, he proposed that people who lived in Italian towns outside Rome itself should become Roman citizens. It was this measure that led to his downfall. He had already succeeded where his brother had failed in being elected tribune for a second year. But when he tried for a third term of office, he found that much of his support had gone because of his plan to make other Italians into citizens of Rome. Romans were unwilling to share their privileges with anyone else. In the end, Gaius suffered the same fate as his brother—he was murdered in a street riot.

There were four aspects of the careers of the Gracchi which were particularly important because they involve themes which were to recur again and again in the history of the next years:

1 Both brothers were tribunes: this office gave its holders the opportunity to have laws passed and was increasingly used for this purpose. Also a tribune could 'veto' any other public business that was going on, and so prevent an opponent from being successful.
2 Gaius tried to help the *equites*. From now on they play an important part in Roman affairs.
3 Gaius fought for equal rights for other Italians—many lives were to be lost before this happened.
4 Both brothers lost their lives in a violent way. There was to be much more violence of the same sort.

After the death of Gaius Gracchus there was still considerable unrest, but soon a very important figure appeared, that of Gaius Marius. He was not a noble and so found that there were many obstacles to his advancement. But he was an extraordinary general, and since Rome was involved in two serious wars at this time, he was able to thwart his opponents. The first war was against an African king called Jugurtha (111–105 B.C.) and the second against Germanic tribes who were at this time migrating from their former homelands and were threatening the northern borders of Italy (105–101). In both these wars Marius was highly successful and by 100 B.C. he had been elected consul for a record six times. He had also taken the opportunity to make sweeping army reforms which greatly improved army efficiency. They also, however, meant that the soldiers tended more and more to look to their general for rewards, rather than to the state. The result was that a general could ask his men to do virtually anything for him, even fight against fellow Romans. We shall see later how some generals used this new power.

The problem of citizenship for Rome's Italian allies had not been solved. By 90 B.C. the Italians had become so frustrated that they resorted to war—the so-called 'Social War' (from *socius* = an ally). A later Roman called Velleius Paterculus has this to say about it:

'So bitter was this Italian war that in two successive years two Roman consuls were slain by the enemy, and the armies of the Roman people were routed in many places. The Italians chose Corfinium as their capital and named it Italica. Then little by little the strength of the Romans was recruited by admitting to citizenship those who had not taken up arms or had not been slow to lay them down again, and Pompeius, Sulla and Marius restored the tottering power of the Roman people.'

So Rome's allies gained what they wanted, and Italy gradually became one country. Of the generals in this war Marius has already been mentioned, Pompeius was the father of Pompey the Great of whom we shall hear more later, and Sulla was the person who dominated the next few years of Roman history.

Soon after the end of the Social War, Sulla was appointed to conduct a war against King Mithridates who was threatening the provinces recently acquired by Rome in the East. There was, however, considerable rivalry between Sulla and Marius, and Marius' supporters succeeded in having this command transferred to him although he was now 70 years old (88 B.C.). Sulla still had the army which he had used in the Social War, and he now took a step which had never before been taken—he marched with his army on Rome itself! Marius and his supporters had to flee and the command was given back to Sulla. Soon after this he set sail for the East to deal with Mithridates. When he had gone, Marius and his friends, especially a man named Cinna, were able to re-establish themselves in Rome, and they set about avenging themselves on their opponents, many of whom were murdered. Fortunately for everyone, Marius died within a matter of weeks, and under Cinna's guidance government was well organised. It meant, however, that Sulla's enemies were in control and, as soon as he had defeated Mithridates (though he did not destroy him completely and we shall hear of him again), Sulla hurried back to Italy. There he set about leading an army against Rome for the second time, was again victorious and had himself appointed dictator (82 B.C.). This is Appian's description of his rule:

'He seems to have been the first to make a formal list of those whom he condemned to death, to offer prizes to assassins and rewards to informers, and to threaten with punishment those who concealed the condemned. . . . Some of these, taken unawares, were killed where they were caught, in their homes, in the streets, or in the temples. Others were hurled through mid air and thrown at Sulla's feet. Others were dragged through the city and trampled on, none of the spectators daring to utter a word of remonstrance against these horrors. Banishment was inflicted upon some, and confiscation upon others. Spies were searching everywhere for those who had fled from the city and those whom they caught they killed.'

Sulla also introduced several measures which were aimed at making sure that once again the real power in the state was in the hands of the noble families—especially those who were his friends. How far he was successful we shall see in the next section. Very soon after his reforms he retired from public life and within a few months was dead. It was now possible to see if the nobles he hoped would run affairs at Rome would in fact be able to do so.

(ii) The Age of Pompey and Caesar

The period of Roman history between the death of Sulla and the death of Caesar is probably better known to historians than any other. At this time lived many Romans whose names are very familiar even today. There was Cicero the great orator to whose speeches and private letters we owe so much of our knowledge of that time; there were the poets Lucretius and Catullus and the historian Sallust; there was Crassus, the richest man in Rome, Pompey who was called 'the Great' and was for a long time the most powerful person in the world, and there was C. Julius Caesar, one of the most remarkable men in the history of the whole world. These people lived when, as we have already seen, the very nature of the state in which they lived was under considerable strain. Because so much was happening at that time, it would not be possible to give an account of everything here, and so we shall look at the life of Rome in these years particularly as it affected the most famous of all the great men of Rome, C. Julius Caesar.

Caesar was born in 100 B.C. and so by the time of Sulla's dictatorship was beginning to take part in public life. In fact his public life was almost over before it had really started! It was proposed that Caesar should become the Priest of Jupiter, called in Latin *Flamen Dialis*. Had this happened he would have been barred from commanding an army and we shall see how important this was to be in his later career. However, when Sulla returned after his defeat of Mithridates in the East he refused to allow Caesar to be appointed. So, oddly enough, Caesar's political opponent ensured that Caesar should have a political career! Indeed, Caesar carried this opposition even further, and the result was that during Sulla's dictatorship he had to leave Rome.

It was not until after the death of Sulla that he really started his political career. There was nothing spectacular about his early years. He made quite a good reputation for himself in the law-courts, he acquired many influential friends, and he started to climb the political ladder which he hoped would lead eventually to the consulship. Very different was the career of Pompey. He was just six years older than Caesar, but already he was the most influential man in Rome. He had aided Sulla with an army which he had inherited from his father at the age of nineteen. Then during the 70's he had fought two more important wars and in 70 B.C. was already consul, although by the strictest application of the law he was still too young. Shortly after this, in 67 B.C., he was granted a huge force to deal with the problem of piracy in the Mediterranean which threatened to make Rome's trade almost impossible.

Some years earlier Caesar had been captured by a band of these pirates who, as Plutarch says, 'even at that time controlled the seas

BUST OF POMPEY   BUST OF CICERO

with their large fleets of ships and innumerable smaller craft.' He then goes on to tell this story:

'First, when the pirates demanded a ransom of twenty talents, Caesar burst out laughing. They did not know, he said, who it was they had captured, and he volunteered to pay fifty! Then when he had sent his followers to raise the money and was left with one friend and two servants among these Cilicians, about the most blood-thirsty people in the world, he treated them so highhandedly that, whenever he wanted to sleep, he would send to them and tell them to stop talking. For thirty-eight days, with the greatest unconcern, he joined in all their games and exercises, just as if he were their leader instead of their prisoner. He also wrote poems and speeches which he read aloud to them and if they failed to admire his work, he would call them to their faces illiterate savages, and would often laughingly threaten to have them all hanged. They were much taken with this and attributed his freedom of speech to a kind of simplicity in his character or boyish playfulness. However, the ransom arrived from Miletus and, as soon as he had paid it and had been set free, he immediately manned some ships and set sail from the harbour of Miletus against the pirates. He found them still there, lying at anchor off the island, and he captured nearly all of them. He took their property as spoils of war and put the men themselves into prison.'

Men like these and many thousands more were the pirates Pompey had to deal with. Such was his efficiency that within a matter of months he had swept the pirates off the seas and virtually solved this problem for Rome. In the very next year (66 B.C.) he was given another great command, this time against Mithridates. This was the king, as was told above, whom Sulla had defeated, but had failed to destroy completely. Soon he was again making trouble for Rome and a general named Lucullus had been appointed to oppose him. Despite some successes he too had not completed the job and now Pompey took over. Once again he was highly successful. Mithridates was completely finished off and Pompey penetrated as far east as Jerusalem. He also organised this whole area in such a way that his arrangements lasted for very many years. When Pompey returned to Rome in 62 B.C. he was clearly more powerful than anyone else.

While Pompey was engaged in these great affairs, Caesar, as we have said, was progressing quietly but surely. In 67 he was quaestor and afterwards went to Spain to help administer that province. Suetonius, who later wrote a biography of Caesar, tells this story of his stay there:

'When he was there, he came to Gades and, noticing a statue of Alexander the Great in the temple of Hercules, he heaved a sigh and—as if out of patience with his own incapacity in having as yet done nothing noteworthy at a time of life when Alexander had already brought the world to his feet—he straightaway asked for his discharge to grasp the first opportunity for greater enterprises at Rome (see also LXI). Furthermore, when he was dismayed by a dream the following night, the soothsayers inspired him with high hopes by their interpretation, which was that he was destined to rule the world.'

When Pompey returned to Rome from the East, he found that many nobles were jealous of his great power and wanted to thwart his hopes. He was unable to carry out the measures he had planned but he did not want to imitate Sulla by using his army against Rome. Caesar had by now been a praetor and hoped soon to be elected consul. The rich Crassus had been unable to gain the power he desired so much. And so these three—Caesar, Crassus, Pompey— joined together to help one another in an alliance which is usually called 'The First Triumvirate' (from *tres* = 'three' and *vir* = 'man'). Because of their power they were able to ensure that Caesar was elected consul for 59 B.C. and afterwards should have Gaul as his province. Pompey and Crassus too had many of their wishes carried out.

One of the best known parts of Caesar's career is the period he spent in Gaul. He himself kept a very full record of all the battles he fought while bringing Gaul into the Roman Empire. He was in Gaul continuously from 58 to 49 B.C. except for a short period when he was invading Britain. The Britons had been helping the Gauls, and Caesar decided to punish them, although at this time he probably did not intend to add Britain to the Empire. Here is a description he himself gives of the Britons:

'The most civilised of all these peoples are those who inhabit Kent, which is entirely a maritime district, and they do not differ much from the Gauls in customs. Most of the inland inhabitants do not sow grain but live on milk and flesh and are dressed in skins. All the Britons, indeed, dye themselves with woad, which produces a bluish colour, and thereby they have a more terrible appearance in battle. They wear their hair long and have every part of their body shaved except their head and upper lip. Groups of ten and twelve have wives in common.'

Caesar was unsuccessful in his expeditions to Britain but won Gaul.

While Caesar was engaged in this way in Gaul, there had been considerable unrest and disorder in Rome. Pompey still exercised great influence, but even he found it virtually impossible to have anything done because his opponents hired mobs to stir up fighting in the streets. Eventually, however, the nobles decided that Pompey was less of a danger to their interests than Caesar, and they tried to win him over. Pompey was unwilling to oppose Caesar, but now both men were increasingly suspicious and wary of each other. Although it is probably true to say that neither of them really wanted to fight, circumstances and the intrigues of Caesar's bitterest enemies eventually brought about the Civil War between the two. Suetonius tells this story about Caesar's final decision to fight:

'As he stood in doubt, this sign was given him. On a sudden there appeared hard by a being of wondrous stature and beauty who sat, and played upon a reed; and when not only the shepherds flocked to hear him, but many of the soldiers left their posts, and among them some of the trumpeters, the apparition snatched a trumpet from one of them, rushed to the river and, sounding the war-note with a mighty blast, strode to the opposite bank. Then Caesar cried: "We take the course which the signs of the gods and the false dealing of our foes point out. The die is cast!"'

The river was called the 'Rubicon' and formed the boundary which Caesar could not legally cross with his army. By crossing it, he was in effect starting the war. We still today keep the expression 'crossing the Rubicon' in talking about a decision which, once made, cannot be reversed.

It would be impossible to tell here all the events of this Civil War. All we can say is that Pompey was defeated and killed and after more fighting against the rest of Pompey's supporters Caesar was appointed Dictator. He passed many laws which he hoped would help to cure Rome of the troubles of the previous century. One other measure he took which has lasted almost unchanged to the present day was his reform of the calendar. It was he who created the calendar we know today. However, Caesar did not live long enough to change as much as he would have wished. Everyone has heard of the Ides of March, 44 B.C. On that day (15th March) Caesar entered the Senate House, and Suetonius describes in this way what happened:

'As he took his seat, the conspirators gathered about him as if to pay their respects, and straightaway Cimber, who had assumed the lead, came nearer as though to ask something; and when Caesar put him off to another time, Cimber caught his toga by both shoulders.

Then one of the Cascas stabbed him from one side just below the throat. As Caesar tried to leap to his feet, he was stopped by another wound. When he saw that he was beset on every side by drawn daggers, he muffled his head in his robe. He was stabbed with twenty-three wounds, uttering not a word, but merely a groan at the first stroke, though some have written that when Marcus Brutus rushed at him, he said in Greek, "You too, my child?" '

Caesar's death did not bring peace to Rome. For many years still there was civil war until Octavian, Caesar's grand-nephew and adopted son, later called Augustus, defeated his main rival Antony and became what we call the first Roman Emperor. He reorganised the government of Rome in a way that was to last for several centuries.

It is at this point that we end our brief introduction to Roman History, but of course, as we have said, Roman power continued for a long time after this. Many of the Emperors are well-known names—Nero, Hadrian, Constantine, for example; and there were many other famous Romans—the poets Vergil, Ovid and Horace; the historians Livy and Tacitus, and many more. The story of these centuries is just as interesting as the one told here, and those who would like to know more can read about it in many good history books.

6 Rome and her Provinces

We have seen how Rome acquired a large empire and now we should briefly look at how she governed it and how she treated the inhabitants of her provinces.

When some foreign territory became a province of the Roman empire, the senate usually appointed a commission of ten men to go to the province, examine the situation and draw up the clauses of what was called the *Lex provinciae*—the law by which the province was to be governed in future. For each individual province the senate then appointed a governor who was a person who had been consul, praetor or quaestor at Rome. In the first instance the appointment would normally be for one year, though this might be extended and in some exceptional cases, for example Pompey and Caesar, it might last over several years. Before he went to his province, each governor had to issue an edict which set out the rules by which he would govern, and he was then legally bound by that edict as well as by the *Lex provinciae*. In addition it was possible for citizens of a province to prosecute a governor in Rome after his term of office if it was felt that he had governed badly.

In theory then the government of the provinces ought to have worked well, because the laws and the edicts were always fair to the provincials. But in practice things often went wrong. There were many reasons for this: one year was not long enough for a man to get to know his province really well; the edict was issued before a governor even saw his province; Romans as a whole were not very interested in the people of the provinces, except where they could be of use; to prosecute a governor successfully after his term of office required a lot of money and powerful friends at Rome. But the largest faults of the system were to be found in the Romans who went to the provinces either as governors or in some business capacity.

To take the governors first. Not all governors were bad, of course, but we have already seen how a political career at Rome could be very expensive; men often had to borrow large sums of money and the normal way to repay these debts was by making money from provincials as a governor. Probably the best known example— and certainly one of the worst—was the praetor C. Verres, who governed Sicily from 73 to 71 B.C. When he returned from Sicily he was brought to trial. In this case the provincials who had been harmed had enough money and friends, and also they had as the prosecutor Cicero, the most able orator of his day. Cicero tells many stories in his speeches against Verres about the criminal behaviour of that man and the rogues who worked for him. Here is one in which Verres tried to rob a man called Pamphilus, though in the end it was Verres' helpers who came off best. Cicero is addressing the jury:

'I remember, gentlemen, a good friend of mine, Pamphilus, telling me that this fellow Verres had used his power as governor to rob him of an exquisitely made ewer of great weight. Pamphilus went home in distress, because he had had taken from him an article inherited from his ancestors which he used to use at festival times and when entertaining friends. Pamphilus went on: "When I was sitting at home and feeling very sorry for myself, along came a messenger from Verres. He told me I had to bring some decorated goblets to the praetor at once. I was stunned, for I had a pair of them. But I gave orders that they should be taken out and brought with me to the praetor's house, for I was afraid of something worse happening. When I arrived the praetor was asleep! But those two brothers who work for Verres were wandering about. When they saw me they said: 'The cups, Pamphilus.' Reluctantly I showed them and they were impressed. I started to complain that I would soon have nothing valuable left if they took these goblets too. When they saw my distress they said 'What will you give us if we don't take them?'

To cut a long story short, they demanded a large bribe which I agreed to give. Just then Verres called, asking for the cups. Those rogues started to tell Verres that from what they had heard they had supposed that Pamphilus' cups were of some value, but now they had turned out to be worthless and quite unworthy of Verres' collection." And Verres believed them!'

Verres did not wait until the trial could be completed—he knew that in his case only one verdict could be reached—and he fled into exile, no doubt still having enough money to live very comfortably for the rest of his life.

As well as the governors, other Romans moved into the provinces with a view to making money. These were mostly *equites*, from which class came the financiers and businessmen of Rome. Provinces had to pay taxes to Rome and in many cases these were collected by groups of Roman equites, who clearly took more than was permitted in order to make a handsome profit. If because of this, or for any other reason, provincials fell into debt, there were always other Roman equites on hand to lend money—but of course at a high rate of interest: we hear of examples of 48% compound interest being charged. In addition to this, the court at Rome which tried provincial governors had, for most of the time we are discussing, juries which were wholly or largely composed of equites and their friends. It is easy to see how the equites could have a very great influence over provincial governors. Cicero himself, who tried to be a good and fair governor, discovered this in his province of Cilicia, and he was unable as a result to carry out all the measures he would have liked. He knew that the equites and their friends would be able to put pressure on him at Rome.

Does all of this mean that Roman provincial government was completely bad? Not quite, even though its faults were numerous, and many of them had to be removed by the Roman emperors, Augustus and his successors. In many ways Romans were less harsh than the original rulers of these countries, many roads were built and general peace was brought—the foundations in fact of Roman civilising influence. Good governors could do a little, even if not as much as they would have wished, and in the end Romanisation meant increased prosperity for all.

Early Roman Education

Up to 250 B.C. when Greek influence began, Roman education was based on the practical needs of rural life, an education adapted to the early Roman agricultural community. Until foreign conquest and the wealth it brought with it transformed Roman life, the average Roman was a soldier-farmer. Hard work, good husbandry, the ability to run a farm were the prime social virtues. The farm was based on the family and its religious and legal connexion with the state. It was in the family that education was given and the child was taught to emulate its parents and become their worthy successor.

To the age of seven it was the mother who formed the child's character and sowed in him the seeds of the basic Roman virtues of *gravitas* (a dignified and serious attitude to life), *pietas* (a sense of duty to family, gods and state), *iustitia* (justice), *constantia* (resolution) and *prudentia* (sound judgement). Then the father took over and by precept and example initiated the boy into his duties as a farmer, a soldier, a citizen. The boy would help on the farm, take part in religious rites and accompany his father on visits to the city. He listened to stories of heroism from Roman history and learned by heart the Twelve Tables of Roman Law. These early Romans never handed over the sacred duty of educating their sons to a hired foreigner or slave schoolmaster. These boys may have had few formal lessons except in reading and counting, but they were well versed in Roman traditions and the privileges and responsibilities of Roman citizenship. They saw the closely-knit life of the family reproduced on broader canvas in the life of the Roman State (*Res Publica*).

Greek Influence

As Rome extended her influence over Italy and beyond it, there were two consequences important for educational development. First, fathers were now absent from Rome for long periods fighting wars or governing provinces and so could not personally supervise their sons' education. This also led to an increase in divorce and frequent break-up of the family unit. Secondly, it brought Rome wealth and acquaintance with the vital and attractive civilisation of Greece. Greek art, philosophy, literature, mythology flooded Rome. It was soon necessary for better-class Romans to be able to speak and read Greek and to send their children to Greek schoolmasters who came to Rome in large numbers. So the old family-centred education largely disappeared.

MASTER AND PUPILS

Three Stages of Education

The elementary stage was from seven to twelve years of age and consisted of learning to read, write and count. The pupil left home at dawn carrying his breakfast to eat on the way. He was accompanied by his *paedagogus*. He was a trusted slave of some education who carried the boy's books, saw to his safety and good conduct in the streets and supervised his homework. School was usually a groundfloor room open to the street. The elementary schoolmaster (*ludi magister*) was nearly always a Greek, poorly paid and often despised by his pupils. He enforced discipline by the ruthless use of cane or whip. A Roman poet complains of the noise the pupils made in the early morning chanting their lessons or yelling when caned and promises the teacher twice his pay if he will take his school somewhere else! Many children never went beyond this first stage.

The second stage, from twelve to sixteen, was supervised by a master called the *grammaticus*. He was better educated than the *ludi magister* and received four times as much pay. The curriculum consisted mainly of grammar and literature—mainly Greek literature, though later Vergil and Horace were also studied. Books were read for grammatical analysis, scansion and background information rather than to inculcate a love of literature for its own sake.

Young men aiming at a public career continued their education after sixteen though at that age most boys put off the toga of childhood (*toga praetexta*), assumed the man's toga (*toga virilis*) and became full Roman citizens. Advanced, university-type education had the sole aim of imparting the art of public speaking and was conducted by a *rhetor* or professor of eloquence. The students were given moral or historical themes which they had to argue against one another. The training was rigorous and highly organised but was directed solely at persuasion and winning the case no matter what quibbles or prevarications were involved.

For and against the System

The primary advantage of Roman education was that it was useful and it was efficient. The Romans were a hard-headed race and they insisted that their children be able to read, write and count with ease. The ability to speak well was not only useful, it was essential for public life. A mastery of Greek language and civilisation was a 'must' for an educated man. By the cane, by repetition, by thorough instruction and gruelling practice Roman schoolmasters at the various grades produced results even from the most unpromising material.

But this educational system was open to serious criticism. Most important was the fact that the pupils seldom felt love or respect for their teachers and so absorbed instruction from them but no real moral guidance or example. It is true that elementary pupils repeated strings of proverbs such as 'The man who keeps his word can get anywhere' or 'The miser is the cause of his own misery' or 'He always wins who uses clemency', but these alone without the inspiration of good parents and teachers could do little. The other main criticism would be of the unimaginative methods and the limited aims of instruction. The *ludi magister* made no attempt to arouse his pupils' interest. The *grammaticus* showed the mechanics of language and composition but seldom tried to inspire a love of literature. The *rhetor* drilled the elements of oratory but had forgotten that a great orator must be a fully integrated and civilised man, not just an efficient talking machine.

School Materials

Pupils wrote on wax tablets framed in light wood. Sometimes several of these were fastened together to form a wax-tablet notebook. An instrument called a *stilus* was used for writing on the wax. It had one end sharp to scratch the letters and the other flat to erase them and smooth the wax surface for re-use.

Later a pupil might write with pen and ink on paper made from the pith of the Egyptian papyrus reed. But this was expensive and he would usually write on the back of paper already used once.

Books were in the form of long strips of papyrus rolled into scrolls. Rectangular columns of writing from top to bottom of the scroll width continued throughout the roll. The reader unrolled the scroll with his right hand to expose a few columns of writing and rolled up with his left as each column was completed. Scrolls were kept in pigeon-holes with tags hanging down to show title and author. In the absence of printing, books were copied by hand by slaves employed for that purpose.

Counting was assisted either by using the fingers or a frame with wires on which beads could be slid or by the use of the *abacus* illustrated below. For a simple explanation of the use of this instrument I quote from Treble and King, *Everyday Life in Rome*, page 60: 'We can disregard the five rods at the right-hand side. They were used only for working fractions of the duodecimal type—i.e. having the denominator a multiple of twelve. The other fourteen rods on the abacus were for dealing with whole numbers. Thus, the rod marked I was for counting units, the next (marked X) for tens, the next for hundreds and so on up to millions, which were counted on the extreme left-hand rod. It will be noticed that the seven longer rods on the left had only four beads, so that it was possible to count on them only as far as 4; 40; 400 . . . as the case might be. The one bead on each short rod stood for five units, tens, hundreds, and so on; and thus the process of counting was made more rapid. Even so it was a difficult instrument to use, especially for division and multiplication.'

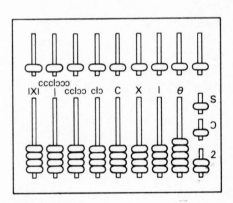

English words derived from Roman Educational System

1 From the use of the fingers (*digiti*) in counting comes the English 'digit', a number from one to ten.

2 From the word 'pebbles' (*calculi*), also used in counting, we get 'calculate'.

3 From the reed *papyrus* comes our word 'paper'.

4 From *liber* (the pith of the papyrus reed) comes the Latin *liber* (a book) and English 'library'.

5 From Latin *volvere* (to unroll the book-scroll) is derived our word 'volume'.

SEE: *Oxford Classical Dictionary* under 'Education', 'Books', 'Abacus'; Warde Fowler, *Social Life at Rome*, Ch. VI; Carcopino, *Daily Life in Ancient Rome*, Ch. V; Treble and King, *Everyday Life in Rome*, Ch. VI.

Origins of Holidays

Like other Mediterranean peoples the Romans were fond of parades, of spectacle, of singing and dancing and all the fun of the fiesta. Most Roman festivals were originally religious in character and go back to the annual cycle of agricultural festivals in Rome's earliest days. As the empire expanded and the city became richer these rustic holidays were extended until they occupied about one hundred days a year. In addition to these fixed festivals, victorious generals and citizens seeking popularity with the people in order to further their political careers put on shows at their own expense. This wooing of the people was necessary because the Roman state consisted of the Senate and Roman People (*Senatus Populusque Romanus*). Though the latter was becoming decadent and idle as a plentiful supply of slaves took over essential work, the people still had power to elect magistrates and so had to be flattered by those ambitious for power.

Roman citizens paid nothing to attend these shows. At first they were free, since they were state religious ceremonies. During the Punic Wars more free shows were added to keep up the morale of the people and soon, as mentioned above, further free holidays were added as a bribe for popular support at elections. Many ambitious men spent their own fortunes and borrowed others in the hope of gaining high office and the governorship of a province where they could recoup their outlay with interest.

Names of some Festivals

Among annual Roman festivals were the *Saturnalia*, starting on December 17th and lasting seven days. This originated as a rustic mid-winter festival of merry-making and some of its customs and much of its spirit survive in our Christmas festivities.

The *Ludi Magni* from September 5th to 19th originally celebrated victories on the field of battle.

Other fixed festivals were the *Ludi Plebeii* (November 4th–17th), *Ludi Apollinares* (July 6th–13th), *Ludi Megalenses* (April 4th–10th) and *Ludi Ceriales* (April 12th–19th).

Chariot Races

The Ludi Magni started with a great procession from the temple of Jupiter on the Capitol to the Circus Maximus where the show connected with the festival was held. The main feature of this was the chariot races (*circenses*). Later, plays were added and later still, combats between armed men and wild animals which seriously reduced the numbers of lions, bears, panthers, etc., in the countries round the Mediterranean. The Circus Maximus held 150,000 people with special seats for senators and a box for the presiding magistrate.

The building was rectangular with semicircular ends. Down the central area—called the *arena* (the Latin word for 'sand') because the ground was covered with sand—ran a marble barrier (the *spina*) which divided the lap of about 1,500 m. (1,600 yards) into two. At each end of the barrier were three pillars to mark the turning-points for the chariots. Seven complete laps constituted a race. On the spina were seven marble objects, sometimes egg-shaped, sometimes carved to represent dolphins, one of which was lifted down at the end of each lap.

The racing chariots, pulled by four horses, were two-wheeled and of light construction. The driver wound the ends of the reins round his body but carried a sharp knife so that he could cut them if he were thrown during the race. The chariots waited in stables (*carceres*) until, at a sign from the senior magistrate, the folding doors were opened and they came forth on the course. There were usually four chariots in a race, though sometimes as many as twelve competed. The main danger was at the turning-points where chariots kept as close as possible to the centre and might either break an axle on the marble spina or collide with another competitor.

As with football clubs today the charioteers wore the colours of the companies which employed and trained them. The colours were white, red, blue or green. The rivalry between the colours and the gambling on the results produced the frantic enthusiasm and excitement now provided by a cup-match or the football pools. The upper classes rather scorned this mob hysteria, saying that the people cheered not the skill of the driver but the colour of his jersey!

Gladiators

It was many years after the start of the annual festivals before exhibitions of gladiators (*munera*) were made part of them. This bloodthirsty, cruel form of entertainment came to be even more popular than chariot racing. Its origin can be traced to the Etruscans, who staged human fights to the death as part of the funeral games to some great chieftain. The blood that was shed soaked into the ground as an offering to the spirit of the dead man. The gladiatorial shows were at first given by private individuals. In 264 B.C. three pairs of gladiators fought at the funeral of M. Brutus. In 174 B.C. at the funeral of T. Flamininus thirty-seven pairs fought. Julius Caesar as aedile exhibited 320 pairs and the Emperor Trajan no less than 5,000 pairs!

CHARIOT RACING

Gladiators were usually either prisoners of war, slaves or condemned criminals. Later, impoverished Roman citizens took up the job and under the Empire men of rank, attracted by the glamour and the danger, volunteered for training. Gladiators were trained in great schools by professional trainers (*lanistae*) to become cool, expert fighters who faced death at every contest but who, with luck and skill, could capture the imagination of the audience and win great popularity and even wealth. For most of them, however, life was short and death quick and violent.

They marched into the arena, saluted the presiding magistrate with the words *Morituri te salutant* (Men about to die salute you) and then separated into fighting pairs. The vanquished gladiator was usually killed by his victor unless he had put up a good fight and was popular with the audience. In that case the spectators waved their handkerchiefs and the president gave the 'thumbs-up' sign which granted the loser his life.

Some gladiators were fully armed and were called *Mirmillones* or *Samnites* according to the type of armour worn. These either fought one another or were pitted against light-armed fighters called *Threces*. A favourite contest was between a heavy-armed man and a gladiator called a *Retiarius* (from *rete* = a net). He was almost naked and carried a net in which he tried to entangle his slower-moving opponent. If successful, he killed him with a long pointed trident.

23

Theatres

Theatrical shows (*Ludi Scaenici*) formed part of the festivals. At first tragedies and comedies of some merit were staged and appreciated, but as time went on and the taste of the people declined plays were written to be read, not acted. Their place was taken by farce with improvised dialogue, topical allusions and accompanied by music and dancing. Popular also were coarse dumb-shows (*pantomimi*) where the story was told by grimaces and eloquent gestures.

The Romans never really took to drama as the Greeks did. The authorities always thought of it as something to be frowned on. Shows were either given in the open air or in temporary wooden buildings. Rome's first permanent theatre was built by Pompey as late as 55 B.C.

SEE: *Oxford Classical Dictionary* under 'Ludi', 'Venationes', 'Gladiators' and 'Circus';　Warde Fowler, *Social Life at Rome*, Ch. X.

ROMAN HOUSES
See diagram opposite.

Far back in the past when the Romans were still an agricultural people most of them lived in a simple hut with a hole in the roof or wall through which the smoke from the fire escaped. This basic form can still be seen in the later Roman house (*domus*). The central part of this preserved the opening to the sky and was called the *atrium* which means 'the black place' (see opposite).

The Domus

This generally had two sections, a Roman section in front and a Greek section behind.

Suppose you have been invited by a wealthy friend to a meal in his house. As you stand in the street outside, you are faced by a blank wall in which there is the front door (*ianua*) and, further along, perhaps round the corner, the side door (*posticum*). You knock and a slave doorkeeper lets you into the vestibule (*vestibulum*). From there you go into the central hall to meet your host. There are no windows. Light comes from a hole in the roof under which is a tank to catch rain water. The walls have painted scenes. The floor is mosaic pavement and along the sides of it stand statues of your host's famous ancestors. On either side are doors to the bedrooms (*cubicula*). As you move back towards the Greek part of the house you see the dining room (*triclinium*) on the left, the main corridor (*fauces*) on the right and beyond it the bedroom kept for important guests. In front

24

THE ROMAN HOUSE

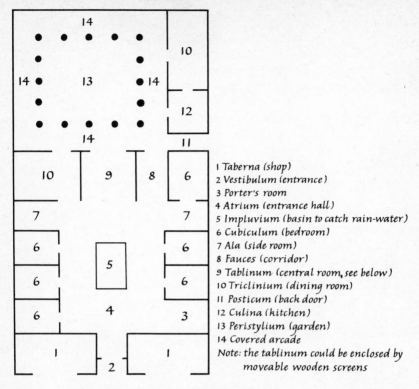

1 Taberna (shop)
2 Vestibulum (entrance)
3 Porter's room
4 Atrium (entrance hall)
5 Impluvium (basin to catch rain-water)
6 Cubiculum (bedroom)
7 Ala (side room)
8 Fauces (corridor)
9 Tablinum (central room, see below)
10 Triclinium (dining room)
11 Posticum (back door)
12 Culina (kitchen)
13 Peristylium (garden)
14 Covered arcade
Note: the tablinum could be enclosed by
      moveable wooden screens

is the central room (*tablinum*). This has ornately carved wooden shutters left open in summer but closed in winter.

Now you are ushered down the corridor into the Greek-type garden (*peristylium*) where the family spend most of their time in hot weather. It has flower beds and shrubs and perhaps a fountain, a marble table and seats. Around it runs a covered arcade. To the right is another dining room used mostly in the summer and beside it the kitchen. The kitchen is out here to keep the cooking smells from the main rooms. Also the slaves are able to bring the food in from the market through the side door. In warm weather one can stroll about either in the open garden or under the shade of the pillared portico.

The furniture in these large houses was luxurious compared with that used by the poor, but by our standards it was fairly meagre. Chairs with arms and a back were used only by women, elderly people or guests. Others sat on the floor or on stools. The table could be of cypress or cedar or of a cheaper wood. At meals people reclined

25

on couches round the table and were attended by the household slaves. Other articles were beds, coverlets, rugs, draperies, cutlery (mainly spoons; knives and forks were not used at table), cups and dishes (metal or earthenware), personal jewelry and kitchen equipment.

Where there were not cavity walls and a central heating furnace in the basement, heat came from charcoal-burning braziers, usually made of brass and very elegant. To start the fire flint and steel were used.

For artificial lighting there were olive oil lamps with wicks of flax or papyrus which protruded out of the lamp spout and hung downwards to cast the light further. The light given was not very bright and, with oil expensive, only the rich could afford multiple lamps in great candelabra. For the poor the rule was 'early to bed'.

Only very wealthy Romans could have private bathrooms in their houses and possibly even lavatories. These were situated near the kitchen to be close to a water supply.

PERISTYLIUM OF THE HOUSE OF THE VETTII, POMPEII

RECONSTRUCTION OF APARTMENT HOUSE AT OSTIA

Insulae

In ancient Rome, however, a separate house like the above was the exception. There were about 1,800 houses in the city but over 46,000 blocks of flats. These were called *insulae* (because they were surrounded by four streets) and in them the majority of Romans lived.

The insulae varied enormously in every way. The better kind might have a *domus* on the ground floor, but more often the ground floor was taken up by shops. Their proprietors lived behind or above the premises, often in a loft-like room reached by a ladder. The rest of the building comprised suites of rooms or single rooms hired out to tenants. The rooms got cheaper and more wretched as one climbed upwards. These vast blocks were often cheaply and badly constructed and so were liable to collapse. The Emperor Augustus was forced to put a height limit of 20 m (66 ft.) on them.

Heating, lighting and sanitation in these blocks were not only inadequate, they were also a source of danger to the inhabitants and to their neighbours. The cheap braziers and lamps could easily fall over or be knocked down in the small dark rooms and a fire, once started, spread quickly in the overcrowded conditions. If you lived on the sixth or seventh floor, just under the tiles, you might easily awake to find the whole building a raging inferno.

Though the Romans were very advanced in bringing good clean water into Rome in aqueducts, it cost a lot to have the supply brought to your house. Usually it was piped to central fountains where the inhabitants had to queue up with buckets. Most people did not bath in their homes but went down the street to the public baths.

With no lavatories in their flats people either went to the public toilets or they used pots and emptied them out of the window into the street! This practice was not uncommon throughout Europe until quite recently. To walk along some of the smaller streets must have been an unpleasant and dangerous business!

Houses in the Country

In the countryside the poor farmers lived in small, dark cottages (*casae*), as also did labourers who hired out their services. The rich farmer had a large farmhouse where, in addition to barns and other work buildings, he had rooms of the same style and luxury as his rich equivalent in the city. There were also country villas (*villae*) where rich city men relaxed after the strain of city life.

Life was certainly pleasant in the house of a man like the millionaire Crassus, but remember that most of Rome's citizens lived in conditions which would not be tolerated today.

SEE: Treble and King, *Everyday Life in Rome*, Ch. III; Carcopino, *Daily Life in Ancient Rome*, pp. 31–59; film-strips: *The Roman House* (Daily Mail Filmstrips).

TRAVEL IN ROMAN TIMES

Importance of Roads

Nowadays the building of roads is often associated with the opening up of new areas for tourism. In Roman times the development of a road network was an important factor in the spread of Rome's empire from Britain to the Middle East. Along the new roads marched armies to conquer and pacify fresh territories. Later the same roads carried Roman officials to govern and dispense justice and also tradesmen to foster commerce and introduce Roman customs and language. Later still, as the area became more settled, the roads would be used by those travelling for pleasure, to visit friends or spend a few weeks in their country villas.

The *Pax Romana* (Roman Peace) and the use of Latin as an international language made travel easier. Long journeys across Europe and North Africa were certainly safer and more frequent under the Roman Empire than up to quite modern times. This fact contributed largely to the rapid spread of Christianity.

ROAD PAVING

Some Main Routes

The cost of building and repairing roads was largely met by the public treasury, though local authorities and those through whose land the road passed also made some contribution.

Under the Republic most road building was in Italy as Rome extended her influence there. Such roads were the Via Appia, the southern highroad to Capua and Brundisium, and the Via Flaminia leading north to Ariminum on the Adriatic. Two great trunk roads were built outside Italy about 130–120 B.C. The Via Domitia ran from the River Rhone to Spain and the Via Egnatia, the highway to the east, ran from Dyrrhachium on the Greek side of the Adriatic via Thessalonica to Byzantium.

Under the emperors most road construction was in the provinces, including the elaborate network that opened up Britain to Roman armies and merchants.

Road Construction

Roman roads, like modern motorways, took the straightest possible route. The Romans were excellent engineers, so that bridging rivers and carrying roads across valleys by means of massive viaducts presented few difficulties. The Pont du Gard aqueduct near Avignon in southern France shows this skill (see illustration over page).

The roads themselves were variously constructed according to the nature of the subsoil and the local material available. The foundation was of earth rammed hard or flagstones or smaller stones. Above this was a layer of rubble or small stones covered with concrete. The

29

cambered top surface would be of basalt or other local stone or, if stone was not available, of rammed gravel or concrete.

Along these roads were milestones, pillars about 2 m (6 ft.) high. These bore the names of the officials who saw to the building or repair of the roads. In Italy distances from Rome were given; in the provinces distances from the nearest large town. In the Forum at Rome the emperor Augustus set up the Golden Milestone which gave the distances from Rome to many important cities in the Empire.

Methods of Travel

As in all ages, the method of travel depended on one's social position. The poor walked or used donkeys; the richer rode on horseback or in various types of carriages. Travel by litter—a sort of sedan chair carried by two or more sturdy slaves—was confined to inside the city or short distances outside it.

The two main types of carriage were the *carpentum* and the *raeda*. The former was two-wheeled and, when horse-drawn, could attain a considerable speed. With changes of horses 160 km (100 miles) a day could be covered. The four-wheeled *raeda* was larger. It held several people with their luggage and provisions for a long journey.

Accommodation

In Roman times there were very few reputable hotels, though the government did provide accommodation for its officials travelling on duty. The ordinary traveller had four choices:

PONT DU GARD

ROMAN BRIDGE AT ARIMINUM (RIMINI)

1 He could stay at an inn (*caupona*). Some of these were good but most were cheap, disreputable and bug-infested, where it was not wise for a customer to make any display of wealth in case he invited robbery or even murder.

2 If his carriage was big enough, he could bed down for the night in it.

3 He could stay in the house of some friend or someone to whom he had been given a letter of introduction.

4 If he were well off, he could stay in one of his own country houses. Cicero had six such houses in the country which he could use for overnight stops on a journey.

The safety of travel varied with the district and the times. High-waymen did attack travellers even on the main roads of Italy but, in general, travel was safer than during the Middle Ages. The rich were accompanied on journeys by an armed retinue of slaves. The poor depended on speed of flight or on the military posts which were stationed at intervals along the main roads.

Travel by Sea

This was less popular than travel by land. There were no passenger ships and so travellers had to wait for a merchant ship going in the required direction. The average merchantman (*navis oneraria*) was a ship of about fifty tons. It was built of wood and, using mainly sail, reached a speed of three to four knots. It was decked, had a small cabin aft and was steered by two large oars at the stern.

During the winter the Mediterranean was too rough for these small vessels and only the brave risked a sea voyage between October and

March. Without compass or sextant, sailors navigated by the stars, normally visible in summer. Ships usually hugged the coast, though some large grain ships used the seasonal winds to go direct from Egypt to Italy in June and back in August. See CV and CIX for St. Paul's use of these ships.

Postal Service

The Roman emperors had an official postal service with posting-houses where the couriers could change horses or sleep. Their speed of travel varied from 80 km (50 miles) to 200 km (150 miles) a day according to the urgency of the message. Private letters could not use this government service without special permission. They were sent by hired couriers (*tabellarii*), often shared among a group of friends. Cicero often mentions that he is writing to a friend because he has heard that a reliable courier is travelling in that direction.

SEE: *Oxford Classical Dictionary* under 'Travel', 'Roads', 'Milestones', 'Carriages' 'Inns', 'Ships,' 'Navigation', 'Postal Service'; film-strip: *People of other Days*, III. Roman Roads (Visual Publications).

ROMAN BRITAIN

Britain was under direct Roman rule for almost four hundred years, but of course most of the buildings and other works of the Romans have long since disappeared. How then do we know what life in Roman Britain was like?

There are two ways. First of all, we know the dates on which various important events took place from the writings of people in different parts of the Roman Empire who were alive at the time. They also tell us something about the customs and way of life of people in Britain. But these references are not very frequent.

Our second way of knowing about Roman Britain is much more important. This is archaeology. Nearly all of the remains of the Romans in Britain are by now buried beneath the ground, and so an archaeologist has the job of digging them up. But he must do this very carefully so that, by studying what he finds, he can build up a picture of the life of people who lived about 2,000 years ago. Some remains can still be seen above the ground. The great fortification called Hadrian's Wall is probably the best-known example. There are others too, including the Roman roads, the course of many of which can still be seen today.

Modern techniques also help the archaeologist. For example, photographs taken from the air at certain times of the year may show

HADRIAN'S WALL: LOOKING WEST OVER HOUSESTEADS FORT

up the outline of remains which cannot be seen from the ground. These can then be excavated and everything that is found noted down. Every stone used in building and every small piece of pottery is useful in giving help to increase our knowledge.

Historical Outline

When the Romans first came to Britain, they found there a people who were mostly Celts and who had originally come from the continent of Europe. They belonged to different Celtic tribes, often unfriendly to one another. They were taller than the average Roman and more powerfully built with fairer skin and hair and with blue eyes. They wore trousers and a tunic. They were not by any means primitive, for they constructed elaborate hill-forts, minted their own coinage and had a settled way of life based on farming.

They had had contact with parts of the Roman Empire through

33

trade before Julius Caesar, in two invasions in 55 and 54 B.C., made the first attempt to bring Britain under Roman rule. Caesar was victorious but he did not stay long and there was no serious attempt to make Britain a Roman province for nearly a hundred years.

Then in A.D. 43 the emperor Claudius invaded Britain. The Britons resisted bravely, but they could not withstand the disciplined advance of the Roman legions. Some tribes co-operated with the Romans and so helped the advance. The Romans gradually established control, moving north through England and into Wales.

The military operations went on long after the death of Claudius and the Romans often had trouble with tribal rebellions. The most famous revolt was that of Boudicca (A.D. 60 or 61). She was queen of a tribe in eastern England called the Iceni. After the death of her husband the king, the Romans treated herself and her daughters very badly and she revolted. Her people and some of her neighbours had been further angered by the financial demands the Romans were making on them. In the rebellion the Romans suffered serious defeats with the loss of many thousands of men before the revolt was finally crushed.

After this the Romans continued to advance until they had penetrated right into Scotland. Remember that this was not a continuous advance, but a series of movements spread over many years. Scotland was not held permanently and the Romans drew back until, in A.D. 122 or 123, the emperor Hadrian began to build his great wall across northern England from coast to coast.

It was 73 miles long, fifteen feet high, with a six-foot battlement on top, and was eight to ten feet broad. On its north side there was a deep ditch and at one mile intervals along its whole length were small forts called 'milecastles' with two turrets between each pair. In these lived a kind of frontier guard, while the regular army lived in larger forts spaced farther apart. A road connected all these forts and the whole area was sealed off as a military zone by a great ditch to the south with earth mounds on either side of it. This ditch, called the *vallum*, later fell into disuse as Britain became more peaceful.

This enormous series of fortifications, much of which is visible today, was intended to be the northern frontier of Roman Britain, and in fact was so for most of the time. But about A.D. 140 the Romans built another wall further north from the Forth to the Clyde. It was called the Antonine Wall. It was only 37 miles long and was made of turf, not stone. The area between the two walls was occupied for about fifty years until trouble in Britain and other parts of the empire made necessary a withdrawal to Hadrian's Wall which once again became the frontier.

Our knowledge of events in the third century A.D. is very scanty. In Britain the century was probably mostly peaceful. By the end of it, however, Britain's security was threatened by pirate attacks on the south-eastern shores. From this period date some of the best-known remains of Roman Britain, the series of massive stone coastal forts in this area, called the Saxon Shore Forts. They were immensely strong, with walls ten feet or more thick.

In A.D. 367 the Saxons, Picts and Scots made a concerted attack and the whole province was thrown into disorder. After a time the emperor Theodosius restored some order, but Britain was never again so completely controlled by the Romans. In the end, in A.D. 410, the emperor Honorius withdrew the Roman garrison and told the Britons to see to their own defence in future. This brought to an end this important chapter in the history of Britain.

Organisation and Life in Britain under the Romans

One of the most important things the Romans did when they took over a country was to build a road system. The Romans attached great importance to this road network and it was built to last. The surfaces of some roads have been excavated and can be seen today. Governors of Britain were responsible for providing surveyors and foremen for road upkeep and, if the army could not provide the labour, local people were recruited for the work.

WITH ITS COLONNADED FORUM, BATHS AND BASILICA AND TYPICAL STREET TRAFFIC, INCLUDING A ROMAN LADY IN A LITTER: A RECONSTRUCTION DRAWING OF VIROCONIUM, THE FOURTH LARGEST ROMAN TOWN IN BRITAIN, AS IT APPEARED IN HADRIAN'S TIME SOME 1800 YEARS AGO

While, of course, the final say in the organisation of the province lay with the governor who was directly responsible to the emperor, there was a considerable amount of local self-government. The four towns called *coloniae*, Eboracum (York), Lindum (Lincoln), Glevum (Gloucester) and Camulodunum (Colchester), whose inhabitants were Roman citizens, modelled themselves on Rome. But smaller towns also had local government. In any case, by an order of the emperor Caracalla in A.D. 212, all inhabitants became Roman citizens.

What was life like in one of the larger towns? Before the Romans arrived, the Britons had not had any town life. Even those places regarded as capitals of the various tribes were not much more than collections of huts. The idea of town life was brought to Britain by veterans of the invasion campaigns who settled there. They settled first at Colchester and with their wives and children and some Britons made up the first real town in Britain. Soon buildings were erected, temples, theatres, administrative buildings. Other towns developed in the same way and soon the largest was London.

As the towns grew, they became centres of trade, and shops were built, often with living accommodation attached. The richest people lived in very impressive houses, with two or more wings and corridors; some had private baths and even flush lavatories. The poor, on the other hand, lived in very simple wooden houses. Public baths were a feature of all towns, the most famous being at Bath with its hot mineral springs. Towns also had a drainage system and in at least one town (Lincoln) there was underground sewerage, every street having its own drain to which each house was linked. In the same way most towns made some provision to dispose of rubbish. A public water supply was provided, not only for the baths, but also as drinking water. Entertainment was available in theatres and amphitheatres. In fact, life in a town in Roman Britain was quite comfortable, especially if one were fairly rich.

In the countryside, the coming of the Romans had no such profound effect. The Romans had no advanced ideas on farming and so the natives continued in their old way. Some parts of the country were taken over as Imperial Estates, which meant that those who farmed the land were tenants of the Emperor. The best known feature of the countryside is the villa system. These large, comfortable houses gradually appeared as ideas of building spread from the towns. In many cases rich farmers abandoned the hut type of house and built a stone villa which was often expanded as time went on. These had a heating system, mosaic floors and painted walls as in Rome. The owners were still farmers—rich farmers—and there were outbuildings around the villas for farm purposes. Poor farmers and labourers still lived in huts which changed little with the passage of time.

This brief account has said nothing about industries, trade, religion and many other aspects of life. Those interested should see the books mentioned below.

SEE: Daily Mail Filmstrips, *The Romans in Britain;* Ordnance Survey map of Roman Britain.

G. Tingay, *From Caesar to the Saxons* (Longman); A. Birley, *Life in Roman Britain* (Batsford); J. A. Richmond, *Roman Britain* (Pelican); D. R. Dudley and G. Webster, *The Roman Conquest of Britain* (Batsford); D. R. Dudley and G. Webster, *The Rebellion of Boudicca* (Routledge).

LXI

Time, place, movement.
Accusative of measurement.

1 For expressions of time see XXXVII.

2 (a) Position *in*, *on* or *at* a place is expressed by the preposition **in** followed by the ablative case.

    in urbe = in the city: **in monte** = on the mountain.

(b) But, if the place is **domus** (home), **rus, ruris** (*n.*) (the countryside) or a town name, a special case called the 'Locative' is used with *no preposition*. The locative of *domus* is **domi** (at home), of *rus* is **ruri** (in the country).

    The locative of town names which are 1st or 2nd declension singular is the same as the genitive; in others it is the same as the ablative.

    Rome = **Roma,** at Rome = **Romae** (gen.):
    Athens = **Athenae** (pl.), at Athens = **Athenis** (abl.).

3 (a) Movement *towards* or *into* a place is **ad** (towards) or **in** (into) followed by the accusative case. Movement *away from* or *out of* is **ab** (from) or **ex** (out of) followed by the ablative case.

    in urbem = into the city: **ab agris** = from the fields.

(b) With *domus*, *rus* and the names of towns the same cases are used but the prepositions are omitted.

    domum = to home: **rus** = to the country: **Romam** = to Rome: **domo** = from home: **Roma** = from Rome.

4 Note that names of *countries* do *not* omit the prepositions.

    in Graecia, ad Britanniam, ex Italia.

5 The measurement indicating height, length, breadth, distance, etc., is put in the accusative case. Note: **pes, pedis** (m.) = a foot.

    murus *decem pedes* **altus** = a wall ten feet high.

6 For *one mile* the Romans used **mille passus** (one thousand paces). Note: **passus, -us** (4) = a pace. For more than one mile use **milia** (thousands) followed by the genitive case. **Tria milia passuum** = three thousands of paces = three miles.

EXERCISES: for numerals, see pages 204–5.

1 Tres dies moratus est. 2 Romam ex agris ibimus. 3 Fluvius decem pedes altus est. 4 Priamus Troiae regnabat. 5 Tertia hora domum veni. 6 Exercitus multa milia passuum contenderat. 7 Ab urbe rus abiit. 8 Puella domi non est. 9 Viginti diebus redibo. 10 Mons mille nongentos (MDCCCC) pedes altus est.

11 Magister unam horam locutus est, sed pueri in sedibus suis dormiebant. 12 Ruri agros videmus, in urbe vias omni genere hominum plenas. 13 A monte duo milia pedum alto in medium campum descendemus. 14 Machinis multos pedes altis urbem tandem expugnabimus. 15 Centum annis non iam vivi erimus.

JULIUS CAESAR: ROMAN LIFE: A TRUE STORY

With the career of Julius Caesar, conqueror of Pompey in the civil war and himself murdered in 44 B.C., the Roman republic comes to an end.

Caesar's heir Octavian, after his victory over Antony at Actium in 31 B.C., founds the Empire and himself becomes the first Princeps with the title 'Augustus'. In this time the city of Rome is rebuilt and the Latin language spreads over the known world.

You will also read the stories of two famous Roman women, Cornelia, who lived under the republic, and Arria, during the empire.

Julius Caesar (i)

C. Julius Caesar omnium ducum Romanorum maximus erat, qui adhuc iuvenis illam virtutem praestabat qua postea Galliam vicit novamque provinciam imperio Romano addidit.

Roma olim in Asiam discesserat, quod oratorem clarissimum Graecum audire volebat. Tum enim iuvenes Romani eloquentiam 5 a magistris Graecis discebant. Dum ad insulam Rhodum hieme navigat, a praedonibus captus est et apud eos multos dies cum paucis servis manere coactus est: reliquos enim servos abire sibique eam pecuniam ferre iusserat quam praedones poscebant. Praedonibus interea multa loquebatur et per iocum[1] 'Vos,' inquit, 'omnes 10 poena gravissima puniam, si unquam liberatus ero.' Servi tandem cum pecunia redierunt: Caesar, ubi quinquaginta talenta praedonibus dedit, liberatus est.

Nec diu moratus est. Statim classem paravit et praedones, qui iam fugiebant, secutus est. Quos ubi cepit et iam in sua potestate habuit, 15 cruciatu maximo, sicut captivus promiserat, occidit.

Paucis post annis Caesar, ubi in Hispaniam quaestor missus est,

[1] per iocum = as a joke.

statuam ibi Alexandri Magni vidit. Illo spectaculo, ut dicunt,
maxime motus est lacrimasque effudit. 'Alexander,' inquit, 'adhuc
iuvenis orbem terrarum iam vicerat, sed ego nihil magnum feci.' 20
Itaque statim Romam rediit seque ad res maiores paravit.

LXII

Julius Caesar (ii)

Victoriarum Caesaris maxima causa fuit celeritas: longissima enim
itinera brevissimo tempore saepe faciebat. Nonnunquam enim, dum
ad exercitum suum properat, iter centum milium passuum[1] uno die
fecit, nec ulli montes, ulli fluvii eum impedire poterant.

Octo fere annos contra Gallos pugnabat Caesar: totam Galliam 5
vicit imperioque Romano addidit. Post eam victoriam iam tempus

[1] The Roman mile was about 1,620 yards.

HEAD OF JULIUS CAESAR   HEAD OF AUGUSTUS

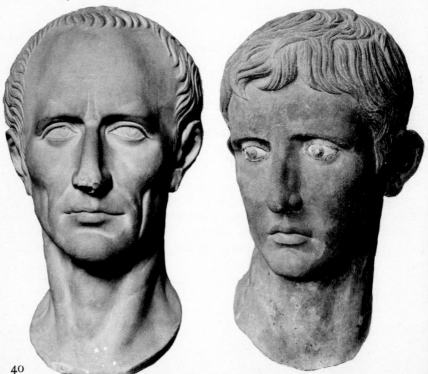

40

erat copias dimittere, sed, quod multos inimicos in urbe[1] habebat, inter quos erant Pompeius magnaque pars senatorum, sine exercitu Romam redire nolebat. Leges autem Romanorum eum copias suas trans Rubiconem fluvium, qui Galliam ab Italia dividebat, ducere 10 vetabant. Itaque, ubi ad Rubiconem venit, diu in ripa moratus est, diu de bello contra Pompeium senatumque deliberavit. Repente se ad milites suos convertit; 'Etiam nunc,' inquit, 'redire possumus: hunc si fluvium transierimus, contra patriam pugnare cogemur.' Tandem voce magna clamavit: 'Iacta alea est.[2] Ibimus, quo 15 inimici nostri nos vocant.' Sine mora cum exercitu fluvium transiit, copias inimicorum superavit, Pompeium ex Italia expulit.

Aliam victoriam, quam in Asia reportavit, tribus clarissimis verbis nuntiavit, 'Veni, vidi, vici'; quibus verbis non solum victoriam sed celeritatem suam monstrare voluit. 20

Clarum etiam est aliud Caesaris dictum. Cenabat cum amicis quibusdam, multaque inter se de multis rebus loquebantur. Forte rogavit quidam: 'Quem finem vitae optimum putas?' Cui statim Caesar, 'Inopinatum,' inquit. Postero die ipse a Bruto ceterisque coniuratis occisus est. 25

LXIII

Actium and Augustus

Post mortem Caesaris bellum civile inter M. Antonium et M. Octavianum, qui postea princeps nomine Augusti erat, gestum est; cuius belli finis proelium navale Actiacum fuit.

Multa Vergilius poeta de hoc proelio, multa de fama Augusti imperiique Romani narrat. Ambo duces ingentem navium multit- 5 udinem comparaverant. Ab altera parte in nave alta stat vir armis insignis, cuius ex facie funduntur flammae et super caput stella fulget. Hic est Augustus Caesar, qui populos Italos in pugnam ducit. Contra eum M. Antonius Aegyptum populosque Orientis ducit; quem sequitur Cleopatra Aegyptiorum regina Antoniique uxor. 10 Classis contra classem navigat, volant tela, mare sanguine fluit. Cleopatra omnes deos Aegypti contra deos Romanos—Neptunum, Venerem, Minervam—invocat. Mars pugnam regit navemque contra navem vertit. Tandem tota Aegyptia classis timore superatur fluviumque Nilum petit: ipsa regina prima e proelio fugit. 15

---

[1] *urbs* often means 'the city of Rome'.   [2] iacta alea est = the die is cast.

Inde Augustus Caesar victor urbem intravit, triumphum ad Capitolium duxit. Ante omnia templa deis sacrificabat, per omnes vias cives laeti imperatorem suum salutabant. Inter captivos, qui ordine longo ducebantur, erant gentes variae ex omni parte orbis terrarum, quas Romani a fluvio Euphrate usque ad Rhenum super- 20 averant.

Hac victoria Augustus non solum belli civilis finem fecit, sed ipse primus princeps totius imperii Romani factus est. Ii, qui post eum idem imperium acceperunt, 'imperatores' vocabantur. Per quattuor saecula a tempore Augusti totus orbis terrarum ab imperatoribus 25 Romanis regebatur.

LXIV

The City of Rome[1]

Audivistis iam, lectores, de origine Romae, de proeliis Romanorum, de claris viris. Nunc pauca de urbe ipsa, de lingua moribusque Romanorum legetis.

Urbs Roma in septem montibus aedificata est, quorum altissimus erat Capitolium. In altera parte Capitolii Arx fuit, in altera Iovis 5 Optimi Maximi templum, quo imperatores Romani triumphos ducebant.

Prope Capitolium in media urbe locum apertum etiam hodie videmus. Is erat Forum Romanorum, quo cives ad mercaturam aliasque res conveniebant. In Foro erat templum Vestae, ubi ignis 10 aeternus a Vestalibus servabatur, et Regia, Pontificis Maximi domus, in qua olim Iulius Caesar habitabat. Basilicae quoque erant, aedificia ingentia, quae magnam civium multitudinem continere poterant. Multis post annis, ubi Romani fidem Christianam acceperunt, basilicae in usum ecclesiarum versae sunt. 15

In Foro haud procul a Capitolio erat Curia, ubi Senatus conveniebat, Rostraque, unde oratores ad populum Romanum orationes habebant. Is locus 'Rostra' vocatus est, quod rostris navium ornatus est, quae bello captae erant.

Erat Romae ingens civium multitudo, quorum plurimi in magnis 20 aedificiis habitabant, quae 'insulae' vocabantur. Hae altissimae erant et ii, qui cubicula superiora habebant, magno labore ascendebant. Erat olim, ut narrat scriptor Romanus, poeta quidam miserrimus qui

[1] See Maps F and G.

42

ducentos gradus cotidie ascendebat. Magnum fuit quoque periculum ignium, quibus totae insulae saepe vastabantur. Inter insulas duce- 25 bant angustae viae, quae plenae erant civium turba omnique genere vehiculorum quorum strepitus cives nocte dormire prohibebat.

ROMAN FORUM

A   AEDES DIVI IVLII
B   AEDES CASTORVM
C · SACRA VIA
D · ROSTRA
E   CLIVOS CAPITOLINVS
F   BASILICA IVLIA
G   AEDES SATVRNI
H   AEDES CONCORDIAE
I   AEDES VESPASIANI
K   AEDES IOVIS
L   TABVLARIVM

The Latin Language

Augustus Caesar non solum urbi Romanae sed toti orbi terrarum pacem dedit. Post victoriam suam portas templi Iani clausit: hoc Romani nunquam facere solebant, nisi omnia bella finita erant paxque erat per totum imperium Romanum facta.

Erant tum intra fines unius imperii multi populi, qui omnes suas 5 linguas habebant. His omnibus Romani non solum pacem sed unam quoque linguam dederunt; quos enim bello vicerunt, eos etiam linguam Latinam discere coegerunt. Sic Galli, Hispani, Afri mox Latine et loqui et legere didicerunt; Aegyptiis, Syriis, Iudaeis ceterisque Orientis gentibus lingua quoque Graeca nota erat. Ii 10 igitur, quibus hae duae linguae erant notae, per omnes imperii Romani provincias facillime iter facere poterant.

Iudaei non solum Latina et Graeca sed Hebraica etiam lingua utebantur: ubi enim Iesus Christus in terra Iudaeorum sub Pontio Pilato cruce periit, scriptum est in cruce litteris Graecis et Latinis et 15 Hebraicis: Hic est Rex Iudaeorum.

Sed ex his tribus linguis primum locum habebat Latina, quod lingua erat Romanorum, quos poeta Vergilius 'rerum dominos gentemque togatam'[1] vocat.

Nobis quoque hodie utilissima est Latina; ii enim qui hanc 20 linguam bene cognoverunt, multo facilius linguas hodiernas, praesertim Gallicam, Italicam, Hispanam, quae originem suam ab antiqua Latina ducunt, discere possunt. Nostra quoque lingua, quam Anglicam vocamus, plurima verba habet quae a Latina ducuntur. Quotiens igitur Anglice vel legimus vel loquimur, lingua 25 Latina adhuc utimur, nec eam linguam 'mortuam' vocare possumus, quae in sermone librisque hodiernis adhuc vivit vigetque.

LXVI

Grammar: Interrogative words.
            Direct questions.

1 One way of asking a question is by means of an interrogative or 'questioning' word. Commonest of these are:

[1] lords of the world, the people of the toga.

quis? quid?	who? what?	quando?	when?
qui, quae, quod? (adj.)	what?	quomodo?	how?
quantus, -a, -um?	how large?	cur?	why?
quot? (indec.)	how many?	ubi?	where?

2 A question asked with one of these words has the same construction in Latin as in English.

> **Quis hoc fecit?** Who did this?
> **Quando venient?** When will they come?

3 The other way of asking a question is by changing the word order in English. He is coming (statement). Is he coming? (question).

4 Such questions in Latin are done in the following ways:

(**a**) If there is no negative, **-ne** is added to the first Latin word to indicate that a question is being asked.

> **Urbem-ne capient?** Will they capture the city?

(**b**) If the question is negative, the **-ne** is added to **non** and **nonne** is put first.

> **Nonne pulchra est?** Isn't she beautiful?

(**c**) **num** is used where the answer 'no' is expected.

> **Num hoc dixit?** Surely he didn't say that?
> (or) He didn't say that, did he?

(**d**) A double question is indicated by **utrum** (whether) followed by **an** (or). The *utrum* is not translated in English.

> **Utrum manebit an abibit?** (Whether) will he stay or go away?

Exercises

1 Quis hoc dixit? **2** Orationem-ne longam habuit? **3** Quot libros habes? **4** Nonne domum rediit? **5** Quando consul factus est? **6** Utrum bellum an pacem amas? **7** Ubi est frater tuus? **8** Num eos laudabitis? **9** Cur Romam ire vis? **10** Quam urbem ceperunt?

11 Utrum Romanorum puellae in ludis an domi docebantur? **12** Quanta est navis quae in portum nostrum prima hora navigavit? **13** Nonne Romani ad stellas homines mittere solebant? **14** Quomodo linguam Latinam facillime discere possum? **15** Romani-ne in urbe aestate manebant?

Roman Schools

Hodie omnes pueri puellaeque in ludis docentur; Romanorum tamen pueri aut domi a parentibus aut in ludis privatis a magistris, qui

45

saepe Graeci erant, docebantur. In ludis pueri Latine legere et scribere, etiam numerare discebant. Puellas matronae domi docebant. 5

Aestate, quod in urbe calor erat gravissimus periculumque morbi maximum, multi parentes, qui urbem relinquere poterant, in oram maritimam ad villas suas cum liberis abibant. Itaque menses Augustus et September pueris Romanis feriae erant. Maiorem partem anni pueri cotidie prima hora in ludum ibant. Gravissime a magistris 10 puniebantur, si male discebant: saepe clamoribus suis vicinos e somno excitabant.

Iuvenis Romanus, si famam sibi in re publica comparare volebat, non solum legere et scribere sed etiam orationes ad populum habere debebat. Itaque in schola grammatica litteras non solum Latinas 15 sed etiam Graecas discebat. Ibi inter multos alios scriptores Homerum, Graecorum maximum poetam, Vergiliumque, maximum Romanorum, legebat. Magister, qui eloquentiam docebat rhetorque vocabatur, maximum honorem inter Romanos habebat.

Discebant Romani etiam arithmeticam, geometriam, astronomiam; sed minus quam nos naturam ad usum suum vertere volebant. 20 Stellas quidem observabant, sed homines ad eas mittere non conabantur; rerum naturam investigabant, sed nullas machinas inveniebant, quibus nos hodie totas urbes delere possumus.

LXVII

A Good Mother

Erant inter Romanos non solum clari viri sed etiam clarae feminae.

Cornelia filia erat Scipionis Africani uxorque Sempronii Gracchi, viri propter virtutem insignis. Qui ubi mortuus est, Cornelia cum duodecim liberis relicta est. Mox Ptolemaeus, rex Aegypti, eam in matrimonium ducere reginamque facere voluit. Sed ea sola manere 5 coniugisque memoriae fidelis esse quam uxor regis fieri maluit.

Inter filios erant duo, Tiberius et Gaius, qui postea magnam sibi in re publica propter eloquentiam famam comparaverunt et ingenio suo et cura matris, quae eos maxima diligentia educaverat.

Olim femina quaedam Corneliae gemmas suas monstrabat. 10 'Nonne pulchrae sunt gemmae meae?' inquit. 'Et tuae ubi sunt? Nonne eas mihi monstrare vis?' Ad haec Cornelia nihil statim respondit sed servum abire filiosque duos vocare iussit. Qui ubi venerunt, 'Ecce,' inquit, 'gemmae meae!'

Ubi Tiberius et Gaius pro patria mortui sunt, semper de eis mater 15
cum amore sed sine lacrimis loquebatur, omnesque qui audiebant
constantiam eius laudabant, qua dolorem suum superare poterat.

Itaque Cornelia exemplum bonae matris erat; cuius ad honorem
Romani, etiam dum vivit, statuam in urbe posuerunt, in qua erat
inscriptum: Cornelia Mater Gracchorum.   20

LXVIII

A Faithful Wife

Arria uxor erat Caecinae Paeti. Unum filium habebant. Forte et
pater et filius simul morbo gravissimo aegri erant et in periculum
mortis venerant. Filius tandem mortuus est, iuvenis et pulcherrimus
et fortissimus, quem maxime amaverant parentes. Arria nihil de
morte eius patri dixit; ipsa omnia curavit, ipsa filium sepelivit. Ubi 5
pater de filio rogaverat, ea respondebat: 'Bene dormivit', 'Cibum
sumpsit'. Inde e cubiculo exibat, se dolori dabat, sola lacrimas
effundebat. Ubi satis fleverat, laeto vultu ad Paetum redibat. Sic
constantia sua vitam viri conservavit.

Postea Paetus cum aliis contra principem Claudium coniuravit et 10
a militibus ad urbem[1] ducebatur. Quo in periculo Arria virum
relinquere nolebat. Militibus 'Me quoque,' inquit, 'Romam cum
viro meo ducite.' Nolebant milites: sed Arria parvam navem
comparavit navemque secuta est, qua ferebatur Paetus.

Ubi Romam venerunt, Claudius magna ira Paetum adloquitur: 15
'Contra me imperiumque meum, homo sceleste, coniuravisti neque
supplicium tantae perfidiae vitabis. Utrum te ipsum occidere vis an
per servos meos cruciatu maximo perire? Delige celeriter: si enim
cras vivus eris, ad mortem miserrimam traheris.'

Tum Arria 'Ego,' inquit, 'cum viro meo moriar et ad mortem 20
viam facilem ipsa prima monstrabo.' Pugionem sumpsit, pectus
suum percussit. Inde ubi pugionem extraxit, viro dedit cum his
verbis: 'Paete, non dolet.'[2]

[1] See Note 1, page 41.   [2] non dolet = it's not painful.

LXIX

A True Story (i)

Quibus fabulis delectabantur Romani? Hic fabulam habetis, cui a scriptore titulus 'Vera Historia' datus est. Scriptor autem Lucianus erat, qui saeculo secundo post Christum scribebat. Sic incipit:

Olim a columnis Herculis secundo vento in Oceanum navem solvi. Cuius navigationis causa erat studium rerum novarum; 5 Oceani enim finem incolasque qui trans Oceanum habitabant invenire volebam. Itaque magnam copiam cibi, aquae, armorum in navem imposui comitesque quinquaginta mecum duxi. Diem noctemque secundo vento in conspectu terrae navigavimus; postridie prima luce augebatur ventus et mare turbabatur, nec iam vela 10 tollere poteramus. Navem igitur ventis dedimus et septuaginta novem dies tempestate iactabamur; octogesimo inde die solem iterum insulamque conspeximus; e nave egressi sumus et longo labore defessi diu in litore iacebamus. Inde triginta viros custodes navis reliqui: ego ipse cum viginti comitibus profectus sum: insulam 15 enim explorare volui.

Ubi haud procul a mari per silvam processimus, columnam vidimus, in qua Graecis litteris scriptum est: 'Huc venerunt Heracles et Bacchus.' Inde ad fluvium latum venimus qui vino fluebat: propter hoc verbis credidimus quae in columna scripta sunt: 'Huc 20 venit Bacchus.'

Postero die, ubi vinum ex fluvio sumpsimus, iterum navem solvimus et ad meridiem navigavimus. Subito coorta est tempestas ingens, quae navem magna vi ex mari in caelum sustulit. Septem dies noctesque per caelum ferebamur nec terram videre poteramus. 25

LXX

A True Story (ii)

Octavo autem die terram magnam in caelo, sicut insulam, luce magna fulgentem vidimus, in quam e nave egressi sumus. Interdiu nihil ibi videre poteramus, sed ubi nox erat multas insulas, alias maiores, alias minores, omnes igni similes haud procul conspeximus. Infra erat alia terra quae urbes, fluvios, maria, silvas, montes 5 habebat. Haec, ut putabamus, nostra Terra erat.

48

Inde ad nos appropinquabant ingentes quidam homines qui avibus vehebantur et nos secum ad regem eius terrae venire iusserunt. Ubi rex nos conspexit, 'Graecine,' inquit, 'vos estis?' Nos respondimus: 'Graeci sumus.' Tum is 'Quomodo,' inquit, 'huc per caelum ven- 10 istis?' Ubi omnia ei de itinere nostro narravimus, 'Ego,' inquit, 'olim homo fui et in Terra habitabam. Nomen mihi erat Endymion. Sed ubi dormiebam, subito huc transportatus sum huiusque terrae rex sum factus. Haec terra, ubi vos nunc estis, Luna est, quam vos in caelo vestro fulgentem videtis.' 15

Itaque in Luna paulisper mansimus, multaque et mira de incolis eius cognovimus. Oculos habent mobiles auresque ingentes. Ubi senescunt, non moriuntur sed velut fumus evanescunt. Speculum quoque habent ingens: si quis id inspicit, omnes urbes omnesque populos velut praesentes videt. In illo speculo ego tum patriam 20 parentesque meos vidi, sed illi fortasse me videre non poterant. Haec vera sunt; is qui non credit, si ipse iter faciet, ipse cognoscet.

LXXI

GRAMMAR: Prohibitions.

1 A prohibition is a negative command. It tells someone *not* to do something. In English it is introduced by 'Do not' or 'Don't'. Do not tell lies. Don't say such things.

2 Prohibitions in Latin are expressed by the imperatives of the verb **nolo** (I am unwilling). The imperatives are **noli** (sing.) and **nolite** (plural). **noli** or **nolite** are followed by the simple infinitive.
Noli hoc facere, puer = Be unwilling to do this, boy = Don't do this, boy.
Nolite fugere, milites = Be unwilling to flee, soldiers = Do not flee, soldiers.

EXERCISES

1 Nolite homines ad lunam mittere. 2 Noli in silvas errare, puella. 3 Nolite hic manere, pueri. 4 Nolite in aquam cadere, liberi. 5 Noli cladem regi nuntiare. 6 Noli milites laudare qui tam male rem gesser- unt. 7 Nolite verba magistri improbissimi audire. 8 Noli in viam currere, puer; est enim periculosissimum. 9 Noli ante primam lucem abire. 10 Cur has fabulas narras? Noli liberos terrere.

Many of the ideas that we take for granted today were either first thought of by the Greeks or developed by them. These include the principles of democracy and freedom, the dramatic arts of tragedy and comedy, systematic history, advances in medicine, and much original thinking in philosophy, science and other branches of knowledge. In a few hundred years in the small area around the Aegean Sea more varied progress was made than at any other time or place in human history.

We owe a debt also to the Romans who eagerly studied Greek thought and literature and preserved much of it for us.

The next ten passages take a quick look at some aspects of the astonishing Greek genius.

Importance of the Greek Victory over Persia

De bello, quod Graeci contra Persas gesserunt, et de victoriis, quas in illo bello reportaverunt, iam scripsimus. Nolite has res contemnere, lectores, quod antiquissimae vobis esse videntur. Multis ante saeculis certe pugnaverunt Graeci Persaeque, sed huius belli eventus etiam hodie videre possumus. Victoria enim sua Graeci libertatem suam 5 totiusque Europae conservaverunt neque tyrannis Persicis parere coacti sunt. Graecorum igitur poetae, scriptores, philosophi sine timore versus, historias, sententias et dicere et scribere poterant et horum ingenio multae artes, de quibus plura postea scribemus, inventae sunt.

10

ODYSSEUS ESCAPING FROM CYCLOPS

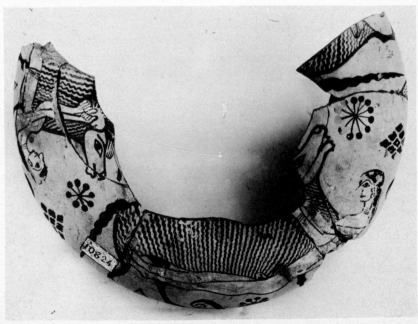

Sed Romanis quoque gratiam habere debemus, qui magno studio res Graecas discebant nobisque eas in libris suis tradiderunt. Romani enim vi et armis Graeciam ceperunt sed litteris artibusque Graecorum victores ipsi capti sunt. Pueri Romani linguam Graecam, sicut nos linguam Latinam, discebant et propter hoc Graecorum 15 opera nonnulla conservata sunt.

'Nos omnes', inquit poeta Germanus,[1] 'Graeci sumus', nam ab eis magna pars litterarum nostrarum initium capit. Nunc pauca audite quae nobis a Graecis tradita sunt. Postea Alexandri Magni historiam legetis, qui Persas superavit, oppida condidit, mores 20 scientiamque Graecorum in ultimas orbis terrarum partes tulit.

LXXII

Greek Imagination and Story-telling

Ab initio rerum Graeci, ubi in speluncis seminudi habitabant, fabulas narrabant. Primo natura eis saeva et inimica esse videbatur et frigore, tempestate, fulmine terrebantur. Hunc timorem non magicis artibus, sicut aliae gentes, sed ingenio suo superaverunt. Deos enim hominibus similes sed maiore statura fingebant: hi non 5 solum vim naturae regere sed etiam homines, qui auxilium rogabant, defendere poterant. Sic maiore spe pericula vitae obibant. Non iam fulmen vis quaedam caeca fuit, sed hoc fulmine Iuppiter deorum hominumque pater improbos puniebat. Non iam sine causa tempestates marinae oriebantur: habitabat enim in medio mari Neptunus 10 Iovis frater, qui undas et regere et excitare poterat.

De rebus minoribus eodem modo fabulae narrabantur. Si pueri in agris rorem prima luce viderunt et matri 'Quid est hoc?' dixerunt, respondit illa: 'Vultis-ne originem huius aquae scire? Venite ad me et fabulam vobis narrabo. In caelo habitat Aurora dea, quae stellas 15 fugat lucemque novam nobis cotidie fert. Erat ei filius Memnon, quem magnopere amabat. Is in bello Troiano ab Achille occisus est. Mater igitur ob filium mortuum tristis mane effundit lacrimas, quae e caelo in terram cadunt et a nobis "ros" vocantur.'

Nonne Graecis gratiam habere debemus, quod fabulas tam miras 20 nobis tradiderunt, quae a liberis omnium gentium semper libentissime leguntur?

[1] Goethe.

51

LXXIII

Homer and Epic Poetry

Has fabulas primo parentes liberis suis ex memoria tradebant sed,
ubi Graeci a Phoenicibus scribere didicerunt, poetae fabulas colligere et multis versibus libros componere inceperunt, quibus facta
deorum hominumque clarorum celebrabant.

Quorum poetarum facile princeps fuit Homerus, qui duo opera 5
egregia condidit. In altero, cuius nomen 'Ilias' est, iram Achillis et
Hectoris mortem narrat, quas res in prima huius libri parte iam
legistis; in altero, quod 'Odyssea' vocatur, pericula narrantur, quae
obiit Ulixes dum Troia domum ad insulam Ithacam redibat.

Condebat Homerus octavo ante Christum saeculo: de vita igitur 10
operibusque eius multa incerta sunt, de quibus viri doctissimi diu
disputant. Quo in loco natus est? Caecus-ne re vera fuit? Quantum[1]
poetis, qui ante se vixerunt, debebat? Sed unum in incerto non est—
Homerum poetarum primum atque clarissimum imitari possumus,
nunquam superare. 15

Ludi magister olim discipulis suis, qui magno labore linguam
Graecam Latinamque discebant, rem sapientissimam dixit: 'labore
omnia bona petuntur, sed pro hoc labore vestro praemium maximum
vobis dabitur—Homerum Vergiliumque legere poteritis!'

Si vos linguam Graecam non discitis, Homeri opera Anglice 20
reddita[2] parvo pretio emere potestis.

LXXIV

The Theatre

Ubi in theatro histriones videtis qui fabulam in scaena agunt,
rogatis fortasse, 'Qui primi fabulas ad scaenam composuerunt?' Qua
de re difficile est responsum dare sed Graeci certe inter primos
artem theatralem invenerunt.

Iuvenes olim Graecorum, qui dies festos celebrabant, saltabant et 5
carmina longa cantabant, in quibus facta deorum egregia narrabantur. Multos per annos carmina eadem eodem modo cantare
solebant, sed tandem unus e iuvenibus, 'Molestum est,' inquit

---

[1] quantum = how much?   [2] Anglice reddita = translated into English.

52

THEATRE OF DIONYSUS AT ATHENS

comitibus, 'haec carmina sic semper cantare. Melius erit, si vos primi scaenam intrabitis; ego sequar et solus rem totam narrabo. 10 Deinde vos me multa rogate, quibus ego responsa dabo. Si hoc modo inter nos carmen dividemus, fabulam non solum narrare sed etiam agere videbimur.' Ab hoc parvo initio ars theatri orta est.

Itaque saltatoribus (qui 'chorus' vocabantur) unus histrio additus est, qui cum duce chori loquebatur. Postea histrionum numerus ad 15 tres auctus est. Chorus primo duodecim, mox quindecim numero erat.

Aeschylus, Sophocles, Euripides poetarum tragicorum clarissimi fuerunt, quorum opera etiam hodie in scaena aguntur.

Romanorum nullus scriptor, qui fabulas tragicas composuit, hos 20 poetas Graecos superare poterat. Sed in Britannia, dum regnabat ibi Elizabetha prima, poeta erat, qui ingenio Graecis pari scribebat. Hic poeta nomen Latinum non habet sed vobis omnibus certe est notissimus.

NOTE: The words 'theatre', 'orchestra', 'drama', 'tragedy', comedy', 'chorus' are all of Greek origin.

LXXV

History

Graecos, qui historiam scripserunt, in duo genera dividere possumus.
Alii enim non solum facta sed etiam mores hominum, oracula deorum, multaque fabulis similiora quam historiae narrare solebant;
alii, qui incerta cum cura investigabant resque leves neglegebant,
opera composuerunt, quibus vera potius quam iucunda scribere 5
conabantur.

Primi generis exemplum est Herodotus, qui 'pater historiae'
vocatur. Scientiae avidus ad multas terras itinera fecit et ubique
incolas multa rogabat—Quae est huius moris origo? Cur sic deis
sacrificatis? Cur Aegyptus certis temporibus Nilo inundatur? 10

Ubi magnam orbis terrarum partem vidit populorumque mores,
leges, artes cognovit, eius belli historiam scripsit quod inter Persas
Graecosque gestum est quodque iam vobis breviter narratum est.

Ex altero scriptorum genere clarissimus erat Thucydides, qui de
eo bello scripsit quod Lacedaemonii cum Atheniensibus gesserunt. 15
Ipse classis Atheniensium dux fuerat sed, quod hostes urbem quan-
dam, Amphipolim nomine, capere non prohibuit, in exilium pulsus
est. In libro eius nullas fabulas, nulla oracula invenietis; sed belli
longi dolores, crudelitas in dies maior, clades gravissima, quam
Athenienses in Sicilia acceperunt, paucis verbis summaque arte 20
narrantur.

Scriptorum Romanorum maximi erant Titus Livius et Cornelius
Tacitus. Ille historiam populi Romani ab initio usque ad Augusti
principis tempora scripsit; hic nobis principum Romanorum
virtutes vitiaque ostendit. Livium cum Herodoto, Tacitum cum 25
Thucydide comparare possumus.

LXXVI

GRAMMAR: Present and Imperfect Subjunctive active and passive of
the four conjugations (see pages 192–3).
Ut in purpose and result clauses.

1 In Latin a positive purpose is indicated by **ut** (in order that)
followed by the present subjunctive (if the main verb is present,

imperative, future or perfect with 'have') or by the imperfect subjunctive (if the main verb is imperfect, pluperfect or perfect without 'have').

Veniet ut me videat (in order that he may see me).
Venerat ut me videret (in order that he might see me).

2 Sometimes a relative pronoun replaces the **ut**:
Milites missi sunt qui castra custodirent (who might guard the camp).

3 Both **1** and **2** above are usually translated by the simple infinitive in English.
Veniet ut me videat = He'll come to see me.
Venerat ut me videret = He had come to see me.
Milites missi sunt qui . . . custodirent = Soldiers were sent to guard . . .

4 If the purpose is negative, Latin always uses **ne** (lest) followed by present or imperfect subjunctive as with **ut**:
Abibit ne me videat.

5 English translates this in various ways:
He will go away lest he may see me.
  that he may not see me.
  so that he may not see me.
  to avoid seeing me.

6 A Result Clause gives the result of the statement made in the main clause. In Latin it is introduced by **ut** (that) followed by a verb in the subjunctive. The subjunctive is present if the result clause verb is present and, usually, imperfect if the result clauses verb is in past time.
Tam fortis est ut nunquam fugiat.
Tam fortiter pugnabat ut semper laudaretur.

7 *Note carefully* that this result clause subjunctive becomes indicative when translated into English.
He is so brave that he never *flees*.
He fought so bravely that he *was* always *praised*.

EXERCISES
1 Pugnant ut patriam servent.   2 Laboravit ut pecuniam compararet.
3 Hoc fecit ne puniretur.   4 Pecuniam dabimus ne puniamur.   5 Venite statim ut templa videatis.   6 Muros aedificabant ne hostes urbem

caperent.   **7** Tam pulchra est ut omnes eam ament.   **8** Tam celeriter currebat ut nemo eum capere posset.   **9** Morbus erat tam gravis ut multi perirent.   **10** Tantum est periculum ut omnes mortem timeant.

11 Roma ad Britanniam iter fecit ut amicum suum adiuvaret.   **12** Statua Minervae tam alta erat ut nautae eam facile videre possent.   **13** Noli verba magistri contemnere ne gravissime puniaris.   **14** Romani tantum exercitum habebant ut hostes in acie pugnare nollent.   **15** Servum meum rus abire iubebo ut frumentum emat.

Architecture: Phidias

Divites quidem Romani, ut postea in hoc libro legetis, domos sibi maximas pulcherrimasque aedificabant: Graeci vero domorum magnificentiam adeo contemnebant ut divitum pauperumque domus plerumque speciem similem haberent. Magnam enim diei partem Graeci foris agebant ut negotia publica privataque gererent 5 et in foro viisque cum amicis loquerentur; domum vesperi redibant ut cenam sumerent et nocte dormirent. Praeterea divitiis suis, ut templa deorum potius quam domos privatas aedificarent, uti malebant.

Urbis Athenarum arx 'Acropolis' vocabatur, in qua non solum 10 muri validissimi erant quibus cives hostium impetus sustinerent sed etiam templa egregia, quorum columnae marmoreae supra urbem

THE PARTHENON

sole fulgentes procul videbantur. Quorum longe pulcherrimum fuit Parthenon, templum Minervae Athenarum custodis; quod templum in altero latere octo, in altero septendecim columnas habebat et 15 statuis multis et egregiis ornatum est. Hoc magna multitudo fabrorum et civium et servorum per multos annos aedificabat, sed toti operi praeerat Phidias artificum Graecorum notissimus.

Idem Phidias in Acropoli statuam Minervae triginta pedes altam ex aere fecit, quam nautae, qui multa milia passuum ab urbe aber- 20 ant, facile conspicere poterant.

Sed omnium Phidiae operum clarissimum erat Iovis simulacrum, quod totum ex auro et ebore factum est et Olympiae in templo Iovis stabat. Cuius simulacri splendor erat tantus et tanta in ore dei maiestas ut omnes qui spectabant divino quodam timore move- 25 rentur.

Statuarum Phidiae nulla nobis relicta est: stat tamen adhuc in colle suo Parthenon et nocte, ubi luna plena illuminatur, gloriam urbis illius antiquae nobis reddere potest.

LXXVII

Archaeology: Schliemann

Ducentos abhinc annos is, qui aut Graecorum aut Romanorum historiam componere volebat, multos libros et antiquos et recentiores summa diligentia legebat, ut illorum temporum facta dictaque cognosceret et de rebus incertis sententiam suam dicere posset. Sed hodie non solum libris adiuvatur historiae scriptor sed etiam labore 5 eorum, qui multis in locis e terra effoderunt temporum antiquorum monumenta quae multa eis, quae in libris invenimus, addunt. Effossa sunt sepulcra, aedificia, tela, quae nos de vita moribusque antiquis multa docent; tabulae marmoreae, in quibus inscriptae sunt leges nobis antea ignotae; totae etiam urbes, quae multos annos in 10 terra sepultae erant.

Initio saeculi undevicesimi[1] in parvo Germaniae oppido puer quidam[2] de libro, quem manu tenebat, cum patre loquebatur:

'Urbs-ne Troia,' inquit, 'a Graecis re vera incensa est, pater, sicut in hoc libro legi?' 15

'Certe,' respondit pater qui dormire volebat.

'Nonne ullum eius vestigium relictum est?'

---

[1] 1829.   [2] Heinrich Schliemann.

57

'Nullum,' inquit pater iam iratus. 'Noli me plura rogare sed in libro tuo quaere responsa.'

Puer igitur tacere coactus est, sed 'Tanta urbs,' sibi inquit, 20 'evanescere non poterat. Ego, ubi vir fiam, in Asiam ibo ut Troiam effodiam.'

Exinde puer duas res facere constituit—linguam Graecam discere ut apud Homerum fabulam Troianam legeret et divitias sibi comparare ut Troiam quaerere posset. 25

Quadraginta post annis mercaturam, per quam dives factus erat, reliquit, feminam Graecam in matrimonium duxit, laeto animo cum ea profectus est ut tandem Troiam suam effoderet.

Viris quidem doctis stultus esse videbatur hic Germanus, qui in scholam grammaticam nunquam iverat et tamen situm Troiae cum 30 uxore librisque Homeri quaerebat. Sed constantia sua Homerique scientia ille Germanus omnes doctos superavit.

In planitie Troiana collem quendam delegit; ibi fossam altissimam duxit. Quo in loco non unam, sed septem urbes invenit, quae alia super aliam aetatibus variis aedificatae erant; gemmas quoque 35 pulcherrimas effodit, quas 'Helenae reginae gemmas' statim vocavit.

LXXVIII

Ancient Medicine: Hippocrates

Primo Graeci, sicut aliae gentes, artibus magicis utebantur ut omnia genera morborum depellerent. Is, qui morbo aeger erat, aut herbis sacris, quas a sacerdotibus lumine lunae colligere iussus erat, remedium quaerebat, aut carminibus precibusque deos placare conabatur quorum ira afflictus erat. Aesculapium medicinae deum 5 saepissime aegri auxilium rogabant; cuius in templo vir aeger in pelle hostiae, quam deo sacrificaverat, per noctem iacebat ut somnio remedium morbi inveniret.

Quae remedia magica Hippocrates Graecus, qui 'pater medicinae' vocatur, contempsit primusque causas morborum cum cura investi- 10 gavit. Cuius tantum erat ingenium tantaque artis medicinae scientia ut etiam hodie medici eisdem remediis, quibus[1] ille, saepe utantur. Aetatis suae medicis Hippocrates non solum remedia sed etiam leges dedit quibus artem suam exercerent—quarum legum multae a medicis hodie observantur. 'Si domum intrabo,' inquit, 'intrabo ut 15

---

[1] idem . . . qui = the same . . . as.

aegros adiuvem: si quid ibi audivero quod aeger celare vult, id aliis non dicam. Si mente pura artem exercuero, famam comparabo; si autem artis meae leges violavero, supplicio gravissimo dignus ero.'

Galenus, qui ex Asia Romam venit medicusque principis Marci Aurelii factus est, ab Hippocrate multa didicit multaque ipse arti 20 medicinae addidit. Is mortuorum corpora discindebat ut partes varias inspiceret librumque de corpore humano scriberet. Quo in libro 'Corporis membra,' inquit, 'tam bene facta sunt, ut nullo modo meliora fieri possint.'

Milites Romani, qui proelio vulnerati erant, primo in tabern- 25 aculis suis iacebant et medici legionis, ut eos curarent, cotidie tabernacula circumire debebant; postea in castris 'valetudinaria'[1] aedificata sunt in quibus omnes simul minore medicorum labore curabantur. Mox in oppidis multis imperii Romani divites pecuniam dederunt ut valetudinaria publica aedificarentur et medici periti 30 deligerentur qui civium morbos sanarent.

LXXIX

Philosophy: Socrates

'Philosophia,' ut scribit Cicero Romanorum scriptor clarissimus, 'nihil aliud est quam studium sapientiae.'

Graecorum philosophi erant viri doctissimi qui de natura rerum, de virtute, de deo multisque aliis rebus multa rogabant. Nihil erat quod non investigabant et saepe, ut cum aliis philosophis loquer- 5 entur, itinera longa faciebant. His viris levissimae esse videbantur fabulae deorum, qui in Olympo habitabant et, sicut homines, rixarum inter se potius quam virtutis avidi erant. Itaque, quod cultum deorum nonnunquam neglegebant, ab inimicis saepe accusabantur.   10

Inter philosophos notissimus erat Socrates Atheniensis, qui a Cicerone 'parens philosophiae' et oraculo Apollinis 'omnium sapientissimus' vocabatur.

Officia quidem publica non neglexit, nam magistratus apud Athenienses erat et olim in proelio vitam Alcibiadis amici sui 15 conservavit.

Studio tamen sapientiae ante omnia se dedit. In foro viisque Athenarum omnes, qui cum eo disputare volebant, praesertim eos,

---

[1] valetudinarium = sick-quarters, hospital.

qui inter cives doctissimi habebantur, adloquebatur ut sententias eorum varias cognosceret. Deinde eis, qui in sententiis errare vide- 20 bantur, errorem ostendebat; quos errores tanta arte invenire poterat ut multi, qui sibi sapientes esse videbantur, iratissimi a colloquio discederent et exinde Socrati inimici fierent.

Ab inimicis tandem accusatus est: 'Peccat Socrates,' inquiunt 'quod non eosdem deos quos urbs nostra habet iuvenesque nostros 25 corrumpit. Si tamen hoc studium suum relinquere volet, tutus ab hoc iudicio abibit: si nolet, morte punietur.'

'Ubi pro patria,' respondit Socrates, 'in acie pugnavi, a loco meo nunquam discessi, neque nunc philosophiam relinquere possum quae mihi omnium studiorum optima videtur. Deus me iussit vera 30 quaerere neque periculi timore iussum divinum neglegam.'

Capitis igitur damnatus est,[1] sed, antequam in carcerem ductus

[1] capitis damnare = to condemn to death.

SOCRATES

DEMOSTHENES

est, iudicibus haec verba egregia dixit: 'Tempus est iam hinc abire;
ego quidem ad mortem abeo, vos autem ut vitam agatis. Utrum ego
an vos ad rem meliorem abitis? Hoc nemo scire potest, nisi deus 35
ipse.'

LXXX

Oratory: Demosthenes

Ubi Demosthenes septem annos natus est, mortuus est pater, qui
fratribus suis, Demosthenis patruis, magnam pecuniae copiam
reliquit quam puero custodirent. Hanc pecuniam patrui, viri
improbi, ad usum suum vertebant ita ut, ubi Demosthenes iam
iuvenis eam poposcit, nihil paene relinqueretur. Quam ob iniuriam 5
iratus patruos furti accusavit et tandem minimum pecuniae partem
recuperavit. Sic primum causas dicere incepit.

Vox tamen eius adhuc tam tenuis erat ut orationes apud populum
habere non auderet. Quam ut clariorem validioremque faceret, ore
calculis pleno domi dicere solebat aut, ubi ad oram maritimam 10
descendit, strepitum undarum voce sua superare conabatur.

Postea, ubi propter eloquentiam famam comparavit, orationes
multas et claras in ecclesia habebat, quibus Athenienses de Philippo, Macedonum rege, admonebat. Philippus enim, Alexandri
Magni pater, regni sui opes magnopere auxerat et contra Graecos, 15
qui inter se pugnabant periculumque commune patriae neglegebant,
bellum parabat.

Tanta vi eloquentiae Philippi iniurias, stultitiam civium suorum
Demosthenes ostendit ut tandem Graeci excitarentur exercitumque
colligerent quo libertatem suam defenderent. Proelio magno, quod 20
ad Chaeroneam commissum est, fortissime pugnaverunt, sed
Philippus victoriam reportavit Graecosque imperio suo addidit.

Demosthenes tamen de patria non desperavit: primum enim ubi
Philippus, deinde ubi Alexander mortuus est, Graecos ad rebellionem
excitavit ut libertatem recuperarent; Macedonum autem copias 25
vincere non poterant.

Capitis tandem a Macedonibus damnatus est[1] orator, sed illos
hostes, quibus per totam vitam summis viribus restiterat, in extrema
vita fefellit; venenum enim sumpsit, quod in stilo suo servabat, et
sic manu sua potius quam hostium periit. 30

[1] See note to LXXIX.

LXXXI

GRAMMAR: All Participles and their simpler usages (see page 195).

1 A participle is an adjective formed from a verb and so agrees with a noun or pronoun. It can also govern an object if the verb it is formed from is transitive.

Having captured the city the soldiers rested.

Having captured is an adjective agreeing with *soldiers* and also governs the noun *city*.

2 Nearly all Latin verbs have a present participle active. This adds **-ans, -ens, -ens** or **-iens** to the present stem according to conjugation.

portans, terrens, regens, veniens.

It is declined like the adjective *ingens* (but see note, para. 2, LXXXIII).

It is translated by the verb with '-ing' added, sometimes preceded by the word 'while'.

portans = carrying (or) while carrying

3 Notice how the participle agrees with its noun or pronoun.

Milites **castra** *munientes* **vidi** = I saw soldiers fortifying camp.

Ambulans **in ripa in aquam cecidi** = While walking on the river bank I fell into the water (*ambulans* agrees with 'I').

4 Most Latin verbs have a future participle active. This changes the *m* of the fourth principal part to *-rus* and is declined like *bonus*.

amaturus, territurus, recturus, auditurus.

Deponent verbs change the *s* of the third principal part to *-rus*:

loquor, loqui, locutus.

Future participle **locuturus.**

It is translated by the words 'about to—'.

In aquam *casuri* **servati sunt** = (When) about to fall into the water they were saved.

5 Latin transitive verbs have a past participle but, except in the case of deponent verbs, this participle is *passive* in meaning. It is formed by changing the *m* of the fourth principal part to *s* and is declined like *bonus*.

62

punitus = having been punished. **visus** = having been seen. NOTE that there is no Latin for 'having punished', 'having seen' and the like.

Ab hostibus victi in urbem fugerunt = Having been defeated by the enemy they fled into the city.

6 Remember that deponent past participles are active in meaning.
mortuus = having died;   **aggressus** = having attacked; **profectus** = having set out;   **locutus** = having spoken.

7 Latin has few participles but uses them freely to replace English clauses beginning with *when, after, since*.

A duce admoniti milites fortius pugnaverunt   can mean *When* or *after* or *since* they were warned by the leader the soldiers fought more bravely.

This is better English than 'having been warned.'

8 Note the following irregularities in participle formation:

(**a**) The verbs *sum* and *possum* have no present participle. The present participle of *eo* (I go) is **iens**, genitive **euntis** = while going.

(**b**) Future participle of *morior* is **moriturus**, of *iuvo* is **iuvaturus**, of *sum* is **futurus**. *Possum* has no participles.

EXERCISE

1 In silva ambulantes feram viderunt.   2 Muros oppugnaturi constiterunt.   3 Saxis impletus murus erat validissimus.   4 Sol ortus lucem terrae dabat.   5 Puella clamoribus militum pugnantium territa est. 6 Amicum in urbem euntem (see **8(a)** above) conspexi.   7 Feras puellam devoraturas fugavi.   8 In carcerem civem accusatum duxerunt.   9 Filiae civium mortuorum lacrimas effundunt.   10 Mane profectus mox domum venit.   11 Ducem secuti victoriam reportavimus.   12 Haec dixit moriens. 13 Viro morituro (see **8(b)** above) auxilium latum est.   14 A magistratibus accusati in urbe manere nolebant.   15 Cives cineribus oppressos sepelivimus.

ROMAN MONUMENTS

Here we read of some of the most famous of the remains of Roman civilisation dating from the period of the Empire, and the historical events connected with them.

As is well known, Pompeii, owing to its being buried in A.D. 79 by an eruption of Vesuvius, and excavated in modern times, has preserved for us the lay-out of an ancient city and the details of its social life.

The Arch of Titus, besides being a fine example of a Roman triumphal arch, also commemorates the destruction of Jerusalem by Titus in A.D. 70, one of the most desperate of Roman sieges, and a decisive event in Jewish history.

The Colosseum recalls the gladiatorial shows with their story of cruelty and heroism, and finally the Arch of Constantine commemorates the emperor responsible for freeing Christianity from persecution and founding Constantinople (A.D. 330).

The Last Days of Pompeii (i)

In ora Campaniae sub monte Vesuvio praebetur hodie oculis nostris spectaculum totius Italiae maxime mirabile. Hic olim erat nota illa urbs Pompeii nomine, quae antiquis temporibus furore montis Vesuvii victa tam alte sepulta est ut mille septingentos fere annos usque ad tempora nostra ignota iaceret. 5

Qualis fuit ea clades, qua deleta est tam clara urbs? Multa de eius exitio narrata invenimus apud Plinium, scriptorem Romanum, qui eo tempore iuvenis annos duodeviginti natus in villa avunculi haud procul Pompeiis habitabat.

Anno post Christum natum septuagesimo nono mense Augusto 10 fiebant per multos dies in ora Campaniae terrae tremores. Sed nihil adhuc timebant cives. Inde die quodam hora fere septima ex monte Vesuvio nubes subito in caelum orta est, velut ingens arbor cum ramis nigris, simulque cineres lapidesque vias domosque urbis implere inceperunt. Diem secuta est nox timore plena: per tenebras 15 flammae ex monte ortae late fulgebant, tantique terrae tremores fiebant ut aedificia ex sedibus suis moverentur. Postero die hora prima adhuc nox erat civiumque, qui solem conspicere non poterant, ingens timor erat. Qui enim in domibus suis manserant, fumo sulphureo peribant; qui vero exierant, lapidibus oppressi in terram 20 cadebant. Mare praeterea tam procul a litore propter terrae tremores repulsum erat, ut navibus fugere non possent.

Tertio die, ubi lux tandem reddita est, omnia mutata erant. Urbs enim tota evanuerat sub cineribus lapidibusque alte sepulta.

LXXXII

Pompeii (ii)

Urbis sepultae usque ad aetatem nostram nihil fere praeter nomen manserat. Inde ducentos fere annos abhinc homines docti, qui

maximo scientiae studio moti monumenta temporum antiquorum
quaerebant, eum locum ubi Pompeii olim fuerant effodere inceperunt, multorumque annorum labore maximaque diligentia mag- 5
nam urbis partem, forum, vias, aedificia, templa paulatim oculis
hominum reddiderunt; quae omnia ita conservata sunt ut nos hodie
vitam Pompeianorum et privatam et publicam, sicut tum erat,
videre possimus.

Nec solum urbs nobis ostenditur sed etiam hominum multorum 10
corpora, qui aut fugientes aut intra suos muros manentes mortui
sunt; quorum infelicium erant ex viginti milibus civium duo fere
milia. Nonnunquam etiam animalia inventa sunt, praesertim canes,
qui cinere oppressi cum dominis suis sepulti sunt.

Nunc, si vultis, lectores, paulisper per vias ambulabimus. Viae sunt 15
plerumque angustae: vehiculis certe antiquo tempore locus non erat
civesque aut pedibus ibant aut a servis lecticis ferebantur. Latioribus
autem in viis et vehiculorum vestigia videmus et saxa lata, quibus
utebantur ii qui vias transire volebant. Ab utraque parte viarum
sunt tabernae, ubi cives vinum, frumentum, cibum omnesque res ad 20
vitam necessarias emere poterant. Multa etiam in muris Latine
inscripta legimus, edicta magistratuum vel poetarum versus vel
etiam puerorum iocos: quorum exemplum hic versus est, quo dominus iratus sic cives suos admonet:

Otiosis locus hic non est: discede morator.[1] 25
Alius civis isque dives amorem suum pecuniae his verbis ostendit:
Ave lucrum![2]

LXXXIII

GRAMMAR: The Ablative Absolute.

1 A participle agreeing with a noun or pronoun in the ablative case
is usually an example of the ablative absolute construction.
   Nave (abl.) **visa** (abl.), **domum rediit.**
Translate the noun or pronoun first without using *by, with, from.*
Next give the participle its usual meaning.
Finally, you may express the idea by a clause beginning with
when, after, since, because, while, as suits the sense.
   The ship having been seen, he returned home = When he had
seen the ship, *or* After seeing the ship.

[1] This is no place for slackers: on your way, lounger!   [2] Hurrah for money!

2 This construction is also found with present or future participles. (Note that the ablative singular of the present participle in the ablative absolute ends in *e*).

Xerxe regnante Persae Graeciam oppugnaverunt.

Xerxes (while) reigning, the Persians attacked Greece = While Xerxes was reigning, *or* In the reign of Xerxes, etc.

Cessuris Romanis, Caesar advenit.

The Romans (being) about to yield, Caesar arrived = When the Romans were about to yield, etc.

3 Since the verb *to be* has no present participle, this must be understood in such examples as:

Caesare duce, Romani Gallos vicerunt.

Caesar (being) leader, the Romans conquered the Gauls = Under the leadership of Caesar, etc.

4 Note that the Ablative Absolute is only used when its noun or pronoun has no grammatical connection with the main clause.

The walls having been built, the citizens were safe.

(no mention of 'walls' in the main clause)

Muris aedificatis (abl. abs.), **cives tuti erant.**

but The walls having been built saved the citizens.

('walls' now the subject of the main verb 'saved')

Muri aedificati (nom.) **cives servaverunt.**

or The walls having been built, we praised them.

('them' = 'the walls')

We praised the having-been-built walls (omit 'them')

Muros aedificatos (acc.) **laudavimus.**

EXERCISE

1 Hostibus oppressis Caesar ad castra rediit. **2** Morbo depulso frater meus cenare poterat. **3** Civibus dormientibus urbs capta est. **4** Periculo contempto milites in pugnam processerunt. **5** Romulo rege Roma urbs parva erat. **6** Fabulam scriptam amicis legit. **7** Ad urbem profecturus patrem meum vidi. **8** Magna parte urbis capta cives diutius resistere non poterant. **9** Vobis in silva sedentibus villa vestra igne deleta est. **10** Hostibus urbem intraturis portae clausae sunt. **11** Cibo sumpto melius pugnare poterimus. **12** Illas puellas prope ripam stantes vidi. **13** Regina Victoria bellum in Africa gestum est. **14** Foro illuminato amicos facile conspicere poteram. **15** Poeta versus componente, uxor eius laborare coacta est.

Pompeii (iii)

Quales domos habebant Pompeiani? Intremus et videamus!
Primum ex via vestibulum,[1] ex vestibulo atrium[1] intramus; magnum
altumque est, tectum habet ad caelum apertum, ita ut imber in
impluvium[1] in medio atrio positum descendat. Haec prima pars erat
domus Romanae; huc clientes cotidie veniebant ut dominum 5
divitem salutarent. Prope atrium erant quoque cubicula ubi familia
dormiebat.

Secunda pars domus Graeco nomine peristylium[1] vocabatur; quo
in medio hortus erat cum fonte, ubi homines iucunde ambulare vel
sedere poterant. Muri interiores pulcherrime ornati sunt, in quibus 10
Graecorum more dei deaeque Romanorum, Mars, Venus, Diana et
alii, hominesque rebus gestis clari, Aeneas Herculesque, animalia,
aves, flores, coloribus clarissimis picti sunt.

Vesperi dominus, negotiis suis in foro finitis, cum familia amicisque
triclinium[1] intrabat, ut cenam a servis paratam sumeret. In medio 15
triclinio mensa erat, ad latera mensae lecti tres, in quibus convivae
non, sicut nos, sedebant sed iacebant. Luxuriose cenabant Pompeiani divites; non tamen cibo solum delectabantur sed etiam
sermonibus hospitum, qui de rebus variis, de amicis, de pecunia, de
ludis, de re publica, etiam, si docti erant, de philosophia multas horas 20
loqui solebant.

[1] For these words see the plan on page 25 and also illustration below.

A ROMAN HOUSE

Sic divites vitam iucundam otiosamque in peristyliis suis agebant, nec subitam cladem mortemque timebant. Vita enim luxuriosa mores bonos Romanorum ita corruperat ut nec virtutem iam curarent nec deos timerent. Quis enim Romanorum Iovem, Venerem, 25 Martem non contemnebat, de quibus tot fabulas levissimas a Graecis traditas in muris suis pictas videbant?

LXXXIV

The Arch of Titus

Nunc Pompeiis relictis Romam redeamus. Ibi quoque multa monumenta videbimus ab antiquo tempore optime conservata. Haud procul a foro stat magnum aedificium: arcus triumphalis est, a senatu populoque Romano aedificatus, ut memoriam victoriae ab imperatore Tito reportatae conservaret. Quae fuit ea victoria? 5 Ipsum monumentum, si propius spectabimus, respondebit: nam in inferiore arcus parte triumphum Romanum videbimus militesque candelabrum ingens portantes, quod olim Hierosolymis a Iudaeis in Templo diligenter custodiebatur. Haec quoque verba in superiore parte monumenti inscripta legimus 10
    SENATUS . POPULUSQUE . ROMANUS
    DIVO . TITO . DIVI . VESPASIANI . F .[1]
Nunc de exitio Hierosolymorum cladibusque Iudaeorum narrabimus. Iudaei, a Cn. Pompeio sexaginta fere annis ante Christum victi, imperium Romanum nunquam patienter ferebant. Semper liberta- 15 tem petebant, semper contra Romanos coniurabant. Tandem annis fere quadraginta post Christi mortem, omnibus iam rebus paratis, bellum contra Romanos susceperunt.

Titus, principis Vespasiani filius, imperio a patre accepto, exercituque ingenti collecto, contra Iudaeos profectus est. Quo de itinere 20 multa in eo libro narrata invenimus, qui a Flavio Iosepho, ipso ex gente Iudaeorum, scriptus est. Ibant ante agmen equites, qui silvas locaque omnia explorarent, ne impetus subitus hostium fieret. Quos sequebantur fabri carrique exercitus impedimenta portantes. In medio agmine ibat dux ipse, quem milites delecti custodiebant. 25 Post eum trahebantur machinae, quibus Romani muros oppugnare solebant. Postremo quattuor legiones cum tribunis centurionibusque contendebant.

His copiis Titus ad urbem Hierosolyma appropinquabat.

[1] 'The Roman Senate and People (dedicated this arch) to the deified Titus, son of the deified Vespasian.' Roman emperors were worshipped as gods after death.

ATRIUM OF SAMNITE HOUSE AT HERCULANEUM

LXXXV

The Destruction of Jerusalem

Urbs Hierosolyma tribus muris turribusque centum pedes altis
defendebatur. Intra has munitiones erat Templum, ab Herode
Magno summa magnificentia aedificatum, cuius partem interiorem,
Deo Iudaeorum sacram, nulli nisi Iudaei unquam intrabant. Nullum
ibi erat simulacrum; Iudaeis enim nefas erat Dei simulacrum facere; 5
id quod Romanis maxime mirabile fuit, qui ipsi nullum templum
sine simulacro dei vel deae habebant, ita ut Iudaei prope soli ex
omnibus gentibus nullum deum habere viderentur.

Incipiunt statim Romani urbem vallo circumdare murosque
machinis oppugnare. Ex omni genere tormentorum saxa plurima 10
ingenti pondere in urbem mittuntur. Primo, quod hostes saxis albis

SPOILS FROM JERUSALEM

plerumque utebantur, custodes ab Iudaeis in muris positi non
solum saxa missa audire sed etiam conspicere poterant. Quo cognito Romani saxa nigra mittere inceperunt, ita ut Iudaei iam non
effugere possent multique cives sic perirent.   15

Machinarum maxima ac potentissima ab ipsis Iudaeis 'Victor'
vocabatur; cuius auxilio quindecim diebus primus murus est captus,
inde quinque post diebus secundus, totaque urbs iam vallo circum-
data erat, ita ut cives fame gravissima premerentur. Tandem ea
turris, qua maxime Templum defendebatur, est capta ipsumque   20
Templum incensum; quo tempore audiebatur mira quaedam vox
velut hominis clamantis 'Hinc discedimus'. Mox victoribus Romanis
omne aurum argentumque, omnia sacra, quae in Templo custodie-
bantur, tradita sunt, Titusque a militibus 'Imperator'[1] salutatus est.
In eo loco, ubi Templum Iudaeorum fuerat, postea collocatum est a 25
principe Hadriano templum Iovi Capitolino dedicatum, in quo
erant simulacra Iovis, Iunonis et Minervae.

Sic urbs ac Templum Iudaeorum eum finem habuerunt quem
Dominus noster discipulis suis multis ante annis praedixerat his
verbis: 'Videtis-ne haec omnia? Venient dies, quibus non relinquetur 30
saxum super saxum quod non delebitur.'

[1] Here stands for the title given to a victorious general.

70

LXXXVI

GRAMMAR: Perfect and Pluperfect Subjunctive active and passive of the four conjugations.
Indirect Commands.
Cum with the subjunctive.

1 For the perfect and pluperfect subjunctive forms see pages 192–3.

2 'Do this', 'Don't do this' are direct commands, one positive, one negative. When these become indirect, that is when they are in reported speech, they are expressed as follows in English:
He ordered me *to do this*. (Indirect form of 'Do this')
He ordered me *not to do this*. (Indirect of 'Don't do this')

3 Latin expresses an indirect command by **ut** (that) or **ne** (lest) followed by the present or imperfect subjunctive.
He orders me to do this = He orders me that I may do this = **Mihi imperat ut hoc faciam.**
He ordered me not to do this = He ordered me lest I might do this = **Mihi imperavit ne hoc facerem.**
This construction is used after such verbs as: *impero, rogo, admoneo, persuadeo, oro, moneo, hortor* to replace the English infinitive.

4 But the verbs *iubeo* (I order) and *veto* (I forbid) are followed by the infinitive in Latin as in English.
He orders me to do this = **Me hoc facere iubet.**
He ordered me not to do this = He forbade me to do this = **Me hoc facere vetuit.**

5 **cum** = *since* or *although* always has a subjunctive in Latin. This subjunctive becomes indicative in English.
cum amicus meus *sis* = since you *are* my friend.
Cum vulneratus *esset*, **se tradere tamen nolebat** = Though he *had* been wounded, still he didn't want to surrender.

6 **cum** = *when* usually has a subjunctive in Latin when the verb is past tense. This subjunctive becomes indicative in English.
cum in foro *sederem* = when I *was sitting* in the forum.
cum ad urbem *venisset* = when he *had come* (or) when he *came* to the city.

7 cum = *when* with present or future time takes indicative. Note that a future indicative is used where English uses a present to refer to future time.

Cum Romae sum, amicos meos video—When I am in Rome, I see my friends. (present time)

Cum tecum *ero*, **felix ero**—When I *am* with you, I shall be happy. (future time)

Exercises

1 Iudices rogabo ut mihi pecuniam dent. **2** Cum multas horas puellam exspectavisset, puer discessit. **3** Pueris imperavi ut mane surgerent. **4** Cum magistro placere nolis, punieris. **5** Caesarem rogavimus ne captivos interficeret. **6** Cum aurum invenietis, divites eritis. **7** Milites suos in proelium procurrere iussit. **8** Cum in ripa ambularem, in aquam cecidi. **9** Sacerdotibus imperat ut deis omnibus sacrificent. **10** Cum urbem capere non possemus, abire coacti sumus.

11 Puero imperavi ut hunc librum legere conaretur. **12** Cum mane surgo, solem orientem video. **13** Dux milites rogabit ne arma hostibus tradant. **14** Cum aeger sim, Romam tamen ibo ut amicos videam. **15** Magna clade accepta milites e castris exire vetabo. **16** Cum in pugnam procurretis, milites, pro patria fortissime pugnate. **17** Servis tuis impera ut cenam statim parent. **18** Cum e monte descendisset, homines multos in planitie sedentes conspexit. **19** Quis te rogavit ut rem tam difficilem susciperes? **20** Cum pecuniam nullam habeatis, ludos videre non potestis.

The Colosseum (i)

Haud procul ab arcu Titi ante oculos nostros surgit ingens aedificium, quod magnitudine cetera Romae antiquae monumenta facile superat. Hoc est Colosseum, quod ab ingenti simulacro principis Neronis, olim prope hunc locum posito, nomen ducit. Amphitheatrum quoque Flavium appellatur, auxilio captivorum Iudaeo- 5 rum a Vespasiano Titoque aedificatum, ut plebem ludis spectaculisque delectarent.

Medium Amphitheatri spatium, ubi spectacula dabantur, 'arena' appellabatur longisque sedum ordinibus undique cingebatur, quae quinquaginta fere milia hominum continere poterant. Imas sedes 10 habebant ludorum iudices et is magistratus qui ludos dabat, virginesque Vestales, rei publicae Romanae sacerdotes. Inter eos primo loco sedebat ipse Caesar.[1] Altius sedebant cives nobiles, senatores, feminae auro gemmisque ornatae. Summas vero sedes habebant plebs Romana, milites, servi. Undique columnae floribus ornatae 15

[1] 'Caesar' is often a general title for Roman emperors.

statuaeque deorum conspiciebantur, undique sermones varii hominum spectacula exspectantium audiebantur. Omnia plena erant voluptate, plena gaudio.

Nunc incipit spectaculum. Exeunt in arenam gladiatores armis instructi. Ante Caesarem armis positis consistunt et clamant: Ave, 20 Caesar, morituri te salutamus! Tum signo dato in pugnam procurrunt. Vir contra virum, viri contra viros pedibus vel ex equis curribusque pugnant. Si gladiator fortiter pugnaverat, praemium accipiebat; si vero populo non placuerat, spectatores, inter eos etiam feminae, imperabant ut interficeretur. Sic saepe iudicio 25 feminarum vel etiam puellarum vir fortissimus mortem obibat.

LXXXVII

The Colosseum (ii)

Dabantur quoque spectacula, quibus viri cum feris feraeque cum feris pugnabant. Ex omni orbis terrarum parte ferae Romam importabantur, ex Aegypto hippopotami, ex Germania apri, ex Africa leones, ex India elephanti. In primis spectaculis, quae in Amphitheatro nuper aedificato data sunt, ut apud scriptores Ro- 5 manos legimus, intra centum viginti dies, quibus ludi celebrabantur, duodecim milia ferarum, gladiatorum milia decem perierunt.

Non solum gladiatores sed etiam ii qui propter scelera damnati erant in arenam ducebantur ut aut gladio armati pugnarent aut inermes a feris laniarentur. Inter hos infelices erant interdum 10 Christiani, qui propter fidem suam a feris devorabantur cum ingenti spectantium furore, qui 'Christianos ad leones' clamabant.

His saevis spectaculis mores populi Romani paulatim corrumpebantur. Tandem initio quinti post Christum saeculi pugnae gladiatorum finem habuerunt. Erat tum Romae Christianus quidam, 15 nomine Telemachus, qui ad urbem ex Asia venerat. Is forte aderat in Amphitheatro, sed crudelitate spectaculi ita motus est ut eam diutius ferre non posset. Dum pugnant gladiatores, ex sede sua in arenam desiluit et inter eos, qui pugnabant, procurrit. Spectatores ira moti, plurimis lapidibus coniectis, virum fortem interfecerunt. Sed 20 Telemachus non frustra mortuus est: ex eo enim tempore nullus unquam gladiator in Amphitheatro pugnavit. Stat tamen adhuc ipsum Colosseum, testis hodie nobis et crudelitatis et virtutis humanae.

Hoc aedificium olim a Romanis urbis aeternae signum habebatur. 25
Fuit enim apud eos dictum:

> Quamdiu stabit Colosseum, stabit et Roma.
> Quando[1] cadet Colosseum, cadet et Roma.
> Quando cadet Roma, cadet et mundus.

[1] *Quando* here is for *cum* = *when*.

THE COLOSSEUM

LXXXVIII

Androcles and the Lion (i)

Dabatur olim Romae magnum spectaculum. Erant multae et saevae ferae, inter eas leo, qui ingenti corpore horrendaque voce animos populi maxime excitabat.

Cum multis aliis hominibus miserrimis, qui contra feras pugnare iussi erant, servus quidam, nomine Androcles, in arenam ductus est. 5

74

Quem cum leo procul conspexisset, primo velut attonitus constitit;
inde, ut canes domino conspecto facere solent, leniter caudam movit,
paulatim appropinquavit, servum timore paene mortuum lingua
mulcere incepit. Tandem servus, timore suo superato, cum leonem
diligenter inspexisset, subito velut amicum salutavit. Omnibus, qui 10
aderant, hac mira hominis leonisque amicitia attonitis, Caesar
Androclem ad se vocatum rogavit. 'Cur,' inquit, 'te solum ex omnibus leo non laniavit?' Deinde servus fabulam miram narravit.

'Ego,' inquit, 'olim, cum dominus meus in Africa habitaret,
crudeliter ab eo cotidie puniebar; cuius crudelitatem cum diutius 15
ferre non possem et mori potius quam sic vivere mallem, in loca
deserta fugere constitui et, cum diu locum ab aestu tutum petivissem,
tandem speluncam magnam et umbrosam inveni. Quo cum leo, uno
pede vulneratus, forte venisset, ego fera visa primo perterritus sum.
Leo autem, qui propter vulnus infirmus erat, mihi nullo modo nocuit, 20
sed, pede sublato ut vulnus monstraret, auxilium meum petere
videbatur.'

LXXXIX

Androcles and the Lion (ii)

'Ego, timore superato, spina ingenti e pede leonis extracta, vulnus
maxima diligentia curavi. Postea nos ambo in eadem spelunca tres
annos una habitabamus eisque animalibus alebamur quae leo
cotidie capiebat.

'Tandem cum hanc vitam diutius ferre non possem, leone quon- 5
dam egresso ut cibum peteret, ipse speluncam reliqui atque itinere
trium dierum facto a militibus quibusdam captus ex Africa Romam
ad dominum meum missus sum; qui statim imperavit ut in arenam
ductus feris traderer. Nunc deorum beneficio huic ipsi leoni obviam
ivi, qui gratiam mihi magnam habere videtur.' 10

Qua fabula audita, cives una voce a Caesare petiverunt ut
Androclem non solum omni poena liberaret sed etiam leonem ei
daret ut rei tam mirae memoria conservaretur. Inde Androcles
liberatus cum leone, quem secum ubique ducebat, omnibus civibus
mirantibus totam urbem, omnes domos tabernasque circumibat. 15
Multi cives pecuniam ei dabant, in leonem flores spargebant; omnes
qui obviam ibant, 'Hic est leo,' inquiunt, 'qui hospes fuit hominis;
hic est homo, qui medicus fuit leonis.'

XC

The Arch of Constantine

Est prope Colosseum arcus triumphalis a senatu ad honorem
principis Constantini aedificatus.

Tertio post Christum saeculo res publica, ab Augusto conservata
atque confirmata, multis discordiis et domesticis et externis vexata
erat, quibus tandem Constantinus finem fecit. Legionibus enim 5
Britanniae praefectus, ex urbe Eboraco cum exercitu profectus, cum
Romam contendisset, haud procul ab urbe ad pontem Milvium
adversarium suum Maxentium superavit, solusque Augustus[1] factus
rei publicae iterum pacem dedit. Qua de victoria haec fabula
narratur. 10

Dormienti ante pugnam Constantino crux in caelo visa est audi-
taque est vox 'Hoc signo vinces', simulque admonitus est ut crucis
signum scutis militum suorum inscriberet. Quo facto, victoria
reportata, Constantinus, sive re vera ipse Christianus erat sive non,

[1] The later emperors all assumed the title 'Augustus' as equivalent to 'emperor'.

ARCH OF CONSTANTINE

Christianos eis legibus liberavit, quibus deos Romanos colere adhuc 15
coacti erant.

Bello civili sic finito, Constantinus, qui rebus militaribus occupatus
raro Romae fuerat, novum imperii Romani caput petere constituit,
unde facilius contra hostes orientales proficisci posset. Quam ob
causam urbem Byzantium a Graecis ad ostium Maris Euxini con- 20
ditam delegit. Hanc urbem, in septem collibus sitam naturaque bene
munitam, foro, basilicis, balneis ornavit novoque nomine Con-
stantinopolim vel Novam Romam vocavit.

Haec urbs mores antiquos linguamque Graecam per mille fere
annos conservavit, tandem saeculo quinto decimo a Turcis capta est. 25

XCI

GRAMMAR: Active and passive Infinitives of the four conjugations
(see pages 195–6).
The Accusative and Infinitive construction.

1 The English infinitive always begins with 'to'. There are six
infinitives, three active three passive, as follows:

	Active	*Passive*
Present	to carry	to be carried
Perfect	to have carried	to have been carried
Future	to be about to carry	to be about to be carried

2 These infinitives are formed in Latin as follows:

Active

Pres.	2nd principal part	**portare (terrere, regere, audire)**
Perf.	Add -*isse* to perf. stem	**portav-isse**
Fut.	Fut. participle + *esse*	**portaturus esse**

Passive

Pres.	Note especially ending for 3rd conjugation	**portari (terreri, regi, audiri)**
Perf.	Perfect ptcple. + *esse*	**portatus esse**
Fut.	4th principal part + *iri*	**portatum iri**

3 Deponent verbs have an active form for their future infinitive.
From *sequor, sequi, secutus esse* the future infinitive is **secuturus
esse** = to be about to follow.

77

4 Only the participles used to form the future active and perfect passive Latin infinitives (*portaturus, portatus*; *secuturus, secutus* above) are declined. The other forms (*portare, portavisse, portari, portatum iri*) never change.

5 When reporting what someone said, thought, believed, etc., English uses a clause (called a Noun Clause) beginning with the conjunction *that*.

They said *that* he would save me. (Reporting the words 'He will save you')

He thought that we were coming. (Reporting the thought 'They are coming')

He believed that I had been punished. (Reporting the belief 'He has been punished' or 'he was punished')

6 This Noun Clause construction is never used in Latin. Latin omits the conjunction *that*, makes the subject of the noun clause *accusative* and the verb of the noun clause *infinitive*. Hence the Latin construction for reporting what someone said, thought, believed, is called the *Accusative and Infinitive*. (Note: English occasionally uses the Latin method. We can say 'I believe this (*acc.*) to be (*inf.*) true')

7 If we change the examples in **5** above from noun clause to accusative and infinitive, we get the following 'Latin English'.

They said him (acc.) *to be about to save* (fut. inf.) *me.*

He thought us (acc.) *to be coming* (pres. inf.).

He believed me (acc.) *to have been punished* (perf. inf. pass.)

This gives the following Latin. Note how the participles agree with the main accusative and how this main accusative comes first and the infinitive last in this construction.

Dixerunt eum me servatur*um* esse.

Putavit nos (acc.) **venire.**

Credidit me punit*um* esse.

8 When the subjects of the two clauses are the same and both are third person, *se* is used, not *eum, eam, eos*.

Caesar dixit **se** venturum esse.

Caesar said that he (Caesar) would come.

If *eum* were used for *se*, it would mean that Caesar said that he (someone else) would come.

9 The accusative and infinitive after *spero* (I hope), *promitto* (I promise), *minor* (I threaten) is usually translated by a simple infinitive.

Spero me eos visurum esse = I hope me to be about to see them = I hope to see them.

But not when the two subjects are different.

Spero te eos visurum esse = I hope you to be about to see them = I hope that you will see them.

Practise forming and translating Latin infinitives before attempting the following exercise.

EXERCISE

1 Puto hostes appropinquare.　**2** Dicit Romanos discessisse.　**3** Credit urbem captum iri.　**4** Dicunt eum dormire.　**5** Putamus te esse fortem. **6** Audio eam punitam esse.　**7** Dixit leones eum interfecturos esse. **8** Putavi matrem meam venire.　**9** Audivimus Romanos victos esse. **10** Non putavimus eos impetum facturos esse.

11 Dixi vos proficisci.　**12** Non credidi eam hostes adiuvisse.　**13** Putat eum nobis nocere.　**14** Putat se nobis nocere.　**15** Dixerunt se laudatos esse.　**16** Puella dixit se venturam esse.　**17** Minati sunt se nos interfecturos esse.　**18** Speramus nos victoriam reportaturos esse.　**19** Cur promisisti te hoc facturum esse?　**20** Androcles dixit se leonem in locis desertis vidisse.　**21** Leo credidit Androclem vulnus suum curaturum esse.　**22** Nolite sperare vos in arena mortem crudelem vitaturos esse. **23** Putant se, non vos, discipulos optimos in ludo esse.　**24** Dixit se profectum esse et paucis diebus ad castra venturum esse.　**25** Cives audiverunt Caesarem interfectum esse et Antonium orationem in foro habere.

ALEXANDER THE GREAT

Alexander became king of Macedonia in Greece at the age of twenty. When he died at the age of thirty-two he had spread his empire eastwards to India, northwards to the steppes of Russia and to Egypt in the south. The story of his success and reckless courage is exciting in itself, but Alexander also founded cities and spread Greek language and culture over a vast area.

The young king who inspired Julius Caesar and, we are told, wept because there were no more worlds to conquer, captures the imagination of all who read about him. His name is still found in magical charms and legends from Greece to the Himalayas.

Operations in Europe (336–335 B.C.)

Cum Philippus Macedonum rex, qui finitimis omnibus superatis bellum contra Persas gerere parabat, ab inimico quodam interfectus

79

esset, in regnum successit Alexander filius eius, iuvenis tum viginti annos natus. Hic statim in pericula maxima venit: gentes enim a Philippo victae sperabant se rebellione facta libertatem suam facile 5 recuperaturos esse. Alexander autem se patre dignum praebuit, nam tanta celeritate in hostium fines contendit ut nemo resistere posset et omnes sine proelio eum victorem salutarent.

Deinde Alexander concilio Graecorum convocato nuntiavit se in Asiam exercitum magnum ducturum esse ut Dario e regno expulso 10 in eius locum ipse succederet. 'Achilles olim,' inquit, 'e gente mea miles fortissimus, in Asia famam bello comparavit: cuius exemplo ego in Asiam profectus hos barbaros puniam qui, tribus incursionibus in Graeciam factis, maioribus nostris iniurias gravissimas intulerunt.' Quae cum dixisset, Graeci magno clamore sublato 15 Alexandrum belli ducem delegerunt et se copias daturos esse promiserunt.

Sed proximo anno, cum urbis Thebarum civibus falso nuntiatum esset Alexandrum in Thracia occisum esse, Thebani armis sumptis in Macedones, qui arcem Thebarum tenebant, impetum fecerunt. 20 Quo audito Alexander Thracia relicta itinere celerrimo Thebas venit. Proelio atrocissimo sex milibus Thebanorum occisis, reliqui in servitutem abducti sunt. Tum Alexander ob rebellionem iratus imperavit ut omnia urbis aedificia funditus delerentur. Unam solam domum servavisse dicitur, in qua habitaverat Pindarus poeta. 25

Quo exemplo tristissimo Graecia tandem pacata, Alexander in Asiam proficisci poterat.

XCII

The Conquest of Asia Minor (334 B.C.)

Antipatro legato cum magna parte exercitus in Macedonia relicto ut Europam defenderet, Alexander, antequam ad Asiam profectus est, bona sua omnia inter amicos divisit. Tum Perdiccas Alexandri amicus 'Omnia,' inquit, 'rex, nobis dedisti. Quid tibi ipsi reliquum est?' 'Spes,' respondit Alexander. Quo audito Perdiccas nihil 5 accipere volebat: 'Ego,' inquit, 'qui tecum ad bellum proficiscor, hanc spem tuam potius quam divitias tuas mecum ferre malo.'

Copiis suis in Asiam traiectis, Alexander ipse, cum ad litus Troianum navigavisset, primus e nave in terram desiluit. Inde ad eum locum, ubi Troia antiqua fuerat, progressus Priamo sacrificavit, 10 ut iram eius a se averteret. Deinde ad Achillis tumulum properavit;

80

HEAD OF PHILIP

in quo coronam posuit et 'Te Achillem,' inquit, 'generis mei auctorem, ad hoc bellum socium meum voco.'

Interea Persae, magno numero peditum equitumque collecto, ad flumen Granicum instructi adventum hostium exspectabant. Equites 15 Persarum in media acie collocati fluminis ripam altam et arduam defendebant. Quod ubi vidit Alexander equitibus suis imperavit ut impetu per aquam facto ripam adversam ascenderent; ipse primus in medios hostium ordines equo vectus est. Atrox ibi proelium erat. Alexandrum, quem armis insignem multi hostes petebant, servavit 20 Clitus eius amicus: Persam enim quemdam, qui regem gladio transfixurus erat, occidit. Hostium tandem equites terga verterunt: mox pedites eorum, quos a fronte phalanx, a latere equites victores aggrediebantur, multis interfectis salutem fuga petierunt.

Alexander, cum a flumine Granico in Lydiam contendisset, 25 Sardes, eius regionis caput, urbem divitem et muris validis munitam, sine proelio occupavit. Urbium maritimarum aliae ab incolis traditae, aliae vi expugnatae sunt. Initio hiemis, nonnullis legatis in Macedoniam missis qui novas copias inde ducerent, ipse Gordii hiemare constituit. 30

Persian Defeat at Issus (333 B.C.)

Alexander, antequam Gordio castra movit, Iovis templum intrat. Vehiculum ibi, quo Gordius Phrygiae rex antiquus vectus esse dicebatur, conspexit; cuius vehiculi iugum nodis tanta arte factis deligatum erat ut nemo eos solvere posset. Incolae autem eius loci dicebant eum, qui illos nodos solvisset, totius Asiae imperium 5 habiturum esse. Quibus verbis motus rex, diu vincula solvere frustra conatus, gladio tandem sumpto omnes nodos discidit et sic ostendit se eodem gladio, quo nodos solvisset, Darii regno potiturum esse.

Inde multa milia passuum progressus ad urbem Tarsum tanta celeritate venit ut Persae adventu eius subito perterriti, urbem 1 incendere frustra conati, fugerent. Aestas tum erat et Alexander longo itinere defessus in flumine Cydno, quod per mediam urbem fluebat, natare constituit. Sed aquam ingressus tam gravi morbo repente affectus est ut omnes putarent eum moriturum esse. Erat

inter medicos ex Macedonia regem secutos Philippus quidam medi- 15
cinae peritissimus, qui dixit se morbum sanare posse. Dum is remedium parat, litteras accepit Alexander in quibus scriptum est hunc
medicum a Dario auro corruptum esse. Sed Philippo adeo confidebat
ut, litteris ei datis, remedium paratum simul exhauriret. Nec vana
fuit fides: brevissimo enim tempore morbus sanatus est. 20

Darius, quingentis milibus peditum et centum milibus equitum
collectis, flumen Euphratem transgressus, ad Issum in parva
planitie cum Macedonibus proelium commisit. In exercitu Persarum
erant triginta milia Graecorum qui primum impetum Macedonum
summa virtute sustinebant; quibus proelio atrocissimo deletis, tota 25
Persarum acies terga vertit. Darius ipse et scuto et veste regia abiectis
primus e proelio fugit, salutis suae tam avidus ut Alexander, castris
hostium potitus, matrem eius et uxorem et duas filias ibi relictas
inveniret.

ALEXANDER AND DARIUS AT THE BATTLE OF ISSUS
(MOSAIC FROM POMPEII)

Capture of Tyre and Gaza (332 B.C.)

Tanta victoria reportata, Alexander in medios hostium fines statim contendere et Darium, qui exercitum novum nondum collegerat, e regno expellere poterat. Sed, quod scivit Persas nondum mari victos oram maritimam vastaturos et novas copias ad se venire prohibituros esse,[1] constituit ad meridiem iter facere ut Syriae 5 Phoeniciaeque portus omnes occuparet et ex Aegypto Persarum praesidia expelleret.

Phoeniciae urbs potentissima erat Tyrus, et navibus et muris et situ ipso egregie munita. In insula enim posita freto quingentos passus lato a continente dividebatur. Quam ut caperet, Alexander, 10 cui tum nullae naves erant, opus omnium difficillimum suscepit. Ingenti militum labore saxis et arboribus undique collectis, molem trans fretum aedificare incepit ut insulam continenti iungeret et tormentis in mole collocatis muros oppugnaret. Hoc opus impediebat et mare ventis turbatum et hostium nautae qui e navibus tela in 15 fabros mittebant; neque, cum tandem moles usque ad insulam aedificata esset, murum centum quinquaginta pedes altum ullo modo diruere poterant.

[1] *prohibeo* usually with infinitive in Latin.

HEAD OF ALEXANDER

Desperante Alexandro, advenerunt naves e Graecia et insula Cypro missae, quae Tyrios classem suam intra portum continere 20 coegerunt. Quas in naves tormentis impositis et urbe undique summa vi oppugnata, murus uno in loco deletus est. Hic Macedonum milites delecti e navibus egressi, Alexandro ipso duce,[1] in urbem impetum fecerunt. Octo milibus Tyriorum occisis, septimo mense urbs expugnata est. 25

Deinde Tyro profectus ad urbem Gazam contendit, quam defendebat Betis vir Dario fidissimus. Multos dies Persae fortiter resistebant sed tandem muris dirutis Macedones urbem intraverunt. In hoc proelio Alexander, ut solebat, inter primos pugnabat et sagitta et saxo e catapulta misso vulneratus est. 30

Gaza capta, Persae, qui in Aegypto erant, cum non iam effugere possent neque putarent Darium sibi auxilium missurum esse, Alexandro victori se tradere constituerunt.

XCV

Alexander in Egypt (331 B.C.)

Alexander, copiis Gaza motis, septimo die ad Aegyptum appropinquabat. Quem Aegyptii, qui crudeliter se atque superbe a Persis regi credebant, victorem venientem laeti salutabant; neque Persarum imperator resistere conatus est sed se suaque omnia Alexandro tradidit. 5

Aegypti reges antiqui 'Hammonis dei filii' vocabantur: Alexander igitur Memphi[2] Aegyptiorum rex creatus, adire Hammonis oraculum constituit ut a deo ipso 'filius' vocaretur. Difficillimum fuit illud iter regi comitibusque suis, qui per altam arenam sole torridam aegre progredientes et aestum et aquae inopiam vix patiebantur. 10 Cum ad oraculi sedem vastis arenis undique circumventam venissent, miro modo omnia mutata esse viderunt. Incolarum enim casae silvis tectae sunt quas alebant multi fontes. Macedonibus itinere defessis gratissimum erat in umbra arborum iacere. Tum regem adeuntem sacerdos oraculi 'filium' appellavit dixitque hoc nomen 15 Alexandro a patre Hammone dari: respondit Alexander se nomen datum accipere.

Deinde ab oraculo regressus, cum ad locum haud procul ab insula

---

[1] See LXXXIII, para. 3.   [2] 'at Memphis', the capital of the Pharaohs.

Pharo venisset, urbem novam ibi condere constituit, quam ex nomine auctoris 'Alexandriam' vocavit. Cum continentem insulae 20 mole mille passus longa iunxisset, duos portus fecit qui magnum navium numerum continere poterant. Haec urbs non solum omnium ab Alexandro conditarum urbium est notissima sed etiam hodie Aegypti portus maximus est.

Volebat Alexander in interiorem Aegypti partem usque ad Aeth- 25 iopiam iter facere, sed, cum audivisset Darium copias ingentes in Babylonia colligere, duobus legatis Aegypto praefectis et quattuor milibus militum relictis qui eam regionem defenderent, ipse in Syriam contendere properavit.

XCVI

GRAMMAR: Conditional Sentences.

1 A conditional sentence is one which says that if one thing is so, then another must be so.

If you had done this (then inevitably) you would have been punished.

2 There are six main types of conditional sentence in English. In the first three the possibility suggested by the 'if' clause is felt as a real one, in the second three the possibility is vaguer and less likely.

Real Possibility

A (i) Present time
   If you are doing this, you are doing wrong.
   (ii) Past time
   If you did this, you did wrong.
   (iii) Future time
   If you do this, you will do wrong.

Vaguer Possibility

B (i) Present time
   If you were doing this (now), you would be doing wrong.
   (ii) Past time
   If you had done this, you would have done wrong.
   (iii) Future time
   If you were to do this, you would do wrong.

86

3 In Latin the first three, A (i–iii), are as in English, except that in A (iii) the future (or future-perfect) indicative is used instead of the English present. (Note: Latin for 'I do wrong' is *pecco*(1)).

A (i) **Si hoc facis, peccas.**
   (ii) **Si hoc fecisti, peccavisti.**
   (iii) **Si hoc facies (feceris), peccabis.**

4 In types B (i–iii) Latin uses the subjunctive mood for both verbs in the sentence: in B (i) two imperfect subjunctives, in B (ii) two pluperfect subjunctives and in B (iii) two present subjunctives. Note carefully from the English for B (i–iii) in **2** above how these Latin subjunctives must be translated.

B (i) **Si hoc faceres, peccares.**
   (ii) **Si hoc fecisses, peccavisses.**
   (iii) **Si hoc facias, pecces.**

5 The Latin for 'if . . . not' is usually *nisi* (unless).
   Nisi hoc fecisses, punitus esses.
   If you had not done this, you would have been punished.

In the examples that follow decide from the Latin which type the sentence is, A (i–iii) or B (i–iii), and then translate accordingly (see **2** above).

EXERCISE

1 Si statim venies, librum tibi dabo.   **2** Si pecuniam accepisses, te culpavissem.   **3** Si hoc dicant, culpentur.   **4** Si hunc librum legit, linguam Latinam discit.   **5** Si heri advenisset, reginam vidisset.   **6** Si nunc proelium committant, vincantur.   **7** Si tu adesses, nos laeti essemus.   **8** Si impetum sustinebunt, gloriam magnam comparabunt. **9** Si in tabernaculo suo mansisset, non vulneratus esset.   **10** Si Romam iter fecerunt, Capitolium certe viderunt.   **11** Si auxilium roget, cum magnis copiis statim veniamus.   **12** Si hanc urbem capietis, nolite cives interficere.   **13** Nisi hoc statim facies, puer, magister te gravissime puniet.   **14** Si in aquam cecidisset, nemo eum servavisset.   **15** Si hoc me roges, respondere nolim.   **16** Nisi eis pecuniam monstravissemus, nos non aggressi essent.   **17** Si in Graecia nunc habitaremus, non frigore afficeremur.   **18** Si ad Indiam navigem, gemmas multas ibi inveniam.   **19** Nisi Androcles leonem antea curavisset, ab eo certe laniatus esset.   **20** Si ad Colosseum ibis, multa crudelia spectabis.   **21** Si tanta pericula non timet, honore magno dignus est.   **22** Si hos nodos solvas, Alexander, totius Asiae imperium habeas.   **23** Nisi diu in sole stetissent, non aegri fuissent.   **24** Si puellis nocere conatus es, supplicio dignus eras.   **25** Si huc adveneris, labor tuus mox finem habebit.

Veritus ne Darius in interiorem regni sui partem fugeret et Macedones in loca deserta hostes secuti cibi inopia premerentur, Alexander summa celeritate e Syria profectus non solum trans Euphratem exercitum traiecit sed etiam ad Tigrim, flumen rapidissimum, appropinquavit. Hoc quoque flumen transierunt Macedones arma 5 supra capita ferentes; quos si Persae impeditos aggressi essent, totum Graecorum exercitum delevissent.

Tum Alexandro nuntiatum est Darii uxorem[1] itinere longo defessam mortem obiisse. Quo audito rex magno dolore affectus, cum ad tabernaculum Darii matris venisset, non solum lacrimas effudit 10 sed imperavit ut captiva mortua summo honore Persarum more sepeliretur. Dum exsequiae parantur, reginae servus quidam e castris Macedonum elapsus ad Darium pervenit et mortem reginae et exsequiarum magnificentiam nuntiavit.

Inde Darius Alexandri beneficio motus decem legatos misit qui 15 pacem peterent. 'Periculosum est magnum imperium', inquiunt, 'faciliusque est vincere quam regiones victas obtinere. Darius tibi omnia, quae inter Hellespontum et Euphratem sunt, tradere vult et pro matre et filiabus milia triginta talentorum auri dat.'

Quibus auditis Parmenio 'Ego,' inquit, 'si Alexander essem, has 20 condiciones acciperem.' Cui respondit rex: 'et ego pecuniam quam gloriam habere mallem, si Parmenio essem.' Inde legatis 'Nuntiate Dario,' inquit, 'omnia, quae habeat, praemia esse belli: fortunam belli aut mihi aut ei haec praemia cras daturam esse.'

Postero die ad Gaugamelam progressus Alexander cum ingentibus 25 Persarum copiis proelium commisit. Atrox ibi pugna erat sed, cum Darius mortem timens, sicut ad Issum, currum suum in fugam vertisset, Persae maxima caede victi sunt.

Cum victor ad urbem Babylona, muris validissimis munitam processisset, principes sacerdotesque e portis egressi urbem arcemque 30 sine proelio tradiderunt.

XCVII

Susa and Persepolis (331–330 B.C.)

Paucis mensibus exercitui ad quietem datis, Alexander Susa, ubi aestate habitabant reges Persarum, progressus est; cuius urbis in arce ingentes thesauri auri argentique inventi sunt.

[1] See XCIII, last sentence.

Inde rex, quamquam hiems gravissima erat, ad urbem Persepolim procedere constituit, quo in loco audiverat se thesauros etiam 5 maiores capere posse. Hanc urbem defendebant et montes nive altissima tecti et milites, qui ab Ariobarzane post proelium ad Gaugamelam commissum collecti saltus omnes occupaverant.

Alexander, cum ad illum saltum, quem 'Portas Persicas' vocant, venisset, longius progredi non poterat: hostes enim plurima saxa in 10 viam devolvebant magnumque numerum Macedonum interfecerunt. Sed rex a captivo certior factus alteram viam per silvas ad summum iugum ducere, cum militibus delectis nocte profectus, itinere difficillimo facto, se subito supra hostes, qui saltum defendebant, ostendit. Quibus oppressis, per saltum exercitum duxit victorque Perse- 15 polim intravit.

Multas urbes divitissimas Alexander iam ante expugnaverat sed haec urbs divitiis suis omnes alias superavit. Nam ibi centum viginti milia talentorum invenit; quae ut veheret, magnam iumentorum multitudinem colligi iussit.   20

Illa nocte in regia Darii magnum erat convivium, cui intererant feminae quaedam. Ex his una, Thais nomine, admonuit Macedones ut regiam Persarum incenderent qui ipsi tot templa Graecorum incendissent. Tum convivae et verbis feminae et vino excitati, facibus manu correptis, per totam urbem cucurrerunt: Alexander 25 ipse ignem primus iecit: mox regia, cuius magna pars lignea erat, flammis consumebatur. Alii dicunt et regiam et urbem, imperii Persarum caput, funditus deletas esse, alii Alexandrum consilio mutato flammas exstingui iussisse.

XCVIII

GRAMMAR: Indirect Questions.

1 In XCI paras. **5–8**, it was explained that noun clauses beginning with the conjunction *that* are accusative and infinitive in Latin.

2 If the English noun clause begins with some word other than *that*, quite a different construction is used. Here are a few examples of such noun clauses: He asked *who I was.*

when I arrived.
why I did this.
if this was true.

Here the noun clauses begin with *who, when, why, if.*

3 These types of noun clauses are called Indirect Questions because they are the reported form of a direct question.

Direct Question	Reported Form
Where is he?	I asked *where he was.*
What did you do?	I asked *what he had done.*
How will we conquer?	I asked *how we would conquer.*

4 The verb in an indirect question (i.e. a noun clause *not* beginning with *that*) is indicative in English *but always subjunctive mood in Latin.*

He asked who I *was.*   **Rogavit quis** *essem.*

5 The tense of the subjunctive follows the tense of the English indicative, but the following important rule for the use of the four subjunctive tenses should be carefully observed.

(**a**) When the *main* verb is primary (i.e. present, future, perfect with 'have' or 'has', imperative) the subjunctive in the noun clause must be either present or perfect.

Main Verb		Subjunctive in noun clause	
He asks	**Rogat**	they are coming	**veniant**
He will ask	**Rogabit**	why	(present)
He has asked	**Rogavit**	**cur** they have come	**venerint**
Ask	**Roga**	(or) came	(perfect)

(**b**) When the main verb is historic (i.e. perfect without 'have', imperfect, pluperfect) the subjunctive in the noun clause must be either imperfect or pluperfect.

Main Verb		Subjunctive in noun clause	
He asked	**Rogavit**	they were coming	**venirent**
He was asking	**Rogabat**	why	(imperfect)
He had asked	**Rogaverat**	**cur** they had come	**venissent**
		(or) came	(pluperfect)

6 Latin has no future subjunctive, so when the indirect question refers to future time, use the future participle with the present subjunctive of the verb *to be* after a primary main verb or the imperfect subjunctive of *to be* after a historic main verb. Note that the participle, being an adjective, agrees with the subject of the noun clause.

He asks why they *will come.* **Rogat cur venturi sint.**

He asked why they *would come.* **Rogavit cur venturi essent.**
This is difficult from English into Latin, but not when translating from Latin. Merely use *will* or *would* as the tense requires.

7 The Indirect Question construction is found after many main verbs. Some of these are *rogo* (I ask), *scio* (I know), *nescio* (I don't know), *cognosco* (I learn, find out), *audio* (I hear), *nuntio* (I report).

8 Note that the questioning word in an indirect question is the same as for a direct question (see LXVI). Accordingly, *who = quis*, *what = quid*, *when = quando*, *how = quomodo*. In this construction *if* is *num*, not *si*.

He asks *if* this is true. **Rogat *num* hoc verum sit.**

but If this is true, I am glad. (Conditional clause, see XCVI). *Si* **hoc verum est, laetus sum.**

9 As in the examples above, be sure to translate these Latin subjunctives by the corresponding tense of the English indicative.

Scio quis *sit*. = I know who he *is*. (*Not* 'who he may be')

EXERCISE

1 Rogabo quid dicat.   **2** Scivit quid facerem.   **3** Nescit quis hoc fecerit.   **4** Cognoscemus quomodo hoc facturus sit.   **5** Audivi ubi urbem condidissent.   **6** Nuntiaverunt quando Caesar profecturus esset.   **7** Cognovi quid fecisset.   **8** Quomodo scis quid facturi sint?   **9** Rogat quomodo eis persuaserimus.   **10** Sciverunt cur hoc dicerem.   **11** Roga eos num longius progressuri sint.   **12** Nemo cognoscere potest cur Romam eant.   **13** Postero die nuntiatum est cur hoc factum esset.   **14** Nescivit quando novae copiae adventurae essent.   **15** Dic mihi, Caesar, quo equites miseris.   **16** Nemo scire videbatur ad quem portum navis navigaret.   **17** Audivisti-ne quis creatus sit consul?   **18** Omnes rogabant quomodo tantam victoriam reportavisset.   **19** Saepe rogaveram quando ex Africa redituri essent.   **20** Tandem cognovi quid eos huc venire prohibeat.

Death of Darius: Alexander in India (330–326 B.C.)

Interea Darius, qui in urbe Ecbatanis novum exercitum colligere conabatur, cum audivisset Alexandrum contra se profectum esse, Ecbatanis relictis, ad provinciam Bactriam iter facere coepit. Sed in itinere Bessus, eius provinciae procurator, Darium in vincula coniectum et tandem pugione transfixum prope viam morientem reliquit. 5 Quem cum Alexander invenisset, Persepolim missum in sepulcro regum Persarum summo honore sepeliri iussit.

Deinde Alexander, cum per multas terras contendisset multasque gentes bello vicisset, ad Indiam appropinquavit, quam ultimam orbis terrarum partem proximamque Oceano esse putabat. 10

Erat ibi princeps Indorum Porus nomine, qui multos viros magnumque elephantorum numerum contra Macedones duxit. Is proelio superatus dextroque humero vulneratus animo tamen invicto ex acie elephanto vehebatur. Cuius virtute motus Alexander, nuntiis missis qui principi persuaderent ut rediret, ipse obviam Poro 15 equo vectus est. 'Dic mihi,' inquit Alexander, 'quid putes me victorem in te victum statuere debere.' Respondit Porus: 'Me regem vicisti; da mihi honorem quo dignus sum.' Tum Alexander non solum aegrum curavit sed etiam in amicorum numerum accepit regnumque maius dedit quam ante tenuerat. 20

Deinde ad flumen Hyphasem progressus Alexander illas regiones explorare volebat, quae circum Gangem iacent. Sed Macedonibus multis proeliis defessis et in loca ignota ire timentibus, ut longius procederent, nullo modo persuadere poterat. Itaque invitus consilium suum omisit et, duodecim aris in ripa Hyphasis fluminis 25 aedificatis, duodecim Olympi deis sacrificavit, qui eum incolumem usque ad extremos orbis terrarum fines duxerant.

XCIX

Voyage of Nearchus: Death of Alexander (325–323 B.C.)

Alexander, cum longius progredi non posset, alia via Babylona redire constituit. Regressus igitur ad flumen Indum, secundo flumine nave vectus, ad urbem Pataliorum pervenit, qui prope ostium Indi habitabant.

Deinde Nearcho imperavit ut, classe coacta, ab India ad ostium 5 fluminis Tigridis navigaret, ut, hac via explorata, mercatores Graeci ad Indiam facilius pervenire possent. Ipse dum milites per loca deserta ducebat, primo cibi inopia, deinde fame adeo premi coeperunt ut iumenta atque etiam equos caesos edere cogerentur. Hoc in itinere plures viros amisit Alexander quam in omnibus 10 proeliis suis.

Alexandro Babylona regresso obviam venerunt legati Etruscorum et Carthaginiensium atque etiam ex urbibus Hispaniae missi ut eum salutarent qui dimidium orbis terrarum iam vicisset.

Cum Alexander consilium caperet ut Arabiam quoque imperio 15 suo adderet, morbo gravissimo affectus est. Sex diebus adeo morbus vires eius exhausit ut vix loqui posset. Interea milites multis lacrimis rogabant ut in conspectu ducis sui venire sinerentur. Quos ut rex conspexit, legatis suis 'Quomodo,' inquit, 'cum ego mortuus ero, regem invenietis talibus viris dignum?' Rogantibus cui regnum 20 relinqueret respondit: 'Ei qui est optimus, sed video magnum certamen ob eam rem parari.' Mox mortem obiit nondum triginta tres annos natus is qui ab Graecia usque ad Indiam semper victor processerat.

C

Alexander and his Empire

De vita factisque Alexandri Magni semper disputaverunt historiae scriptores. Alii dicunt eum insano gloriae caedisque studio per Asiam cucurrisse: affirmant alii Alexandrum non solum Persas superare voluisse sed etiam Europam cum Asia pace longa coniungere.

Primo certe, cum in Asiam copias suas duceret, nihil aliud volebat 5 quam Darium e regno expellere et Persas Graecis semper inimicos vi et armis diripere: sed, victoria ad Gaugamelam reportata Darioque mortuo, consilium novum capere incepit. Rex enim Persarum factus Graecos barbarosque in unam gentem contrahere constituit. Itaque oppida multa condidit, quorum incolae lingua Graeca Graecisque 10 moribus utebantur, et Macedonibus suis persuasit ut feminas Persarum in matrimonium ducerent: ipse uxorem Persicam duxit, Persicam vestem induit, provinciis imperii sui et Persas et Graecos praefecit.

Sed, Alexandro mortuo, imperium eius quadraginta annos bello 15 vastatum in tres partes tandem divisum est, quarum una Macedonia, alia Aegyptus, tertia Asia erat. Secundo ante Christum saeculo Romani, Carthaginiensibis victis, ad orientem se verterunt: mox Graeciam totam et Aegyptum et magnam Asiae partem imperio suo addiderunt. 20

Alexander vivus velut deus colebatur et victoriis consiliisque suis effecit ut[1] Graecorum litterae artesque usque ad ultimos Seres pervenirent et libri sacri fidei nostrae lingua Graeca scriberentur.

[1] 'he brought it about that'.

CI

ST. PAUL'S JOURNEY TO ROME

Of all the journeys of St. Paul recorded in the *Acts of the Apostles*, the most absorbing is his final voyage to Rome about A.D. 60 to face his trial before Nero. Written by St. Paul's friend and companion St. Luke, who accompanied him at least on part of the voyage, it not only gives us a vivid idea of Roman government in the provinces, but is also a first-hand account of ancient travel by land and sea. Above all, for the Christian, it records the devotion of a great missionary of the Faith and the obstacles he had to overcome from Jews and pagans alike.

Arrest at Jerusalem

Aestas erat anni quinquagesimi octavi post Christum natum. Hierosolymis Templum plenum erat multitudine Iudaeorum, qui ex omni parte orbis terrarum huc convenerant ut Deum colerent—inter eos vir quidam nomine Paulus.

Fit subito tumultus magnus; concurrit turba hominum, qui Paulo 5 comprehenso conclamant: 'Hic est vir qui homines contra populum et Legem Iudaeorum docet.' Quibus auditis, tota urbe commota, cum plures Iudaei concurrissent, Paulum e Templo traxerunt portisque clausis eum interficere conati sunt.

Erat tum in turre Antonia, quae vicina Templo erat, praesidium 10 Romanum, cui praefectus erat tribunus militum, nomine Claudius Lysias; qui, certior factus totam urbem commotam esse, statim cum militibus centurionibusque ad Templum descendit. Iudaei, Romanis visis, Paulum liberaverunt et tribunus, cum appropinquavisset, eum comprehensum duobus vinculis deligari iussit. Inde captivum 15 rogavit quis esset et quid fecisset, sed, cum propter clamores Iudaeorum nihil audiri posset, eum in turrem duci iussit. Milites, cum ad gradus qui ad turrem ducebant venissent, Paulum propter iram populi manibus portare coacti sunt. Sequebantur enim Iudaei clamantes: 'Interfice eum.' 20

Tum Paulus tribuno Graeca lingua 'Licet-ne mihi,' inquit, 'tibi aliquid dicere?' Et ille 'Graece-ne loqui,' inquit, 'scis? Nonne es Aegyptius ille, qui nuper cum quattuor milibus sceleratorum hominum tumultum fecit?' Cui Paulus: 'Ego vir sum Iudaeus, in urbe Tarso natus, haud ignotae urbis civis. Oro te ut mihi liceat apud 25 populum orationem habere.'

Inde Paulus, cum in gradibus constitisset, silentio facto, populum lingua Hebraica adlocutus est.

CII

'I am a Roman Citizen'

Paulus igitur 'Iudaei,' inquit, 'audite me. Ego Iudaeus sum, in Lege Iudaeorum educatus. Olim Christianos, quos Dei inimicos esse putabam, persequebar; viros feminasque in vincula coniectos ad mortem tradebam. Forte Damascum iter faciebam, a Iudaeis iussus omnes Christianos ibi habitantes Hierosolyma reducere: cum haud 5 procul ab urbe essem, subito e caelo lux ingens circum me effulsit. Ego in terram concidi vocemque audivi dicentem: "Saule,[1] Saule, cur me persequeris?" Ego respondi: "Quis es, Domine?" Et ille mihi: "Ego sum Iesus quem tu persequeris." Ego "Quid," inquam, "faciam, Domine?" Et mihi Dominus: "Surge, contende Damascum; 10 ibi cognosces quid tu facere debeas." Et ego illa luce clarissima caecus a comitibus meis manu ductus, Damascum veni.'

Cum Paulus, his et multis aliis dictis, narravisset quomodo verbis Domini paruisset et ipse Christianus factus esset, Iudaei tumultu iterum facto conclamaverunt ut interficeretur. Inde tribunus eum 15 in turrem reduci et verberari iussit, ut cognosceret quam ob causam Iudaei sic contra eum clamarent.

Sed Paulus centurioni, qui eum verberare parabat, 'Num vobis,' inquit, 'licet virum Romanum atque innocentem verberare?' Quo audito centurio, cum ad tribunum venisset, 'Scis-ne,' inquit, 'quid 20 facias? Hic enim vir se Romanum esse dicit.' Tum tribunus Paulo 'Dic mihi,' inquit; 'tu-ne Romanus es?' Cui Paulus respondit: 'Romanus ego natus sum civis.' Tum tribunus, cum cognovisset eum civem Romanum esse, timore affectus est quod eum deligaverat.

CIII

Paul is sent to the Roman Governor

Postero die Paulus iterum a tribuno ad Iudaeos productus eodemque clamore acceptus iterum in turrem reductus est. Ea autem nocte Dominus ei apparuit et 'Bono,' inquit, 'animo es;[2] testis fuisti mihi Hierosolymis, mox testis eris mihi Romae.'

---

[1] His name was 'Saul' before his conversion.
[2] 'Be of good courage'.

Interim Iudaeorum quidam, numero quadraginta viri, consilium 5
ceperunt Paulum interficere. De quo consilio tribunus certior factus,
duobus centurionibus ad se vocatis, 'Parate,' inquit, 'ducentos
milites, septuaginta equites, ducentos expeditos, ut tertia noctis
vigilia Caesaream iter faciant. Et equos[1] parate, quibus Paulus ad
Felicem, provinciae Iudaeae procuratorem, tutus ducatur.' Scripsit 10
quoque epistolam hanc:

Claudius Lysias optimo procuratori salutem.[2]

Hunc virum a Iudaeis captum ac paene ab eis interfectum ego
militibus missis e periculo conservavi, certior factus eum esse
Romanum. Cum scire vellem quam ob causam Iudaei eum accus- 15
arent, eum ad eos produxi: cognovi eum ob Legem Iudaeorum viol-
atam ab eis accusari, sed nihil morte vel vinculis dignum fecisse.
Nunc certior factus Iudaeos contra eum coniuravisse, statim ad te
eum misi Iudaeisque imperavi ut apud te eum accusent. Vale.

Milites igitur Paulum usque ad urbem Antipatrida nocte duxerunt 20
posteroque die, equitibus eum Caesaream ducere iussis, ipsi ad
turrem Antoniam redierunt.

CIV

Paul appeals to the Roman Emperor

Equites cum Caesaream pervenissent epistolam Paulumque procuratori Felici tradiderunt. Is epistola lecta cum Paulum rogavisset
ex qua provincia esset et cognovisset eum ex Cilicia esse 'Audiam
te,' inquit, 'cum Iudaei huc venerint.' Inde eum in regia Herodis
custodiri iussit. 5

Quinque post diebus Iudaei pervenerunt ut Paulum apud Felicem
accusarent. Quos cum Felix audivisset nec ullam culpam in Paulo
invenire posset, eum centurioni in custodiam tradidit. Inde saepe
cum Paulo locutus est, sed, quod sperabat se pecuniam ab eo
accepturum esse, nec damnavit eum nec liberavit, sed diu in custodia 10
tenebat.

Duobus post annis Felix ex Iudaea Romam revocatus est, eiusque
in locum novus procurator, nomine Porcius Festus, successit; qui
cum Caesaream pervenisset, Paulum vocatum iterum se contra
Iudaeos defendere iussit. Tandem cum Paulus affirmaret se nihil 15

---

[1] i.e. relays of horses for the long journey.
[2] Supply *dat* and translate 'sends greetings'.

contra Legem Iudaeorum, nihil contra Caesarem fecisse, Festus, quod Iudaeis placere volebat, Paulo 'Vis-ne,' inquit, 'Hierosolyma redire ibique apud me causam dicere?'

Cui Paulus: 'Iudaeis non nocui, id quod tu bene scis. Si dignus morte sum, poenam libenter accipio; si vero sum innocens, nemo 20 me Iudaeis tradere potest. Caesarem appello.' Tum Festus respondit 'Caesarem appellavisti; ad Caesarem ibis.'

CV

Paul sets out by Ship for Rome

NOTE: the first person plural is often used because the story is being told by St. Paul's travelling companion, St. Luke.

Cum autem tempus Paulo esset in Italiam navigare, centurioni, Iulio nomine, cum aliis captivis traditus est, nosque omnes navem conscendimus, quae ad provinciam Asiam navigatura erat. Mox e portu Caesarea profecti, postero die Sidonem pervenimus. Ibi centurio se tam benignum praebuit ut Paulum ad amicos ire et se 5 reficere sineret. Inde Sidone profecti, ventos adversos nacti, primo ad Cyprum, inde ad Myram, Lyciae portum, cursum tenuimus.

ROMAN SHIPS

Ibi centurio, cum aliam navem[1] invenisset, quae ab Alexandria in Italiam navigabat, nos eam conscendere iussit. Cum multos dies inde navigavissemus, ad Cretam appropinquavimus et ad locum eius 10 insulae pervenimus, qui Boni Portus[2] vocabatur.

Auctumnus iam erat, quo tempore anni periculosum est navigare; Paulus igitur comites suos his verbis admonuit: 'Viri,' inquit, 'video navigationem nostram non solum navi nostrae sed etiam nobis ipsis periculosissimam futuram esse.' Sed centurio, qui gubernatori 15 magistroque navis potius quam Paulo credere malebat, cum in hoc portu tam parvo hiemare nollet, statim inde navigare constituit et ad Phoenicem pervenire conari ut ibi hiemaremus. Hic portus in ea parte Cretae erat, quae ad Africam spectabat.

CVI

GRAMMAR: Predicative Dative.

1 Certain Latin nouns are found in the dative case expressing the Object for Which or the Effect for Which. Among these nouns are *praesidium* (protection), *auxilium* (help), *subsidium* (support), *salus* (safety), *usus* (use), *donum* (gift).
This dative is found mostly with the verbs *esse* (to be), *relinquere* (to leave), *mittere* (to send) and *dare* (to give).

2 These datives are literally translated by the preposition *as*, but this literal translation must usually be changed to give better English.
Legionem castris praesidio reliquit = He left a legion as a protection for the camp = to defend the camp.
Equites Labieno auxilio misit = He sent cavalry as a help to Labienus = to help Labienus.
Hoc mihi saluti erat = This was as a safety to me = This proved my safety.

3 An adjective is seldom used with this dative. When one is used it is nearly always *magnus*.
Hoc mihi magno usui erit = This will be as a great use to me = This will be very useful to me.

---

[1] Probably a ship on the grain run from Egypt to Italy. See page 32 and illustration on page 97.
[2] Translate: 'Fair Havens'.

98

1 Hoc contra morbos magno remedio fuit. 2 Hoc candelabrum pulcherrimum mihi dono datum est. 3 Dixit disciplinam usui esse civitati. 4 Si nuntium ad Caesarem mittes, hoc omnibus civibus saluti erit. 5 Caesarem rogavimus ut Labienus auxilio nobis mitteretur. 6 Servus fidelis domino suo auxilio est. 7 Virtus ducis magno exemplo militibus fuit. 8 Una cohors equitibus subsidio missa est. 9 Quid patri nostro dono dabimus? 10 Labienum cum equitibus praesidio urbi captae reliquit.

A Storm at Sea

Tum ubi Notus nobis leniter adflare coepit, nautae, qui omnia nunc sibi secunda esse putabant, cum navem solvissent, prope oram Cretae navigare coeperunt.

Mox autem ventus nomine Euraquilo a Creta subito ortus navem nostram corripuit, nosque, quod adversus tempestatem navigare non 5 poteramus, nave vento data, per undas ferebamur. Inde cum ad insulam parvam, Claudae nomine, vento delati essemus, veriti ne in Syrtim deferremur, nautae vela demiserunt.

Postero die cum tempestate ingenti iactaremur, nautae navem leviorem facere coeperunt, tertioque die nos quoque ipsi manibus 10 nostris armamenta navis in mare proiecimus.

Cum autem complures iam dies nec sol nec stellae viderentur nec minor fieret tempestas famesque praeterea magna esset, iam omnem spem salutis amittere coepimus. Tum Paulus, cum in mediis omnibus constitisset, 'Viri,' inquit, 'si me audivissetis, a Creta navem non 15 solvissetis neque in hoc tantum periculum venissetis. Nunc vero vos admoneo ut bono animo sitis; nemo enim e vobis, sed sola navis delebitur. Apparuit enim mihi hac nocte angelus Domini cuius minister sum ac dixit: "Noli timere, Paule; tu certe ante Caesarem stabis. Ecce, Deus tibi vitam omnium eorum dedit, qui tecum navi- 20 gant." Bono igitur animo este, viri. Ego enim credo id futurum esse quod mihi a Deo dictum sit.'

CVII

Land is sighted

Sic per mare tempestate ferebamur. Tandem cum nox quarta decima adesset, media fere nocte nautae, quod altitudinem maris minorem fieri sentiebant, nos ad aliquam terram appropinquare putabant, veritique ne in saxa deferrentur, quattuor ancoris de puppe in mare iactis, diem exspectabant. Complures autem e nautis, cum e nave 5 effugere constituissent, lintrem in mare demittere coeperunt. Tum Paulus centurioni militibusque 'Nisi hi viri,' inquit, 'in nave manebunt, vos incolumes esse non poteritis.' Inde nautae verbis Pauli moti consilium suum omiserunt.

Dum omnes sic diem exspectant, admonuit Paulus omnes ut cibum 10 ederent. 'Vos,' inquit, 'dies iam quattuordecim exspectatis nec cibum ullum sumitis. Suadeo igitur vobis ut aliquid edatis: hoc enim nobis saluti erit.' Quibus dictis, pane manu sumpto in conspectu omnium Deo gratias egit coepitque edere; quod ceteri et ipsi libenter fecerunt. Erant in nave ducenti septuaginta sex homines: qui cum omnes 15 Pauli exemplo satis cibi sumpsissent, frumentum reliquum in mare proiecerunt ut navem leviorem facerent.

Prima autem luce nautae, terra visa, nesciebant quidem quae esset ea terra, sed litus conspiciebant, in quod sperabant se navem impellere posse.

20

CVIII

The Landing on Malta

Itaque ancoris praecisis, velo sublato ventisque dato, ad terram appropinquare coeperunt tandemque navem in litus impulerunt. Et prora quidem in litore immota manebat, puppis vero vi undarum afflictabatur.

Militum autem consilium fuit captivos interficere, ne quis ex eis 5 se in mare coniceret atque effugeret. Sed centurio, cum Paulum conservare vellet, eos hoc facere prohibuit. Inde eos qui natare poterant primos in mare desilire atque ad litus evadere iussit, reliquos autem fragmentis navis se sustinentes sequi. Sic omnes incolumes in litus evasimus.

10

Quo cum venissemus, cognovimus nomen insulae Melitam esse; cuius incolae nos libenter acceperunt, ignemque fecerunt ut tuti contra imbres frigusque essemus.

Cum autem Paulus lignum collectum in ignem coniecisset, subito serpens, quae propter calorem exierat, manum eius corripuit; quod 15 cum barbari conspexissent, inter se dicebant: 'Certe hic homo scelestus quidam est, qui e mari conservatus tamen poenam effugere non potuit.' Sed Paulus, serpente in ignem excussa, nihil mali passus est. At illi, cum is non statim mortuus concidisset, id quod se visuros esse speraverant, sententia mutata, dicebant eum esse deum. 20

CIX

From Malta to Rome

Princeps autem Melitae Publius quidam erat, qui agros multos in ea insula habebat. Is nos domum suam invitatos tres dies benigne curavit. Tum forte Publii pater aeger iacebat; ad quem Paulus cum intravisset Deoque precatus manus ei imposuisset, morbum sanavit. Quo audito ceteri quoque incolae, qui variis morbis aegri erant, cum 5 ad Paulum venissent, sanati sunt. Nos igitur in magno honore habebant, resque, quae nobis ad iter nostrum necessariae erant, praebuerunt.

Tribus autem post mensibus navem Alexandrinam conscendimus, quae in insula Melita hiemaverat, cuius insigne erat Castor et 10 Pollux[1]. Profecti igitur cum Syracusas venissemus, ibi tres dies morati, Rhegium pervenimus. Postero die Notum secundum nacti duobus diebus venimus Puteolos, Ibi cum fratres[2] invenissemus, invitati sumus ut apud eos septem dies maneremus. Inde Romam profecti sumus: tum fratres, qui Romae habitabant, cum de nobis 15 audivissent, obviam nobis usque ad Appii Forum et Tres Tabernas venerunt. Quibus visis Paulus gratias Deo egit bonoque animo erat.

Haec sunt quae de itinere Pauli narrat nobis comes eius Lucas. Nunc ipsi eum iter suum finientem Romamque appropinquantem sequamur. 20

CX

Paul in Rome

Illa via, qua nunc Paulus cum comitibus suis Romam contendit, Via Appia est, maxima et clarissima omnium viarum, quibus omnes Italiae regiones provinciaeque longinquae imperii Romani cum ipsa urbe coniunctae sunt. Plena est viatoribus omnis generis, qui

---

[1] Twin deities, the patron gods of ancient sailors.
[2] 'brethren', fellow Christians.

ROADS AND TRAVELLERS

ad urbem vel ex urbe properant, consules, praetores, legati, legiones, 5
equitum turmae, cives Romani, qui vel lecticis vel raedis in villas
suas in ora Campaniae aedificatas vehuntur. Inter talem turbam
Paulus, Iudaeus ignotus, cum paucis comitibus ad finem itineris sui
appropinquat: absunt enim Tres Tabernae ab urbe triginta tria fere
milia passuum.   1

Ab utraque parte viae conspiciuntur primum domus hortique,
inde propius urbem sepulcra civium, quae more antiquo extra
moenia urbis aedificata sunt. Iam viatores nostri ad portam Capenam
recto itinere procedunt urbemque ipsam intrant; mox Via Sacra eos
ad Forum Capitoliumque ducit. A sinistra parte Viae Sacrae in 1
Monte Palatino Palatium est Neronis Caesaris.

Nunc centurio Iulius, officio suo perfecto, captivum suum Praefecto
Praetorio,[1] qui tum legionibus Caesaris in urbe praeerat, tradere
properavit. Cum Paulus diu Romae mansisset nec Iudaei ad urbem
venissent ut eum accusarent, a custodia liberatus multa alia itinera 2
fecit, sed tandem iterum apud eundem Neronem Caesarem accusatus
mortem pro fide sua obiit. Ipse de fine vitae suae, quem tum exspec-
tabat, ad amicum suum Timotheum haec verba scribit:
Bonum certamen certavi, cursum consummavi, fidem servavi.[2]

[1] 'The Prefect of the Praetorian Guard', the commander of the legions kept at
Rome under the Emperor's personal control.
[2] 'I have fought the good fight, I have finished the course, I have kept the faith.'

CXI

Grammar: Gerund and Gerundive.

1 A gerund is a verbal noun which names the action of the verb. In English this is formed by adding *-ing*.

2 The Latin gerund is formed by changing the *s* of the present participle to *-dum*. It is declined like *bellum*.

regens—regendum: audiens—audiendum

3 The gerund is not used in Latin as subject or as direct object of a verb. In such cases Latin uses the infinitive as a neuter noun.
Learning (gerund subject) is difficult.
Discere (infinitive) **est difficile** (neuter adjective).
I like swimming (gerund direct object).
Amo natare (infinitive).

4 Latin uses the gerund in the accusative case after a preposition and in the genitive, dative or ablative case.
natus ad regendum = born for ruling.
ars regendi = the art of ruling.
regendo dives factus est = he became rich by ruling.

5 It is most frequently found after *ad* = 'for (the purpose of)' or with *causa* = 'for the sake of'. *Causa* takes the genitive case and is placed after the noun it governs.
tempus idoneum ad pugnandum = a time suitable for fighting.
Dormiendi causa huc veni = I came here for the sake of sleeping (i.e. to sleep).

6 The gerundive, which is not found in English, is a passive adjective formed from a verb by changing the *s* of the present participle to *-dus*. It is declined like *bonus*. It means 'requiring to be —ed', '(something) that must be —ed'.
servans—servandus, -a, -um = requiring to be saved
custodiens—custodiendus, -a, -um = requiring to be guarded

7 One of the main uses of the gerundive is to replace the gerund in expressions with *ad* and *causa* where the gerund has an object. *Ad*

and *causa* are made to govern this object and the gerundive is made to agree with the object.

ad servandum (gerund accusative) **muros** (accusative governed by the gerund)
for the purpose of saving the walls
becomes
ad muros (accusative governed by *ad*) **servandos** (gerundive agreeing with *muros*)
for the purpose of the walls requiring to be saved.
Similarly
urbem (accusative governed by gerund) **servandi** (gerund genitive governed by *causa*) **causa**
for the sake of saving the city
becomes
urbis (genitive governed by *causa*) **servandae** (gerundive agreeing with *urbis*) **causa**
for the sake of the city requiring to be saved.
It cannot be definitely stated that **ad servandum muros** and **urbem servandi causa** are incorrect but such usages are rare in good Latin prose and should be avoided.

8 Note: The paragraphs above are difficult. For translation purposes the following simple rule should be learned and followed:
When gerunds or gerundives are accusative after a preposition, genitive, dative or ablative, they are always translated by the English verb in *-ing*.

ad muros aedific*andos* = for (the purpose of) build*ing* walls
amor lege*ndi* = love of read*ing*
libris lege*ndis* = by read*ing* books

EXERCISES

1 Natando ad alteram ripam pervenit. 2 Parendo legibus famam comparavit. 3 Studio pugnandi Romani clari facti sunt. 4 Ars imperandi non facile discitur. 5 In urbem currendo patrem tuum videbis. 6 Hic puer magnum amorem dormiendi habet.

7 Ad bene vivendum vita est brevissima. 8 Amicis placendi causa hoc fecit. 9 Ad mane redeundum (from 'redeo') mane profectus est. 10 Hoc discendi causa multam pecuniam dedit. 11 Puto eum ad regendum natum esse. 12 Dicit se dormiendi causa cubiculo uti.

13 Legati pacis petendae causa missi sunt. 14 Dicit hostes ad urbem expugnandam venire. 15 Rei publicae servandae causa Senatus hoc fecit. 16 Ad impetus sustinendos hoc usui erit. 17 Ad copias instruendas Labienum misit. 18 Supplicii vitandi causa ex urbe fugit.

We are told in the *Gallic War*, written by Caesar himself, that he went to Britain because the Britons had helped the Gauls in their wars against him, and also to explore the island and learn what he could of its people. We cannot be sure whether he intended to establish a permanent Roman settlement. If that was his intention, he did not succeed. The invasions had no permanent result and, after them, our early ancestors were left unmolested by the Romans for nearly a hundred years.

The invasion of 55 B.C. was merely a reconnaissance in force; that of 54 B.C. was on a much larger scale, and during it Roman troops advanced across the River Thames into Middlesex, Hertfordshire and Essex and stormed Cassivellaunus' capital, about five miles from the modern St. Albans.

FIRST INVASION 55 B.C.

Reasons for the Invasion: Preparations

Exigua parte aestatis reliqua Caesar tamen in Britanniam proficisci constituit, quod in omnibus fere Gallicis bellis hostibus nostris inde auxilia missa esse sciebat et, si tempus anni ad bellum gerendum deficeret, tamen magno sibi usui fore[1] arbitrabatur, si modo insulam 5 adisset et genus hominum perspexisset et portus cognovisset; quae omnia fere Gallis erant incognita. Nemo enim praeter mercatores Britanniam adiit, neque eis ipsis quicquam praeter oram maritimam atque eas regiones quae sunt contra Galliam notum est. Itaque vocatis ad se undique mercatoribus, neque quanta esset insulae 10 magnitudo, neque quae aut quantae nationes incolerent, neque quibus moribus uterentur, cognoscere poterat.

Ad haec cognoscenda C. Volusenum cum navi longa mittit. Huic imperat ut exploratis omnibus rebus ad se quam primum redeat. Ipse cum omnibus copiis in Morinos proficiscitur, quod inde erat 15 brevissimus in Britanniam traiectus. Huc naves undique ex finitimis regionibus et classem quam superiore aestate aedificaverat iubet convenire. Interim, consilio eius cognito et per mercatores lato ad Britannos, a compluribus insulae civitatibus ad eum legati veniunt qui dicant se velle et obsides dare et imperio populi Romani 20 parere. Quibus auditis, hortatus ut in ea sententia manerent, eos domum mittit.

---

[1] *fore* = another form of future infinitive of *to be*.

CXII

GRAMMAR: Gerundives of Obligation.

1 A gerundive agreeing with a noun or pronoun in the nominative case or agreeing with the main accusative in the accusative and infinitive construction is translated by *must be, should be, has to be, ought to be.*

> **Urbs delenda est** = The city is requiring to be destroyed = The city must be destroyed.
> **Dixit pueros puniendos esse** = He said the boys to be requiring to be punished = He said that the boys ought to be punished.

2 In this construction the person who must do the thing is put in the dative case, instead of the usual *ab* with the ablative.

> **Dixit hoc** *mihi* **faciendum esse** = He said this to be requiring to be done *by me* = He said that I must do this.

3 When the verb is intransitive or governs the dative case, this gerundive is neuter singular agreeing with the pronoun *it*.

> **Nobis proficiscendum est** = It is requiring to be set out by us = We must set out.
> **Legibus parendum est** = It is requiring to be obeyed to the laws = The laws must be obeyed.

EXERCISES

1 Pecunia statim invenienda est.   2 Impetus hostium sustinendus est.
3 Captivi in carcerem trahendi erant.   4 Pax petenda erit.   5 Dixit castra munienda esse.   6 Puto liberos non terrendos esse.

7 Castra nobis statim ponenda sunt.   8 Domus mihi mox aedificanda erit.
9 Epistola ei heri scribenda erat.   10 Dux Gallis deligendus est.   11 Dixit servum domino puniendum esse.   12 Puto amicos tuos tibi adiuvandos esse.

13 Regi crudeli parendum est.   14 Huic puellae non credendum est.
15 Civibus persuadendum erit.   16 Domum nobis proficiscendum est.
17 In forum nobis properandum erat.   18 His liberis multas horas dormiendum erit.

The Romans approach the Coast of Kent

His constitutis rebus, nactus idoneam ad navigandum tempestatem, tertia fere vigilia profectus, hora circiter diei quarta cum primis

navibus ad Britanniam advenit atque ibi in omnibus collibus instructas hostium copias armatas conspexit. Cuius loci haec erat natura
ut ex locis superioribus in litus telum mitti facile posset. Hunc 5
ad egrediendum nequaquam idoneum locum arbitratus est; itaque
cum et ventum et aestum uno tempore nactus esset secundum, dato
signo et sublatis ancoris, circiter milia passuum septem ab eo loco
progressus in aperto ac plano litore naves constituit.

At barbari, consilio Romanorum cognito, equitatu et essedariis 10
praemissis, quo plerumque genere in proeliis uti consuerunt, reliquis
copiis secuti nostros navibus egredi prohibebant. Erat ob has causas
summa difficultas, quod naves propter magnitudinem nisi in alto
constitui non poterant, militibus autem Romanis, magno et gravi
onere armorum oppressis, simul et e navibus desiliendum et in 15
fluctibus consistendum et cum hostibus erat pugnandum, cum
Britanni aut ex arido aut paulum in aquam progressi, omnibus
membris expeditis, notissimis locis, audacter tela conicerent.

Quibus rebus nostri perterriti atque huius generis pugnae imperiti,
non eodem studio quo in pedestribus uti proeliis consuerunt ute- 20
bantur.

SOLDIERS READY TO JUMP INTO THE SEA

CXIII

GRAMMAR: Intransitive Verbs in the passive voice.

1 Intransitive verbs are not used in the passive in English. In Latin they are so used, but only impersonally, i.e. with the neuter pronoun *it* as subject.

'They came to the city' can be *either* **ad urbem venerunt** *or* **ad urbem ventum est** (it was come to the city). In the second version the intransitive verb *venio* is used impersonally, with subject *it*.

2 In translation these passive intransitive verbs must be turned to the active voice.

Ferociter pugnabitur (it will be fought fiercely) = They will fight fiercely (or) There will be a fierce battle.

In forum concursum est (it was run together into the market-place) = They ran into the market-place (or) There was a rush to the market-place.

3 This usage is common with the gerundive of obligation, see CXII.

Mane mihi proficiscendum est = It must be set out early by me = I must set out early.

Militibus e navibus desiliendum erat = It had to be jumped down from the ships by the soldiers = The soldiers had to jump down from the ships.

EXERCISE

1 Multas horas acriter pugnabatur.   2 Sic vivebatur in urbe Roma. 3 A Britannis in silvas cursum est.   4 Pueris in ludum properandum erit. 5 Hoc mihi aegre persuasum est.   6 Romanis in fluctibus consistendum erat.   6 Post proelium a victoribus bene dormitum est.   8 A sacerdotibus in templum itum est.   9 Ab omnibus subito clamatum est, 'Patria defendenda est'.   10 Nobis statim discedendum neque iterum redeundum est.

The Brave Standard-bearer: Roman Victory

Nostris militibus cunctantibus, maxime propter altitudinem maris, is qui decimae legionis aquilam ferebat, 'Desilite,' inquit, 'milites, nisi vultis aquilam hostibus prodere: ego certe meum rei publicae atque imperatori officium praestabo.' Hoc cum voce magna dixisset, ex navi desiluit atque in hostes aquilam ferre incepit. Tum 5 nostri inter se hortati universi ex navibus desiluerunt.

Pugnatum est ab utrisque acriter. Nostri tamen, quod neque ordines servare neque signa sequi poterant, magnopere perturbabantur; hostes vero, notis omnibus vadis, incitatis equis nostros impeditos aggrediebantur, plures paucos circumsistebant, alii ab 10 latere in universos tela coniciebant. Quod cum animadvertisset Caesar, scaphas longarum navium militibus compleri iussit et, quos laborantes conspexerat, his auxilium mittebat. Nostri, simul atque in arido constiterunt, in hostes impetum fecerunt atque eos in fugam verterunt; longius tamen sequi non potuerunt, quod equites Romani 15 tempestate impediti ad insulam navigare non potuerant.

Hostes proelio superati, simul atque se ex fuga receperunt, statim ad Caesarem legatos de pace miserunt; obsides daturos quaeque imperavisset se facturos esse promiserunt.

CXIV

The Storm

Eadem nocte erat luna plena, qui dies maritimos aestus maximos in Oceano efficere consuevit, nostrisque id erat incognitum. Ita uno tempore et longas naves, quibus Caesar exercitum transportaverat quàsque in aridum subduxerat, aestus compleverat et naves onerarias, quae ad ancoras erant deligatae, tempestas afflictabat, 5 neque ulla nostris facultas adiuvandi dabatur. Compluribus navibus fractis, cum reliquae essent ad navigandum inutiles, magna totius exercitus perturbatio facta est. Neque enim naves erant aliae quibus reportari possent, et omnia deerant quae ad reficiendas naves erant usui et, quod hiemare in Gallia constituerat, frumentum 10 his in locis in hiemem collectum non erat.

Quibus rebus cognitis, principes Britanniae, qui post proelium ad Caesarem venerant, inter se locuti, cum equites et naves et frumentum Romanis deesse intellegerent, optimum esse putaverunt, rebellione facta, frumento commeatuque nostros prohibere et bellum 15 in hiemem producere, quod, Romanis superatis, neminem postea belli gerendi causa in Britanniam transiturum esse confidebant. Itaque, rursus coniuratione facta, paulatim ex castris discedere ac suos clam ex agris ducere inceperunt.

Sed Caesar, etsi nondum eorum consilia cognoverat, tamen ad 20 omnes casus se parabat. Nam et frumentum ex agris cotidie in castra ferebat et navium, quae deletae erant, materia atque aere ad reliquas reficiendas utebatur.

CXV

Attack on the 7th Legion: Return to Gaul

Dum ea geruntur, legione septima e castris missa, milites qui portas castrorum custodiebant Caesari nuntiaverunt nubem pulveris in ea parte videri quam in partem legio iter fecisset. Caesar arbitratus barbaros consilium novum cepisse, cohortes quae in stationibus erant secum in eam partem proficisci, ex reliquis duas cohortes in 5 stationem succedere, reliquas statim se sequi iussit. Cum paulo longius a castris processisset, suos ab hostibus premi atque aegre impetum sustinere et ex omnibus partibus tela conici animadvertit. Nam hostes nostros subito aggressi, paucis interfectis reliquos perturbaverant, simul equitatu atque essedariis circumdederant. 10

Quibus rebus perturbatis nostris Caesar auxilium tulit: nam eius adventu hostes constiterunt, nostri se ex timore receperunt. Quo facto, ad committendum proelium haud idoneum esse tempus arbitratus, suo se loco continuit et mox in castra legiones reduxit. Secutae sunt complures dies tempestates quae et nostros in castris 15 continerent et hostem a pugna prohiberent. Interea barbari nuntios in omnes partes miserunt et celeriter magna multitudine peditum equitumque coacta ad castra nostra venerunt.

Caesar legiones in acie pro castris constituit. Commisso proelio, nostrorum militum impetum hostes ferre non potuerunt ac terga 20 verterunt. Eodem die legati ab hostibus missi ad Caesarem de pace venerunt. His Caesar imperavit ut obsides in continentem ducerent, quod diutius in Britannia manere et infirmis navibus hieme navigare nolebat.

Ipse idoneam tempestatem nactus paulo post mediam noctem 25 naves solvit; quae omnes incolumes ad continentem pervenerunt.

CXVI

CAESAR AND CASSIVELLAUNUS 54 B.C.

Cassivellaunus harries the Romans as they march inland

Maiores iam undique copiae Britannorum convenerant summamque imperii Cassivellauno permiserant, cuius fines a maritimis civitatibus flumen dividit quod appellatur Tamesis a mari circiter milia passuum octoginta.

Quo duce equites hostium essedariique acriter proelio cum equit- 5
atu nostro in itinere conflixerunt, tamen ut nostri omnibus partibus
superiores fuerint atque eos in silvas collesque compulerint. At illi,
intermisso spatio, imprudentibus nostris atque occupatis in muni-
tione castrorum, subito se ex silvis eiecerunt, impetuque in eos facto
qui erant in statione pro castris collocati, acriter pugnaverunt; 10
duabusque missis subsidio cohortibus a Caesare, novo genere pugnae
perterritis nostris, per medios audacissime Britanni perruperunt
seque inde incolumes receperunt. Eo die Q. Laberius Durus, tribunus militum, interficitur. Illi pluribus submissis cohortibus
repelluntur. 15

Toto hoc in genere pugnae nostri propter gravitatem armorum,
quod neque sequi cedentes poterant neque ab signis discedere aud-
ebant, minus apti erant ad huius generis hostem; equites autem
nostri magno cum periculo proelio dimicabant, quod illi consulto
plerumque cedebant et, cum paulum ab legionibus nostros re- 20
movissent, ex essedis desiliebant et pedibus dispari proelio contendebant.

CXVII

The Britons attack Roman Foragers

Postero die procul a castris hostes in collibus constiterunt, rarique
se ostendere et lenius quam pridie nostros equites proelio lacessere
coeperunt. Sed meridie, cum Caesar pabulandi causa tres legiones
atque omnem equitatum cum C. Trebonio legato misisset, repente
ex omnibus partibus ad pabulatores advolaverunt, sic ut ab signis 5
legionibusque non absisterent. Nostri acriter in eos impetu facto
reppulerunt neque finem sequendi fecerunt, quoad subsidio confisi
equites, cum post se legiones viderent, praecipites hostes egerunt,
magnoque eorum numero interfecto, neque sui colligendi neque
consistendi aut ex essedis desiliendi facultatem dederunt. Ex ea 10
fuga protinus auxilia quae undique convenerant discesserunt, neque
post id tempus unquam summis nobiscum copiis hostes contenderunt.

CXVIII

Caesar crosses the Thames into
Cassivellaunus' Territory

Caesar, cognito consilio eorum, ad flumen Tamesim in fines
Cassivellauni exercitum duxit; quod flumen uno omnino loco
pedibus, atque hoc aegre, transiri potest. Eo cum venisset, animadvertit ad alteram fluminis ripam magnas esse copias hostium instructas. Ripa autem erat acutis sudibus munita, eiusdemque 5
generis sub aqua defixae sudes flumine tegebantur. Eis rebus cognitis a captivis perfugisque, Caesar praemisso equitatu celeriter
legiones subsequi iussit. Sed tanta celeritate atque tanto impetu
milites ierunt, cum capite solo ex aqua exstarent, ut hostes impetum
legionum atque equitum sustinere non possent ripasque dimitterent 10
ac terga verterent.

Inde Cassivellaunus, omni deposita spe contentionis, dimissis
maioribus copiis, milibus circiter quattuor essedariorum relictis,
itinera nostra servabat locisque impeditis ac silvestribus se occultabat, atque eis regionibus quibus nos iter facturos cognoverat pecora 15
atque homines ex agris in silvas compellebat et, cum equitatus
noster praedandi vastandique causa se in agros eiecerat, omnibus
viis essedarios ex silvis emittebat et magno cum periculo nostrorum
equitum cum eis confligebat atque hoc metu nostros latius vagari
prohibebat. 20

CXIX

Caesar storms Cassivellaunus' Capital

Caesar cognoscit non longe ab eo loco oppidum Cassivellauni abesse
silvis paludibusque munitum, quo magnus hominum pecorisque
numerus convenerit. Oppidum autem Britanni vocant, cum silvas
impeditas vallo atque fossa munierunt, quo incursionis hostium
vitandae causa convenire consuerunt. Eo proficiscitur cum legionibus: 5
locum reperit egregie natura atque opere munitum; tamen hunc
duabus ex partibus oppugnare contendit. Hostes paulisper morati
militum nostrorum impetum non tulerunt seque alia ex parte oppidi
eiecerunt. Magnus ibi numerus pecoris repertus, multique in fuga
sunt comprehensi atque interfecti. 10

RECONSTRUCTION OF ROMAN FORT ON HADRIAN'S WALL BUILT IN 2ND
CENTURY A.D.

Dum haec in eis locis geruntur, Cassivellaunus ad Cantium, quod
esse ad mare supra demonstravimus, quibus regionibus quattuor
reges praeerant, nuntios mittit atque eis imperat ut coactis omnibus
copiis castra navalia Romanorum oppugnent. Ei cum ad castra
venissent, nostri eruptione facta, multis eorum interfectis, capto 15
etiam nobili duce Lugotorige, suos incolumes reduxerunt.

CXX

Cassivellaunus surrenders: Caesar returns to Gaul

Cassivellaunus, hoc proelio nuntiato, tot cladibus acceptis, vastatis
finibus, legatos de deditione ad Caesarem mittit. Caesar, cum
constituisset hiemare in continenti propter repentinos Galliae motus
neque multum aestatis superesset, obsides imperat[1] et quid vecti-
galis populo Romano Britannia penderet constituit.   5

[1] *impero* with accusative means 'I demand'.

Obsidibus acceptis, exercitum reducit ad mare. Navibus deductis, quod et captivorum magnum numerum habebat et nonnullae tempestate perierant naves, duobus commeatibus exercitum reportare constituit. Ac sic accidit ut ex tanto navium numero neque hoc neque superiore anno ulla omnino navis, quae milites portaret, amitteretur.

Caesar, cum frustra naves e Gallia missas exspectasset, ne anni tempore a navigatione prohiberetur, necessario angustius milites collocavit ac summa tranquillitate secuta, secunda cum solvisset vigilia, prima luce ad terram advenit omnesque incolumes naves perduxit.

Latin-English Vocabularies

NOTE 1 The principal parts of all irregular verbs and of all verbs of the third conjugation are given. A verb is regular if its parts are like **amo** (1), **terreo** (2), **audio** (4).

2 1st and 5th declension nouns are feminine, 2nd and 4th declension nouns are masculine unless otherwise shown, *but* nouns ending in -**um** are neuter. Genders of all 3rd declension nouns are given.

3 Naturally long vowels, except final vowels, are marked. Some short vowels are marked where they aid pronunciation.

4 Hyphens are frequently used to save space. They do not necessarily indicate stems or division of syllables.

5 Similar meanings are separated by commas, others by semi-colons.

SPECIAL VOCABULARIES

61

praest-o, -āre, praestiti, I show (*a quality*)
ōrāt-or, -ōris, *m.,* orator
disc-o, -ĕre, didici, I learn
hiems, hiĕmis, *f.,* winter
praed-o, -ōnis, *m.,* pirate
apud, *prep. with acc.,* among
loqu-or, -i, locūtus sum, I speak, converse
poena (1), penalty, punishment
moror (1), I delay, wait
cruciātus (4), torture
quaest-or, -ōris, *m.,* quaestor
statua (1), statue
maxime, *adv.,* very much
effund-o, -ĕre, effūdi, effūsum, I pour forth, shed
fac-io, -ĕre, fēci, factum, I do

62

celerit-as, -ātis, *f.,* speed
brev-is, -e, *adj.,* short, brief
nōnnunquam, *adv.,* sometimes
centum, *indec.,* a hundred
mīlia (*gen.* **mīlium**), *n. pl.,* thousands
passus (4), pace
octo, *indec.,* eight
fere, *adv.,* about, almost
dīmitt-o, -ĕre, -mīsi, -missum, I send away, disband
senāt-or, -ōris, *m.,* senator
lex, lēgis, *f.,* law
autem, *conj.,* however, but
dīvĭd-o, -ĕre, -vīsi, -vīsum, I divide, separate
convert-o, -ĕre, -i, -versum, I turn
quo, *adv.,* whither, where
dictum (2), a saying
puto (1), I think
inopīnātus, *adj.,* unexpected
cēter-i, -ae, -a, *adj.,* rest of, other
coniūrātus (2), conspirator

63

cīvīl-is, -e, *adj.,* civil

princ-eps, -ĭpis, *m.,* emperor
nāvāl-is, -e, *adj.,* naval
comparo (1), I prepare
sto, stāre, steti, statum, I stand
fulg-eo, -ēre, fulsi, I shine (*intrans.*)
flu-o, -ĕre, -xi, -xum, I flow
pet-o, -ĕre, -īvi or **-ii, -ītum,** I make for
triumphus (2), triumph
ord-o, -ĭnis, *m.,* line
varius, *adj.,* different
usque ad, *with acc.,* right up to
accip-io, -ĕre, -cēpi, -ceptum, I receive

64

lingua (1), language
septem, *indec.,* seven
apertus, *adj.,* open
conven-io, -īre, -vēni, -ventum, I come together; meet
servo (1), I watch
domus (2 & 4), *f.,* house, home
basilica (1), hall
aedificium (2), building
contin-eo, -ēre, -ui, -tentum, I hold; contain
ūsus (4), use
ecclēsia (1), church
haud, *adv.,* not
unde, *adv.,* from where
ōrātiōnem habēre, to deliver a speech
rostrum (2), beak (*of a ship*); *in pl.,* platform
orno (1), I adorn, decorate
cubiculum (2), bedroom
super-ior, -iōris, *adj.,* upper
script-or, -ōris, *c.,* writer
ducent-i, -ae, -a, *adj.,* two hundred
gradus (4), step
vehiculum (2), vehicle
prohibeo (2) *with inf.,* I prevent

65

claud-o, -ĕre, clausi, clausum, I close, shut

sŏl-eo, -ēre, sŏlitus sum, I am accustomed
fīnes, *m. pl.*, boundaries
ūtor, ūti, ūsus sum, *with abl.*, I use
crux, crucis, *f.*, cross
sub, *prep. with abl.*, under
littera (1), letter of alphabet
cognosc-o, -ĕre, -nōvi, -nĭtum, I learn, find out
multo, *adv.*, much
hŏdiernus, *adj.*, of today
praesertim, *adv.*, especially
dūc-o, -ĕre, duxi, ductum, I derive
antīquus, *adj.*, old, ancient
quotiens, *adv.*, whenever
serm-o, -ōnis, *m.*, conversation
vīv-o, -ĕre, vixi, victum, I live, am alive
vigeo (2), I thrive

66

lūdus (2), school
doc-eo, -ēre, -ui, doctum, I teach
prīvātus, *adj.*, private
numero (1), I count
mātrōna (1), married woman
aest-as, -ātis, *f.*, summer
cal-or, -ōris, *m.*, heat
morbus (2), disease, sickness
fēri-ae, -ārum (1) *pl.*, holidays
malus, *adj.*, bad
vīcīnus (2), neighbour
schŏla grammatica (1), grammar school
litter-ae, -ārum (1) *pl.*, literature
rhēt-or, -ŏris, *m.*, teacher of rhetoric
arithmētica (1), arithmetic
geōmetria (1), geometry
astronomia (1), astronomy
mĭnus, *adv.*, less
nātūra (1), nature
quidem, *adv.*, indeed
investīgo (1), I investigate

67

morior, mori, mortuus sum, I die
duŏdecim, *indec.*, twelve
con-iunx, -iŭgis, *m. or f.*, husband; wife
fidēl-is, -e, *adj.*, faithful
dīligentia (1), carefulness
gemma (1), jewel

constantia (1), endurance
dol-or, -ōris, *m.*, grief
māt-er, -ris, *f.*, mother
inscrīb-o, -ĕre, -scripsi, -scriptum, I inscribe

68

aeg-er, -ra, -rum, *adj.*, sick
cūro (1), I look after
fl-eo, -ēre, flēvi, flētum, I weep
vultus (4), face, countenance
conservo (1), I preserve, save
vir, viri (2), husband
adloqu-or, -i, adlocūtus sum, I address, speak to
tantus, *adj.*, so great, such
perfidia (1), treachery
utrum . . . an, whether . . . or
per, *prep. with acc.*, at the hands of
pugi-o, -ōnis, *m.*, dagger
pect-us, -ŏris, *n.*, breast
percut-io, -ĕre, -cussi, -cussum, I strike, pierce
extrah-o, -ĕre, -traxi, -tractum, I draw out, withdraw

69

titulus (2), title
vērus, *adj.*, true
histŏria (1), story; history
secundus, *adj.*, second
columna (1), pillar
nāvem solvĕre, to set sail
nāvigāti-o, -ōnis, *f.*, voyage
studium (2), desire
cōpia (1), supply
impōn-o, -ĕre, -pŏsui, -pŏsitum, I put in
com-es, -itis, *m.*, companion
conspectus (4), sight
postridie, *adv.*, on the next day
aug-eo, -ēre, auxi, auctum, I increase (*trans.*)
turbo (1), I stir up
septuāginta, *indec.*, seventy
nŏvem, *indec.*, nine
octōgēsimus, *adj.*, eightieth
e nāve ēgredi, to disembark (*intrans.*)
līt-us, -ŏris, *n.*, shore
iac-eo, -ēre, -ui, I lie
trīginta, *indec.*, thirty

cust-os, -ōdis, *m.*, guard
proficisc-or, -i, profectus sum, I set
  out
explōro (1), I explore
inde, *adv.*, from there
merīdies (5), south
coor-ior, -īri, coortus sum, I arise
toll-o, -ĕre, sustuli, sublatum, I
  raise

70
octāvus, *adj.*, eighth
fulg-ens, -entis, *adj.*, shining
interdiu, *adv.*, by day
infra, *adv.*, below
veh-o, -ĕre, vexi, vectum, I convey;
  (*pass.*) I ride
transporto (1), I transport
lūna (1), moon
mōbil-is, -e, *adj.*, moveable
senesc-o, -ĕre, senui, I grow old
velut, *adv.*, just like
fūmus (2), smoke
ēvānesc-o, -ĕre, ēvānui, I vanish
speculum (2), mirror
quis, quid (*after* **si, nisi, ne**), anyone, anything
inspic-io, -ĕre, -spexi, -spectum, I
  look into
prae-sens, -sentis, *adj.*, present
fortasse, *adv.*, perhaps

71
vĭd-eor, -ēri, vīsus sum, I seem; am
  seen
certē, *adv.*, certainly
ēventus (4), result, outcome
tyrannus (2), tyrant
philosophus (2), philosopher
versus (4), verse
sententia (1), opinion
trād-o, -ĕre, -idi, -itum, I hand
  down
ŏp-us, -ĕris, *n.*, work
cap-io, -ĕre, cēpi, captum, I take
oppidum (2), town
scientia (1), knowledge

72
spēlunca (1), cave
seminūdus, *adj.*, half naked
frīg-us, -ŏris, *n.*, cold

fulm-en, -ĭnis, *n.*, lightning
magicus, *adj.*, magical, magic
statūra (1), stature, height
ob-ĕo, -īre, -ii *or* **-īvi, -ĭtum,** I meet,
  face
marīnus, *adj.*, of the sea, marine
fing-o, -ĕre, finxi, fictum, I invent
caecus, *adj.*, blind
or-ior, -īri, ortus sum, I arise, rise
rōs, rōris, *m.*, dew
quis, quid, *interrog. pron.*, who? what?
scio (4), I know; I know how (to)

73
compōn-o, -ĕre, -posui, -positum, I
  compose
factum (2), deed
princ-eps, -ĭpis, *m.*, chief
ēgregius, *adj.*, excellent, extraordinary
cond-o, -ĕre, -idi, -itum, I compose
nōnus, *adj.*, ninth
incertus, *adj.*, uncertain, doubtful
doctus, *adj.*, learned
dispŭto (1), I argue, dispute
nasc-or, -i, nātus sum, I am born
rē vēra, really, actually
imitor (1), I imitate, copy
discipulus (2), pupil
pro, *prep. with abl.*, in return for
pretium (2), price
em-o, -ĕre, ēmi, emptum, I buy

74
theātrum (2), theatre
histri-o, -ōnis, *m.*, actor
fābula (1), a play
scaena (1), stage
difficil-is, -e, *adj.*, difficult
responsum (2), answer
theātrāl-is, -e, *adj.*, theatrical
dies festi, *m. pl.*, festivals
salto (1), I dance
carm-en, -ĭnis, *n.*, song; chant
canto (1), I sing
molestus, *adj.*, tedious
saltāt-or, -ōris, *m.*, dancer
chŏrus (2), chorus
quindecim, *indec.*, fifteen
tragicus, *adj.*, tragic
regno (1), I reign, rule
pār, (*gen.* **păris),** *adj.*, equal

75

ōrāculum (2), oracle
lĕv-is, -e, *adj.,* light; trifling
negleg-o, -ĕre, -lexi, -lectum, I pass
over; neglect
iūcundus, *adj.,* pleasant
avidus, *adj. with gen.,* eager for
ubīque, *adv.,* everywhere
certus, *adj.,* fixed, definite
flūm-en, -ĭnis, *n.,* river
inundo (1), I flood (*trans.*)
exilium (2), exile
pell-o, -ĕre, pepuli, pulsum, I
drive
crūdēlit-as, -ātis, *f.,* cruelty
in dies, day by day
summus, *adj.,* very great; utmost
vitium (2), vice
ostend-o, -ĕre, -i, ostentum, I show,
reveal
comparo (1), I compare

76

dīves (*gen.* **dīvĭtis**), *adj.,* rich
magnificentia (1), magnificence
adeo, *adv.,* so much
ut, *with subj.,* in order that; that; so
that
paup-er (*gen.* **-ĕris**), *adj.,* poor
plērumque, *adv.,* generally
species (5), appearance
fŏrīs, *adv.,* out of doors
negōtium (2), business
ger-o, -ĕre, gessi, gestum, I conduct
vesperi, *adv.,* in the evening
cēna (1), dinner
praeterea, *adv.,* in addition
arx, arcis, *f.,* citadel
marmoreus, *adj.,* made of marble
supra, *adv. or prep. with acc.,* above
longē, *adv.,* by far; far
lăt-us, -ĕris, *n.,* side, flank
septendecim, *indec.,* seventeen
praesum, -esse, -fui, *with dat.,* I am
in charge of; rule over
artif-ex, -ĭcis, *m.,* artist
aes, aeris, *n.,* bronze
absum, abesse, afui, I am distant
simulācrum (2), image
aurum (2), gold
ebur, ebŏris, *n.,* ivory
splend-or, -ōris, *m.,* splendour

ōs, ōris, *n.,* face; mouth
māiest-as, -ātis, *f.,* majesty, dignity
dīvīnus, *adj.,* divine
illūmino (1), I light, illuminate
redd-o, -ĕre, -idi, -itum, I give back,
restore

77

abhinc, *adv. with acc.,* ago
rec-ens (*gen.* **-entis**), *adj.,* recent
sententiam dīcĕre, to state an opinion
effŏd-io, -ĕre, -fōdi, -fossum, I dig
up
monumentum (2), memorial
sepulcrum (2), tomb
tabula (1), tablet
ignōtus, *adj.,* unknown
undēvīcēsimus, *adj.,* nineteenth
vestīgium (2), trace
quaer-o, -ĕre, -sīvi, -sītum, I seek,
look for
taceo (2), I am silent
exinde, *adv.,* from then on
apud, *prep. with acc.,* in the works of
quadrāginta, *indec.,* forty
stultus, *adj.,* foolish
sĭtus (4), site
plānities (5), plain
duc-o, -ĕre, duxi, ductum, I dig (*a
ditch*)
aet-as, -ātis, *f.,* age

78

dēpell-o, -ĕre, -pŭli, -pulsum, I
dispel, drive away
herba (1), herb
lūm-en, -ĭnis, *n.,* light
remĕdium (2), remedy
prĕces, *f. pl.,* prayers
plāco (1), I appease, placate
afflīg-o, -ĕre, -flixi, -flictum, I afflict
medicīna (1), medicine
pell-is, -is, *f.,* skin, hide
hostia (1), victim, offering
somnium (2), a dream
medicīnus, *adj.,* of medicine
medicus (2), doctor
exerc-eo, -ēre, -ui, -itum, I practise
cēlo (1), I hide, conceal
mens, mentis, *f.,* mind
pūrus, *adj.,* pure

dignus, *adj. with abl.*, worthy of
membrum (2), part (*of body*), limb
circum-ĕo, -īre, -ii or **-īvi, -ĭtum,** I go round; visit
sāno (1), I heal, cure

79
philosophia (1), philosophy
studium (2), study; desire
sapientia (1), wisdom
virt-ūs, -ūtis, *f.*, virtue
rixa (1), quarrel
cultus (4), worship
accuso (1), I accuse
sapi-ens (*gen.* **-entis**), *adj.*, wise
magistrātus (4), magistrate
habeo (2), I consider
erro (1), I make a mistake
err-or, -ōris, *m.*, mistake
colloquium (2), conversation
pecco (1), I sin, do wrong
corrump-o, -ĕre, -rūpi, -ruptum, I corrupt
iūdicium (2), trial
iussum (2), order
antequam, *conj.*, before
carc-er, -ĕris, *m.*, prison
iūdices, *m. pl.*, jury

80
patruus (2), uncle
improbus, *adj.*, wicked
ita ut, so that
furtum (2), theft
recupero (1), I recover, get back
causam dīcĕre, to plead a case
tenu-is, -e, *adj.*, thin
apud, *prep. with acc.*, before, in the presence of
aud-eo, -ēre, ausus sum, I dare
clārus, *adj.*, clear
calculus (2), pebble
ecclēsia (1), Athenian parliament
ŏpes, ŏpum, *f. pl.*, resources
commūn-is, -e, *adj.*, common
stultitia (1), folly
rebelli-o, -ōnis, *f.*, renewal of war
resist-o, -ĕre, restiti, *with dat.*, I resist (*a person*)
extrēmus, *adj.*, end of
fall-o, -ĕre, fefelli, falsum, I deceive, cheat

venēnum (2), poison
stilus (2), pen

81
maxime, *adv.*, most, especially
mīrābil-is, -e, *adj.*, marvellous
fur-or, -ōris, *m.*, fury
mille, *indec.*, one thousand
septingent-i, -ae, -a, *adj.*, seven hundred
quāl-is, -e, *adj.*, what sort of?
exitium (2), destruction
duodēvīginti, *indec.*, eighteen
avunculus (2), uncle
septuāgēsimus, *adj.*, seventieth
trem-or, -ōris, *m.*, tremor, shaking
septimus, *adj.*, seventh
rāmus (2), branch
cin-is, -ĕris, *m.*, ash
lap-is, -ĭdis, *m.*, stone
impl-eo, -ēre, -ēvi, -ētum, I fill
tenebr-ae, -ārum (1), *pl.*, darkness
lātē, *adv.*, far and wide
sēd-es, -is, *f.*, foundation
sulphureus, *adj.*, of sulphur
vēro, *adv.*, however
opprim-o, -ĕre, -pressi, -pressum, I crush, weigh down

82
praeter, *prep. with acc.*, except
paulātim, *adv.*, gradually
ita, *adv.*, so, in such a way
infēl-ix (*gen.* **-īcis**), *adj.*, unfortunate
anim-al, -ālis, *n.*, animal
can-is, -is, *c.*, dog
lectīca (1), a litter
uterque, utraque, utrumque, *adj.*, each, both
pars, partis, *f.*, side
taberna (1), shop
necessārius, *adj.*, necessary
ēdictum (2), edict, regulation
iŏcus (2), joke

83
prīmum, *adv.*, first
tectum (2), roof
imb-er, -ris, *m.*, rain
pōn-o, -ĕre, posui, positum, I place
dēscend-o, -ĕre, -i, dēscensum, I come down

cli-ens, -entis, *m.*, dependent, caller
dominus (2), owner, master
familia (1), household
hortus (2), garden
fons, fontis, *m.*, fountain
vel, *conj.*, or
sed-eo, -ēre, sēdi, sessum, I sit
inter-ior (*gen.* -iōris), *adj.*, interior
mōs, mōris, *m.*, fashion
dea (1), goddess
rēs gestae, *f. pl.*, exploits
flōs, flōris, *m.*, flower
col-or, -ōris, *m.*, colour
clārus, *adj.*, bright
ping-o, -ĕre, pinxi, pictum, I paint
fŏrum (2), forum, market-place
mensa (1), table
ad, *prep. with acc.*, at
lectus (2), couch
convīva (1) *c.*, guest
iac-eo, -ēre, -ui, I recline
luxuriōsus, *adj.*, luxurious
hosp-es, -ĭtis, *c.*, guest
lūdus (2), game
ōtiōsus, *adj.*, at leisure, leisurely
ag-o, -ĕre, ēgi, actum, I spend (*time*)
subitus, *adj.*, sudden
clād-es, -is, *f.*, disaster
timeo (2), I fear
nec . . . nec, neither . . . nor
cūro (1), I care for
contemn-o, -ĕre, -tempsi, -temp-
tum, I despise
tot, *indec. adj.*, so many

84
conservo (1), I preserve
arcus (4), arch
triumphāl-is, -e, *adj.*, triumphal
imperāt-or, -ōris, *m.*, emperor
specto (1), I look at, look
nam, *conj.*, for
infer-ior (*gen.* -iōris), *adj.*, lower
candēlābrum (2), candle-stick
porto (1), I carry
dīlig-ens (*gen.* -entis), *adj.*, careful
custōdio (4), I guard
sexāginta, *indec.*, sixty
ante, *prep. with acc.*, before
imperium (2), rule
patienter, *adv.*, patiently
lībert-as, -ātis, *f.*, liberty, freedom

suscip-io, -ĕre, -cēpi, -ceptum, I
undertake
fīlius (2), son
collĭg-o, -ĕre, -lēgi, -lectum, I
collect
equĭtes, *m. pl.*, cavalry
nē, *conj.*, lest
impetus (4), attack
host-is, -is, *c.*, enemy
fīo, fīeri, factus sum, to happen,
take place
fab-er, -ri, *m.*, engineer
carrus (2), waggon
impedīment-a, -ōrum, *n. pl.*, baggage
agm-en, -ĭnis, *n.*, army (*on the march*)
postrēmo, *adv.*, finally
legi-o, -ōnis, *f.*, legion
tribūnus (2), tribune
centuri-o, -ōnis, *m.*, centurion
contend-o, -ĕre, -i, I march

85
turr-is, -is, *f.*, tower
pēs, pĕdis, *m.*, foot
dēfend-o, -ĕre, -i, -fensum, I defend
mūniti-o, -ōnis, *f.*, fortification
sac-er, -ra, -rum, *adj.*, sacred
nĕfas, *indec.*, forbidden
prope, *adv.*, almost
vallum (2), rampart
circum-do, -dăre, -dĕdi, -dătum, I
surround
torment-a, -ōrum, *n. pl.*, artillery
pond-us, -ĕris, *n.*, weight
primo, *adv.*, at first
albus, *adj.*, white
nig-er, -ra, -rum, *adj.*, black
effŭg-io, -ĕre, -fūgi, I escape
pŏt-ens (*gen.* -entis), *adj.*, powerful
quinque, *indec.*, five
fam-es, -is, *f.*, hunger, starvation
prem-o, -ĕre, pressi, pressum, I
press; oppress
incend-o, -ĕre, -i, -censum, I burn
(*trans.*)
hinc, *adv.*, from here
argentum (2), silver
trad-o, -ĕre, -idi, -itum, I hand over,
surrender
collŏco (1), I place, set
dēdico (1), I dedicate

ante, *adv.*, before, previously
praedīc-o, -ĕre, -dixi, -dictum, I predict, foretell

86

surg-o, -ĕre, surrexi, surrectum, I rise
magnitūd-o, -ĭnis, *f.*, size
supero (1), I surpass, excel
appello (1), I name, call
plebs, plēbis, *f.*, the common people
spectāculum (2), show, spectacle
spatium (2), space, area
arēna (1), arena
sēd-es, -is, *f.*, seat
undique, *adv.*, on all sides
cing-o, -ĕre, cinxi, cinctum, I surround
īmus, *adj.*, lowest
iūd-ex, -ĭcis, *m.*, judge
virg-o, -ĭnis, *f.*, virgin, maiden
sacerd-ōs, -ōtis, *m.*, priest
nōbil-is, -e, *adj.*, high-born, noble
summus, *adj.*, highest
exspecto (1), I await, wait for
volupt-as, -ātis, *f.*, pleasure
gaudium (2), joy
gladiāt-or, -ōris, *m.*, gladiator
instru-o, -ĕre, -xi, -ctum I equip
avē!, hail!
signum (2), signal
prōcurr-o, -ĕre, -curri, -cursum, I run forward
pedibus, on foot
equus (2), horse
currus (4), chariot
praemium (2), reward
placeo (2) *with dat.*, I please
spectāt-or, -ōris, *c.*, spectator
impero (1) *with dat.*, I order
interfic-io, -ĕre, -fēci, -fectum, I kill
iūdicium (2), judgement
mortem obīre, to meet one's death

87

importo (1), I import, bring in
hippopotamus (2), hippopotamus
ap-er, -ri (2), wild boar
le-o, -ōnis, *m.*, lion
elephantus (2), elephant
nūper, *adv.*, recently

celebro (1), I celebrate
decem, *indec.*, ten
propter, *prep. with acc.*, on account of
scel-us, -ĕris, *n.*, crime
damno (1), I condemn
gladius (2), sword
armātus, *adj.*, armed
inerm-is, -e, *adj.*, unarmed
lanio (1), I tear in pieces
interdum, *adv.*, at times
fur-or, -ōris, *m.*, excitement
saevus, *adj.*, cruel, fierce
mōres, *m. pl.*, character
initium (2), beginning
quintus, *adj.*, fifth
adsum, adesse, adfui, I am present
dēsil-io, -īre, -ui, -ultum, I jump down
conic-io, -ĕre, -iēci, -iectum, I throw
frustra, *adv.*, in vain
test-is, -is, *c.*, a witness
hūmānus, *adj.*, human
signum (2), sign
quamdiu, *adv.*, as long as
et, *conj.*, also
cad-o, -ĕre, cecĭdi, cāsum, I fall
mundus (2), universe, world

88

corp-us, -ŏris, *n.*, body
horrendus, *adj.*, fearsome
animus (2), mind
excĭto (1), I excite
cum, *conj.*, when
velut, *adv.*, as if
attonitus, *adj.*, astonished
dominus (2), master
lēn-is, -e, *adj.*, gentle
cauda (1), tail
paene, *adv.*, almost
lingua (1), tongue
mulc-eo, -ēre, mulsi, mulsum, I lick
inspic-io, -ĕre, -spexi, -spectum, I examine
amīcitia (1), friendship
cur, *adv.*, why?
deinde, *adv.*, then, next
crūdēl-is, -e, *adj.*, cruel
fero, ferre, tuli, lātum, I bear, endure

potius, *adv.*, rather
dēsertus, *adj.*, deserted, lonely
constitu-o, -ěre, -i, -tum, I decide
aestus (4), heat
tūtus, *adj.*, safe
pet-o, -ěre, -īvi *or* **-ii, -ītum,** I seek
umbrōsus, *adj.*, shady
vulnero (1), I wound
perterreo (2), I frighten
vuln-us, -ěris, *n.*, wound
infirmus, *adj.*, weak
mǒdus (2), way, manner
noceo (2) *with dat.*, I hurt, harm

89
spīna (1), a thorn
ūna, *adv.*, together
alo, alěre, alui, altum, I feed
cap-io, -ěre, cēpi, captum, I capture
quondam, *adv.*, once
beneficium (2), kindness
obviam īre, *with dat.*, to meet, go to meet
grātiam habēre, to feel thankful
tam, *adv.*, so
mīror (1), I am amazed
sparg-o, -ěre, sparsi, sparsum, I scatter
hosp-es, -ǐtis, *m.*, host

90
tertius, *adj.*, third
confirmo (1), I establish
discordia (1), quarrel
domesticus, *adj.*, at home, domestic
externus, *adj.*, foreign, abroad
vexo (1), I distress, worry
praefic-io, -ěre, -fēci, -fectum, I put in command
pons, pontis, *m.*, bridge
adversārius (2), adversary, enemy
admoneo (2), I warn
scūtum (2), shield
sīve . . . sīve, whether . . . or
col-o, -ěre, colui, cultum, I worship
adhūc, *adv.*, up to that time
mīlitār-is, -e, *adj.*, military
occupor (1), *passive*, I am busy, occupied
rāro, *adv.*, rarely
cap-ut, -ǐtis, *n.*, capital
orientāl-is, -e, *adj.*, eastern, of the east

ob, *prep. with acc.*, because of
ostium (2), entrance, mouth
cond-o, -ěre, -idi, -itum, I found (*a city*)
coll-is, -is, *m.*, hill
sǐtus, *adj.*, situated
munio (4), I fortify, defend
balne-ae, -ārum (1) *pl.*, public baths
mōs, mōris, *m.*, a custom
decimus, *adj.*, tenth

91
fīnitimus (2), neighbour
regnum (2), kingdom
succēd-o, -ěre, -cessi, -cessum, I succeed to
spēro (1), I hope
praebeo (2), I show (*myself*)
nēmo (*acc.* **nēminem,** *gen.* **nullius**), no one
concilium (2), meeting
convoco (1), I call together, call
comparo (1), I win, gain
barbarus (2), a barbarian
incursi-o, -ōnis, *f.*, invasion
māiōres, *m. pl.*, ancestors
iniūria (1), injury
infero, inferre, intuli, inlātum, I inflict
proximus, *adj.*, next
falso, *adv.*, falsely
sūm-o, -ěre, sumpsi, sumptum, I take up
ten-eo, -ēre, -ui, tentum, I hold
atr-ox (*gen.* **-ōcis**), *adj.*, fierce
sex, *indec.*, six
servit-us, -ūtis, *f.*, slavery
abdūc-o, -ěre, -duxi, -ductum, I lead away
īrātus, *adj.*, angry
funditus, *adv.*, utterly
trist-is, -e, *adj.*, sad
pāco (1), I pacify

92
lēgātus (2), legate, senior officer
bon-a, -ōrum, *n. pl.*, goods, possessions
relǐquus, *adj.*, remaining, left
spēs (5), hope
dīviti-ae, -ārum (1) *pl.*, riches
trāic-io, -ěre, -iēci, -iectum, I lead across

124

prōgred-ior, -i, -gressus sum, I advance, go on

āvert-o, -ĕre, -i, āversum, I avert, turn away

tumulus (2), tomb

corōna (1), crown

gen-us, -ĕris, *n.,* race

auct-or, -ōris, *m.,* founder

socius (2), ally

pedites, *m. pl.,* infantry

instru-o, -ĕre, -struxi, -structum, I draw up

adventus (4), approach

acies (5), line-of-battle

collŏco (1), I station

arduus, *adj.,* steep

adversus, *adj.,* opposite

ord-o, -ĭnis, *m.,* rank

transfīg-o, -ĕre, -fixi, -fixum, I pierce

tergum vertĕre, to turn the back, flee

frons, frontis, *f.,* front

phal-anx, -angis, *f.,* the phalanx

aggred-ior, -i, aggressus sum, I attack

sal-us, -ūtis, *f.,* safety

fuga (1), flight

regi-o, -ōnis, *f.,* region, district

occupo (1), I seize, take possession of

marĭtĭmus, *adj.,* maritime, coastal

vis (*acc.* **vim,** *abl.* **vi),** *f.,* force

expugno (1), I capture, take by storm

nōnnull-i, -ae, -a, *adj.,* some

nŏvae cōpiae, *f. pl.,* reinforcements

inde, *adv.,* from there

hiemo (1), I spend the winter

93

castr-a, -ōrum (2), *pl.,* camp

iŭgum (2), yoke

nōdus (2), knot

ars, artis, *f.,* art, skill

dēligo (1), I fasten, bind

solv-o, -ĕre, -i, solūtum, I loosen

vinculum (2), fastening

dīscind-o, -ĕre, -cidi, -cissum, I cut apart

pot-ior, -īri, -ītus sum, *with abl.,* I get possession of

nato (1), I swim

ingred-ior, -i, -gressus sum, I enter

affic-io, -ĕre, -fēci, -fectum, I affect

perītus, *adj. with gen.,* skilled (in)

litter-ae, -ārum (1) *pl.,* letter

confīd-o, -ĕre, -fīsus sum, *with dat.* or *abl.,* I trust

exhaur-io, -īre, -hausi, -haustum, I drain, drink

vānus, *adj.,* vain

quingent-i, -ae, -a, *adj.,* five hundred

transgred-ior, -i, -gressus sum, I cross

committ-o, -ĕre, -mīsi, -missum, I join (*battle*)

sustin-eo, -ēre, -ui, sustentum, I withstand, resist

vest-is, -is, *f.,* dress

rēgius, *adj.,* royal

abic-io, -ĕre, -iēci, -iectum, I throw away

94

nōndum, *adv.,* not yet

portus (4), harbour

praesidium (2), garrison

frĕtum (2), strait, channel

contin-ens, -entis, *f.,* mainland

arb-or, -ŏris, *f.,* tree

mōl-es, -is, *f.,* mole, causeway

iung-o, -ĕre, iunxi, iunctum, I join

nauta (1) *m.,* sailor

fab-er, -rī (2), workman

mitt-o, -ĕre, mīsi, missum, I launch, hurl

dīru-o, -ĕre, -i, -utum, I breach (*a wall*)

dēspēro (1), I despair

advĕn-io, -īre, -vēni, -ventum, I arrive

contin-eo, -ēre, -ui, -tentum, I keep, hold

impōn-o, -ĕre, -posui, -positum, I place on

fīdus, *adj.,* faithful

sagitta (1), arrow

catapulta (1), catapult, artillery

cum, *conj.,* since

nōn iam, no longer

95

superbus, *adj.,* proud

ad-ĕo, -īre, -ii *or* **-īvi, -ĭtum,** I go to, approach

altus, *adj.*, deep
arēna (1), sand
torridus, *adj.*, scorched
aegre, *adv.*, with difficulty
inŏpia (1), shortage, scarcity
vix, *adv.*, scarcely
pat-ior, -i, passus sum, I endure
vastus, *adj.*, vast
circumvĕn-io, -īre, -vēni, -ventum, I surround
mūto (1), I change
cǎsa (1), hut
teg-o, -ĕre, texi, tectum, I cover
fons, fontis, *m.*, well, spring
grātus, *adj.*, pleasing
umbra (1), shade
accip-io, -ĕre, -cēpi, -ceptum, I accept
regred-ior, -i, -gressus sum, I return
mille passūs, 1,000 paces, one Roman mile

96
vereor (2), I fear
rapidus, *adj.*, swift
impedītus, *adj.*, not ready for battle
tabernāculum (2), tent
captīva (1), a female prisoner
exsequi-ae, -ārum (1) *pl.*, funeral
ēlāb-or, -i, ēlapsus sum, I slip away
pervĕn-io, -īre, -vēni, -ventum, I reach, arrive (at)
interrogo (1), I ask
lēgātus (2), envoy
perīculōsus, *adj.*, dangerous
obtin-eo, -ēre, -ui, -tentum, I hold, retain
condici-o, -ōnis, *f.*, condition
glōria (1), glory
fortūna (1), luck, chance
princ-eps, -ĭpis, *m.*, chieftain, chief

97
qui-es, -ētis, *f.*, rest
thēsaurus (2), treasure
quamquam, *conj.*, although
nix, nĭvis, *f.*, snow
saltus (4), pass
longius, *adv.*, further
dēvolv-o, -ĕre, -i, -volūtum, I roll down

certiōrem facĕre, to inform
alter, -a, -um, *adj.*, another (*of two*)
iŭgum (2), ridge
dūc-o, -ĕre, duxi, ductum, I lead
veh-o, -ĕre, vexi, vectum, I carry, convey
iūmentum (2), baggage animal
rēgia (1), palace
convīvium (2), feast, banquet
intersum, -esse, -fui, *with dat.*, I take part in
admoneo (2), I urge
fax, facis, *f.*, torch
manus (4), *f.*, hand
corrip-io, -ĕre, -ripui, -reptum, I snatch up, seize
curr-o, -ĕre, cucurri, cursum, I run
iac-io, -ĕre, iēci, iactum, I throw
ligneus, *adj.*, made of wood
consūm-o, -ĕre, -sumpsi, -sumptum, I consume
consilium (2), plan
exstingu-o, -ĕre, -stinxi, -stinctum, I put out, extinguish

98
coepi, coepisse, I begin
prōcūrāt-or, -ōris, *m.*, governor
vinculum (2), chain
ultimus, *adj.*, farthest
proximus, *adj.*, nearest
dext-er, -ra, -rum, *adj.*, right
humerus (2), shoulder
animus (2), courage
invictus, *adj.*, undaunted
nuntius (2), messenger
persuād-eo, -ēre, -suāsi, -suāsum, *with dat.*, I persuade
obviam, *with dat.*, to meet
statu-o, -ĕre, -i, statūtum, I decide
circum, *prep. with acc.*, around
invītus, *adj.*, unwilling
omitt-o, -ĕre, -mīsi, -missum, I give up
āra (1), altar
incolum-is, -e, *adj.*, unharmed

99
secundo flūmine, down-stream
cōg-o, -ĕre, coēgi, coactum, I collect
mercāt-or, -ōris, *m.*, merchant
atque, *conj.*, and

caed-o, -ĕre, cecīdi, caesum, I slaughter
ĕdo, edere, ēdi, ēsum, I eat
āmitt-o, -ĕre, -mīsi, -missum, I lose
dīmidium (2), half
consilium capĕre, to form a plan
vīres, *f. pl.*, strength
exhaur-io, -īre, -hausi, -haustum, I exhaust
sin-o, -ĕre, sīvi, sĭtum, I allow
ut, *with indic.*, when
tāl-is, -e, *adj.*, such
certām-en, -ĭnis, *n.*, contest, struggle

100
insānus, *adj.*, mad
affirmo (1), I declare, state
coniung-o, -ĕre, -iunxi, -iunctum, I join
inimīcus, *adj.*, hostile, unfriendly
dīrip-io, -ĕre, -ui, -reptum, I plunder
contrah-o, -ĕre, -traxi, -tractum, I bring together
indu-o, -ĕre, -i, -dūtum, I put on
effic-io, -ĕre, -fēci, -fectum, I cause

101
quinquāgēsimus, *adj.*, fiftieth
tumultus (4), uproar, riot
concurr-o, -ĕre, -curri, -cursum, I come together
comprehend-o, -ĕre, -i, -prehensum I seize, arrest
conclāmo (1), I cry out
commŏv-eo, -ēre, -mōvi, -mōtum, I disturb
vīcīnus, *adj.*, nearby, neighbouring
licet, it is allowed
aliquis, aliquid, *pron.*, someone, something
scio (4), I know how (to)
ōro (1), I beg
consist-o, -ĕre, -stiti, I stand

102
persequ-or, -i, -secūtus sum, I persecute
trād-o, -ĕre, -didi, -ditum, I hand over
redūc-o, -ĕre, -duxi, -ductum, I bring back

effulg-eo, -ēre, -fulsi, I shine forth
concĭd-o, -ĕre, -cĭdi, I fall down
Dominus (2), the Lord
tū, *pron.*, you (*sing.*)
inquam, I said
contend-o, -ĕre, -i, I hasten
pāreo (2) *with dat.*, I obey
verbero (1), I whip, beat
num, surely . . . not?
innoc-ens (*gen.* -entis), *adj.*, innocent

103
prōdūc-o, -ĕre, -duxi, -ductum, I bring forward
appāreo (2), I appear
interim, *adv.*, meanwhile
expedītus (2), light-armed soldier
vigilia (1), watch
violo (1), I violate, break
valē, *imperative*, good-bye

104
epistola (1), a letter
culpa (1), fault; blame
custōdia (1), custody
revōco (1), I recall
libenter, *adv.*, willingly
appello (1), I appeal to

105
conscend-o, -ĕre, -i, -scensum, I board (*a ship*)
benignus, *adj.*, kind
se reficĕre, to refresh oneself
adversus, *adj.*, adverse
nancisc-or, -i, nactus sum, I meet with
cursus (4), course
auctumnus (2), autumn
admoneo (2), I warn
gubernāt-or, -ōris, *m.*, helmsman
magist-er, -ri (2), captain (of a ship)
spectāre ad, to face

106
nŏtus (2), south wind
adflo (1), I blow
ōra (1), shore, coast
adversus, *prep. with acc.*, against
unda (1), wave
dē-fero, -ferre, -tuli, -lātum, I carry away, carry

dēmitt-o, -ĕre, -mīsi, -missum, I lower

lĕv-is, -e, *adj.*, light

armament-a, -ōrum, *n. pl.*, tackle, gear

prŏic-io, -ĕre, -iēci, -iectum, I throw away

complūres, *adj. pl.*, several

vĭd-eor, -ēri, vīsus sum, I am seen

angelus (2), angel

minist-er, -ri (2), servant

107

quartus, *adj.*, fourth

altitūd-o, -ĭnis, *f.*, depth

sent-io, -īre, sensi, sensum, I feel, realise

ancŏra (1), anchor

pupp-is, -is, *f.*, stern

lint-er, -ris, *f.*, small boat

quattuordecim, *indec.*, fourteen

suād-eo, -ēre, suāsi, suāsum, *with dat.*, I advise

pān-is, -is, *m.*, bread

grātias agĕre, to give thanks

frūmentum (2), corn

nescio (4), I do not know

impell-o, -ĕre, -pūli, -pulsum, I drive, drive on

108

praecīd-o, -ĕre, -cīdi, -cīsum, I cut, cut short

prŏra (1), prow, bow

immōtus, *adj.*, motionless

afflicto (1), I dash; damage

ēvād-o, -ĕre, -vāsi, -vāsum, I escape

fragmentum (2), broken piece, fragment

sustin-eo, -ēre, -ui, -tentum, I support, hold up

lignum (2), wood

serp-ens, -entis, *f.*, serpent

barbarus (2), a native

excut-io, -ĕre, -cussi, -cussum, I shake off

mălum (2), harm, evil

at, *conj.*, but

109

agr-i, -ōrum (2) *pl.*, estates

invīto (1), I invite

precor (1), I pray

habeo (2), I hold

praebeo (2), I provide

insign-ĕ, -is, *n.*, emblem

nancisc-or, -i. nactus sum, I obtain

frāt-er, -ris, *m.*, brother

110

longinquus, *adj.*, distant

viāt-or, -ōris, *c.*, traveller

cons-ul, -ŭlis, *m.*, consul

praet-or, -ōris, *m.*, praetor

turma (1), squadron

raeda (1), carriage

extra, *prep. with acc.*, outside

moen-ia, -ium, *n. pl.*, walls

rectus, *adj.*, direct, straight

sinist-er, -ra, -rum, *adj.*, left

officium (2), duty

perfic-io, -ĕre, -fēci, -fectum, I complete

111

exiguus, *adj.*, very small

auxili-a, -ōrum, *n. pl.*, reinforcements

dēfic-io, -ĕre, -fēci, -fectum, to be too short

arbitror (1), I think

mŏdo, *adv.*, only

perspic-io, -ĕre, -spexi, -spectum, I examine, study

incognitus, *adj.*, unknown

quisquam, quicquam, *pron.*, anyone, anything

contra, *prep. with acc.*, opposite, facing

quantus, *adj.*, how great

aut, *conj.*, or

nāti-o, -ōnis, *f.*, tribe

incŏl-o, -ĕre, -ui, I inhabit, dwell in

nāvis longa, warship

quam prīmum, as soon as possible

trāiectus (4), crossing

fīnitimus, *adj.*, neighbouring

super-ior (*gen.* -iōris), *adj.*, previous

cīvit-as, -ātis, *f.*, state

obs-es, -ĭdis, *c.*, hostage

hortor (1), I encourage, exhort

112

idōneus, *adj.*, suitable

tempest-as, -ātis, *f.*, weather

circiter, *adv.*, about

mitt-o, -ĕre, mīsi, missum, I hurl
nēquāquam, *adv.*, not at all
aestus (4), tide
plānus, *adj.*, level
constitu-o, -ĕre, -i, -stitūtum, I
station
equitātus (4), cavalry
essedārius (2), charioteer
praemitt-o, -ĕre, -mīsi, -missum,
I send ahead
consuesc-o, -ĕre, -suēvi, -suētum,
I am accustomed
difficult-as, -ātis, *f.*, difficulty
grav-is, -e, *adj.*, heavy
ŏn-us, -ĕris, *n.*, weight
fluctus (4), wave
āridum (2), dry land
paulum, *adv.*, a little
expedītus, *adj.*, unencumbered
aud-ax (*gen.* **-ācis**), *adj.*, bold
imperītus, *adj. with gen.*, inexperi-
enced in
studium (2), enthusiasm
pedest-er, -ris, -e, *adj.*, of infantry

113
cunctor (1), I hesitate
aquila (1), eagle; standard
prōd-o, -ĕre, -idi, -itum, I betray,
hand over
officium praestāre, to do one's duty
ūniversi, *pl. adj.*, all together
acriter, *adv.*, keenly, fiercely
servo (1), I keep
signum (2), flag, standard
magnŏpere, *adv.*, greatly
perturbo (1), I confuse, frighten
vadum (2), shallow place
incĭto (1), I urge on
circumsist-o, -ĕre, -stĕti, I surround
animadvert-o, -ĕre, -verti, -versum,
I notice
scapha (1), skiff, small boat
compl-eo, -ēre, -plēvi, -plētum, I fill
labōro (1), I am in difficulties
simul atque, as soon as
longius, *adv.*, too far
sē recipĕre, to recover

114
subdūc-o, -ĕre, -duxi, -ductum, I
draw up (*a ship*)

nāvis onerāria, merchant ship
facult-as, -ātis, *f.*, chance, opportunity
adiŭv-o, -āre, -iūvi, -iūtum, I help
frang-o, -ĕre, frēgi, fractum, I
break, smash
inūtil-is, -e, *adj.*, useless
perturbāti-o, -ōnis, *f.*, confusion
reporto (1), I bring back
dēsum, dēesse, dēfui, I am short,
lacking
refic-io, -ĕre, -fēci, -fectum, I repair
in, *prep. with acc.*, for
intelleg-o, -ĕre, -lexi, -lectum, I
realise, understand
commeātus (4), provisions
prōdūc-o, -ĕre, -duxi, -ductum, I
prolong
causa, *prep. with gen.* (*follows its noun*),
for the sake of
rursus, *adv.*, again
clam, *adv.*, secretly
etsi, *conj.*, although
cāsus (4), chance
mātĕria (1), timber

115
ger-o, -ĕre, gessi, gestum, I do
nūb-es, -is, *f.*, cloud
pulv-is, -ĕris, *m.*, dust
pars, partis, *f.*, direction
coh-ors, -ortis, *f.*, cohort, regiment
stati-o, -ōnis, *f.*, picket, guard-post
sē continēre, to stay
pro, *prep. with abl.*, in front of

116
summa imperii, chief command
permitt-o, -ĕre, -mīsi, -missum, I
entrust
octōginta, *indec.*, eighty
conflīg-o, -ĕre, -flixi, -flictum, I
clash, fight
super-ior (*gen.* **-iōris**), *adj.*, superior
compell-o, -ĕre, -puli, -pulsum, I
drive
intermitt-o, -ĕre, -mīsi, -missum,
I allow to pass
spatium (2), interval
imprūd-ens (*gen.* **-entis**), *adj.*, off
one's guard
sē ēicĕre, to rush out

subsidium (2), reinforcement
perrump-o, -ĕre, -rūpi, -ruptum, I
   break through
sē recipĕre, to retreat
submitt-o, -ĕre, -mīsi, -missum, I
   send to help
repell-o, -ĕre, -pŭli, -ulsum, I
   drive back
gravit-as, -ātis, *f.*, weight
cēd-o, -ĕre, cessi, cessum, I yield,
   give way
aptus ad, *adj.*, fit to deal with
dīmĭco (1), I fight
consulto, *adv.*, in purpose
remov-eo, -ēre, -mōvi, -mōtum, I
   draw away, remove
essedum (2), war-chariot
dispar (*gen.* dispăris), *adj.*, unequal
contend-o, -ĕre, -i, I fight

117
rāri, *adj. pl.*, in small groups
prīdie, *adv.*, on the day before
lacess-o, -ĕre, -īvi or -ii, -ītum, I
   provoke
merīdies (5), midday
pābulor (1), I forage, get food
advŏlo (1), I rush towards
absist-o, -ĕre, -stiti, I keep away
   from
quoad, *conj.*, until
post, *prep. with acc.*, behind
praec-eps (*gen.* -ĭpitis), *adj.*, headlong
ag-o, -ĕre, ēgi, actum, I drive
ex, *prep. with abl.*, after
prōtinus, *adv.*, at once

118
omnīno, *adv.*, in all
eo, *adv.*, to there
acūtus, *adj.*, sharp
sud-is, -is, *f.*, stake
sub, *prep. with abl.*, under
dēfīg-o, -ĕre, -fixi, -fixum, I fasten,
   fix in
perfŭga (1) *m.*, deserter
impetus (4), rush, violence

subsequ-or, -i, -secūtus sum, I
   follow up
exst-o, -āre, I stand out, project
dīmitt-o, -ĕre, -mīsi, -missum, I
   give up; send away
dēpōn-o, -ĕre, -posui, -positum, I
   lay aside, abandon
contenti-o, -ōnis, *f.*, struggle, fighting
servo (1), I watch
impedītus, *adj.*, impenetrable
silvestr-is, -e, *adj.*, wooded
occulto (1), I hide
pec-us, -ŏris, *n.*, herd; cattle
praedor (1), I plunder
ēmitt-o, -ĕre, -mīsi, -missum, I
   send out
metus (4), fear
vagor (1), I stray, wander

119
pal-us, -ūdis, *f.*, marsh
fossa (1), ditch
reper-io, -īre, reppĕri, repertum, I
   find
dēmonstro (1), I show, explain
ērupti-o, -ōnis, *f.*, sortie

120
accip-io, -ĕre, -cēpi, -ceptum, I
   suffer (*a defeat*)
dēditi-o, -ōnis, *f.*, surrender
repentīnus, *adj.*, sudden
mōtus (4), disturbance, rising
multum, *adv.*, much
supersum, -esse, -fui, I am left
vectīg-al, -ālis, *n.*, tax, tribute
pend-o, -ĕre, pependi, pensum, I
   pay
dēdūc-o, -ĕre, -duxi, -ductum, I
   launch
commeātus (4), relay
accidit ut, it happened that
necessārio, *adv.*, necessarily
angustus, *adj.*, crowded
tranquillit-as, -ātis, *f.*, calm
perdūc-o, -ĕre, -duxi, -ductum, I
   bring across

GENERAL VOCABULARY

ā *or* **ab,** *prep. with abl.*, from; by
abdūc-o, -ĕre, -duxi, -ductum, I lead off, lead away
ab-ĕo, -īre, -ii *or* **-īvi, -ĭtum,** I go away, depart
abhinc, *adv.*, ago
abic-io, -ĕre, -iēci, -iectum, I throw away
absist-o, -ĕre, -stiti, I keep away from
absum, abesse, āfui, I am distant
ac, *see* **atque**
accĭdit ut, it happened that
accip-io, -ĕre, -cēpi, -ceptum, I receive; accept; suffer (*a defeat*)
accūso (1), I accuse
acies (5), line-of-battle
ācrĭter, *adv.*, keenly, fiercely
acūtus, *adj.*, sharp
ad, *prep. with acc.*, to, towards; near, at; for
add-o, -ĕre, -didi, -ditum, I add
ad-ĕo, -īre, -ii *or* **-īvi, -ĭtum,** I go to, approach
adĕo, *adv.*, so much
adflo (1), I blow
adhūc, *adv.*, still; up to this time
adiŭv-o, -āre, -iūvi, -iūtum, I help
adloqu-or, -i, -locūtus sum, I address, speak to
admoneo (2), I warn; urge
adsum, adesse, adfui, I am present
adven-io, -īre, -vēni, -ventum, I arrive, reach
adventus (4), approach, arrival
adversārius (2), adversary, enemy
adversus, *adj.*, opposite; adverse
adversus, *prep. with acc.*, against
advŏlo (1), I rush towards
aedificium (2), building
aedifico (1), I build
aeg-er, -ra, -rum, *adj.*, sick
aegrē, *adv.*, with difficulty
aes, aeris, *n.*, bronze
aest-as, -ātis, *f.*, summer
aestus (4), heat; tide

aet-as, -ātis, *f.*, age
aeternus, *adj.*, eternal, everlasting
affic-io, -ĕre, -fēci, -fectum, I affect
affirmo (1), I declare, state
afflicto (1), I dash, damage
afflīg-o, -ĕre, -flixi, -flictum, I afflict
ager, agri (2), field; *plur.* estates
aggred-ior, -i, aggressus sum, I attack
agm-en, -ĭnis, *n.*, army (*on the march*)
ago, agĕre, ēgi, actum, I drive; act; spend (*time*)
grātias agĕre, to give thanks
albus, *adj.*, white
aliqui, aliqua, aliquod, *adj.*, some
aliquis, aliquid, *pron.*, someone, something
alius, *adj.*, other, another
alii . . . alii, some . . . others
alo, alĕre, alui, altum, I feed, nourish
alter, -a, -um, *adj.*, one *or* the other (*of two*); another
altitūd-o, -ĭnis, *f.*, depth
altus, *adj.*, high; deep
amb-o, -ae, -o, *adj.*, both
ambulo (1), I walk, stroll
amīcitia (1), friendship
amīcus (2), friend
āmitt-o, -ĕre, -mīsi, -missum, I lose
amo (1), I love; like
am-or, -ōris, *m.*, love
ancŏra (1), anchor
angelus (2), angel
angustus, *adj.*, narrow; crowded
animadvert-o, -ĕre, -verti, -versum, I notice
anim-al, -ālis, *n.*, animal
animus (2), mind; courage
annus (2), year
ante, *prep. with acc.*, before; in front of
antea *or* **ante,** *adv.*, before, previously
antequam, *conj.*, before
antīquus, *adj.*, old, ancient
aper, apri (2), wild boar
apertus, *adj.*, open

appāreo (2), I appear
appello (1), I name; call; appeal to
apprŏpinquo (1), *with* **ad**, I approach
aptus, *adj. with dat.*, suitable for
apud, *prep. with acc.*, among; in the works of; in the presence of
aqua (1), water
aquila (1), eagle; standard
āra (1), altar
arbitror (1), I think
arb-or, -ŏris, *f.*, tree
arcus (4), arch
arduus, *adj.*, steep
arēna (1), arena; sand
argentum (2), silver
āridum (2), dry land
arithmētica (1), arithmetic
arm-a, -ōrum (2) *pl.*, arms
armāment-a, -ōrum (2) *pl.*, tackle, gear
armātus, *adj.*, armed
ars, artis, *f.*, art, skill
artif-ex, -ĭcis, *m.*, artist, designer
arx, arcis, *f.*, citadel
ascend-o, -ĕre, -i, ascensum, I climb, ascend
astronomia (1), astronomy
at, *conj.*, but
atque *or* **ac,** *conj.*, and
atr-ox (*gen.* **-ōcis**), *adj.*, fierce
attonitus, *adj.*, astonished
auct-or, -ōris, *m.*, author; founder
auctumnus (2), autumn
aud-ax (*gen.* **-ācis**), *adj.*, bold
aud-eo, -ēre, ausus sum, I dare
audio (4), I hear, listen to
aug-eo, -ēre, auxi, auctum, I increase
aur-is, -is, *f.*, ear
aurum (2), gold
aut, *conj.*, or
 aut . . . aut, either . . . or
autem, *conj.*, however, but; moreover
auxilium (2), help
 auxilia, *n. pl.*, reinforcements
avē, *imperative*, hail!
āvert-o, -ĕre, āverti, āversum, I avert, turn away
avidus, *adj. with gen.*, eager for
av-is, -is, *f.*, bird
avunculus (2), uncle

balne-ae, -ārum (1) *pl.*, public baths

barbarus (2), barbarian; native
basilica (1), hall
bellum (2), war
bene, *adv.*, well
beneficium (2), kindness
benignus, *adj.*, kind
bon-a, -ōrum (2) *pl.*, goods, possessions
bonus, *adj.*, good
brev-is, -e, *adj.*, short, brief

cad-o, -ĕre, cecĭdi, cāsum, I fall
caecus, *adj.*, blind
caed-es, -is, *f.*, slaughter
caed-o, -ĕre, cecīdi, caesum, I slaughter
caelum (2), sky, heavens
calculus (2), pebble
cal-or, -ōris, *m.*, heat
candēlābrum (2), candelabrum, candle-stick
can-is, -is, *c.*, dog
canto (1), I sing
cap-io, -ĕre, cēpi, captum, I capture; take
 consilium capĕre, to form a plan
captīva (1), female prisoner
captīvus (2), prisoner
cap-ut, -ĭtis, *n.*, head; capital
carc-er, -ĕris, *m.*, prison
carm-en, -ĭnis, *n.*, song; chant
carrus (2), waggon
casa (1), hut
castr-a, -ōrum (2) *pl.*, camp
cāsus (4), chance
catapulta (1), catapult, artillery
cauda (1), tail.
causa (1), reason, cause; law-suit
 causam dīcĕre, to plead a case
 causa, *prep. with gen.* (*follows its noun*), for the sake of
cēd-o, -ĕre, cessi, cessum, I yield, give way
celebro (1), I celebrate; praise
celer, -is, -e, *adj.*, swift, quick
celerit-as, -ātis, *f.*, speed
cēlo (1), I hide, conceal
cēna (1), dinner
cēno (1), I dine
centum, *indecl.*, a hundred
centuri-o, -ōnis, *m.*, centurion, sergeant
certām-en, -ĭnis, *n.*, contest, struggle

certē, *adv.*, certainly
certus, *adj.*, fixed, definite
  certiōrem facĕre, to inform
cēter-i, -ae, -a, *adj.*, rest of
chŏrus (2), chorus
cibus (2), food
cing-o, -ĕre, cinxi, cinctum, I surround
cin-is, -ĕris, *m.*, ash
circiter, *adv.*, about
circum, *prep. with acc.*, around, round
circum-do, -dăre, -dĕdi, -dătum, I surround
circum-ĕo, -īre, -ii *or* -īvi, -ĭtum, I go round, visit
circumsist-o, -ĕre, -stĕti, I stand around, surround
circumven-io, -īre, -vēni, -ventum, I surround
cīvīl-is, -e, *adj.*, civil
cīv-is, -is, *c.*, citizen
cīvit-as, -ātis, *f.*, state
clād-es, -is, *f.*, defeat; disaster
clam, *adv.*, secretly
clāmo (1), I shout; exclaim
clām-or, -ōris, *m.*, shout, cry
clārus, *adj.*, famous; clear, bright
class-is, -is, *f.*, fleet
claud-o, -ĕre, clausi, clausum, I close, shut
cli-ens, -entis, *m.*, dependent, caller
coepi, coepisse, I begin
cognosc-o, -ĕre, -nōvi, -ĭtum, I learn, find out
cōg-o, -ĕre, coēgi, coactum, I compel; collect
cohors, cohortis, *f.*, cohort, regiment
collĭg-o, -ĕre, -lēgi, -lectum, I collect
coll-is, -is, *m.*, hill
collŏco (1), I place, set, station
colloquium (2), conversation
col-o, -ĕre, colui, cultum, I worship
col-or, -ōris, *m.*, colour
columna (1), pillar
com-es, -ĭtis, *c.*, companion, comrade
commeātus (4), provisions; relay
committ-o, -ĕre, -mīsi, -missum, I join (*battle*)
commŏv-eo, -ēre, -mōvi, -mōtum, I disturb
commūn-is, -e, *adj.*, common

KL

comparo (1), I compare
comparo (1), I win, gain; prepare
compell-o, -ĕre, -pŭli, -pulsum, I drive
compl-eo, -ēre, -plēvi, -plētum, I fill
complūres, *adj. pl.*, several
compōn-o, -ĕre, -posui, -positum, I compose, put together
comprehend-o, -ĕre, -i, -prehensum I seize, arrest
concĭd-o, -ĕre, -cĭdi, I fall down
concilium (2), meeting
conclāmo (1), I cry out
concurr-o, -ĕre, -curri, -cursum, I come together
condici-o, -ōnis, *f.*, condition
cond-o, -ĕre, -didi, -ditum, I found (*a city*); compose
confĭd-o, -ĕre, -fīsus sum, *with dat. or abl.*, I trust; believe
confirmo (1), I establish
conflīg-o, -ĕre, -flixi, -flictum, I clash, fight
conic-io, -ĕre, -iēci, -iectum, I throw
coniung-o, -ĕre, -iunxi, -iunctum, I join
coniunx, coniŭgīs, *m. or f.*, husband *or* wife
coniūrāti-o, -ōnis, *f.*, plot, conspiracy
coniūrātus (2), conspirator
coniūro (1), I plot, conspire
cōnor (1), I try
conscend-o, -ĕre, -scendi, -scensum I board (*a ship*)
conservo (1), I preserve; save
consilium (2), plan
  consilium capĕre, to form a plan
consist-o, -ĕre, -stiti, I stand; halt
conspectus (4), sight
conspic-io, -ĕre, -spexi, -spectum, I catch sight of; see
constantia (1), determination; endurance
constitu-o, -ĕre, -stitui, -stitūtum, I decide; station
consuesc-o, -ĕre, -suēvi, -suētum, I become accustomed: *in perf.* I am accustomed
cons-ul, -ŭlis, *m.*, consul
consulto, *adv.*, on purpose

consūm-o, -ĕre, -sumpsi, -sumptum, I consume

contemn-o, -ĕre, -tempsi, -temptum, I despise

contend-o, -ĕre, -i, I hasten; march; fight

contenti-o, -ōnis, f., struggle, fighting

contin-ens, -entis, f., mainland

contin-eo, -ēre, -ui, -tentum, I hold, contain; keep
   se continēre, to stay

contra, prep. with acc., against; opposite

contrah-o, -ĕre, -traxi, -tractum, I bring together

conven-io, -īre, -vēni, -ventum, I come together; meet

convert-o, -ĕre, -i, conversum, I turn

convīva (1) c., guest

convīvium (2), feast, banquet

convŏco (1), I call together, call

coor-ior, -īri, coortus sum, I arise

cōpia (1), amount

cōpi-ae, -ārum (1) pl., forces
   cōpiae nŏvae, reinforcements

corōna (1), crown

corp-us, -ŏris, n., body

corrip-io, -ĕre, -ripui, -reptum, I snatch up, seize

corrump-o, -ĕre, -rūpi, -ruptum, I corrupt; bribe

cotīdie, adv., daily

cras, adv., tomorrow

crēd-o, -ĕre, -ĭdi, -ĭtum, I believe

creo (1), I elect

cruciātus (4), torture

crūdēl-is, -e, adj., cruel

crūdēlit-as, -ātis, f., cruelty

crux, crucis, f., cross

cubiculum (2), bed-room

culpa (1), fault; blame

cultus (4), worship

cum, prep. with abl., along with, with

cum, conj., when; since; although

cunctor (1), I hesitate

cur, adv., why?

cūra (1), care

cūro (1), I look after, see to; care for

curr-o, -ĕre, cucurri, cursum, I run

currus (4), chariot

cursus (4), course

custōdia (1), custody

custōdio (4), I guard

cust-os, -ōdis, m., guardian

damno (1), I condemn

dē, prep. with abl., about, concerning

dea (1), goddess

dēbeo (2), I owe; ought, have to

decem, indecl., ten

decimus, adj., tenth

dēdico (1), I dedicate

dēditi-o, -ōnis, f., surrender

dēdūc-o, -ĕre, -duxi, -ductum, I launch

dēfend-o, -ĕre, -i, -fensum, I defend

dēfero, -ferre, -tuli, -lātum, I carry away, carry

dēfessus, adj., tired

dēfic-io, -ĕre, -fēci, -fectum, I fail; am too short

dēfīg-o, -ĕre, -fixi, -fixum, I fasten, fix in

deinde, adv., then, next

dēlecto (1), I delight, charm

dēl-eo, -ēre, -ēvi, -ētum, I destroy

dēlībero (1), I deliberate, take counsel

dēligo (1), I fasten; bind

dēlig-o, -ĕre, -lēgi, -lectum, I choose

dēmitt-o, -ĕre, -mīsi, -missum, I lower

dēmonstro (1), I show, explain

dēpell-o, -ĕre, -pŭli, -pulsum, I dispel, drive away

dēpōn-o, -ĕre, -posui, -positum, I lay aside, abandon

dēscend-o, -ĕre, -i, -scensum, I descend, come down

dēsertus, adj., deserted, lonely

dēsil-io, -īre, -ui, -sultum, I jump down

dēspēro (1), I despair

dēsum, dēesse, dēfui, I am short, lacking

deus (2), god

dēvolv-o, -ĕre, -i, -volūtum, I roll down (trans.)

dēvŏro (1), I devour

dext-er, -ra, -rum, adj., right

dīc-o, -ĕre, dixi, dictum, I speak; say; tell
   causam dīcĕre, to plead a lawcase
   sententiam dīcĕre, to state an opinion

dictum (2), saying
dies (5) *m.*, day
 in dies, day by day
difficil-is, -e, *adj.*, difficult
difficult-as, -ātis, *f.*, difficulty
dignus, *adj. with abl.*, worthy of
dīlig-ens (*gen.* **-entis**), *adj.*, careful
dīligentia (1), diligence, carefulness
dīmĭco (1), I fight
dīmidium (2), half
dīmitt-o, -ĕre, -mīsi, -missum, I
 give up; send away, disband
dīrip-io, -ĕre, -ui, -reptum, I
 plunder
dīru-o, -ĕre, -i, -rutum, I breach
 (*a wall*)
discēd-o, -ĕre, -cessi, -cessum, I go
 away, depart
discind-o, -ĕre, -scidi, -scissum, I
 cut apart
discipulus (2), pupil; disciple
disc-o, -ĕre, dĭdĭci, I learn
discordia (1), quarrel
dispar (*gen.* **dispăris**), *adj.*, unequal
dispŭto (1), I argue, dispute
diu, *adv.*, for a long time
dīves (*gen.* **dīvĭtis**), *adj.*, rich
dīvĭd-o, -ĕre, -vīsi, -vīsum, I divide;
 separate
dīvīnus, *adj.*, divine
dīviti-ae, -ārum (1) *pl.*, riches
do, dăre, dĕdi, dătum, I give
doc-eo, -ēre, -ui, doctum, I teach
doctus, *adj.*, learned
dol-or, -ōris, *m.*, grief; suffering
domesticus, *adj.*, at home, domestic
dominus (2), master; owner; Lord
domus (2 & 4) *f.*, house, home
dormio (4), I sleep
ducent-i, -ae, -a, *adj.*, two hundred
dūc-o, -ĕre, duxi, ductum, I lead;
 dig (*a ditch*); derive
 in mātrimōnium dūcĕre, to marry
 (*trans.*)
dum, *conj.*, while
duo, duae, duo, *adj.*, two
duodecim, *indecl.*, twelve
duodēvīginti, *indecl.*, eighteen
dux, dŭcis, *m.*, leader, general

ē *or* **ex,** *prep. with abl.*, from; of; after
ebur, ebŏris, *n.*, ivory

eccĕ, behold!
ecclēsia (1), church; Athenian parliament
ēdictum (2), edict, regulation
ĕdo, ĕdĕre, ēdi, ēsum, I eat
ēdūco (1), I rear, bring up
effic-io, -ĕre, -fēci, -fectum, I cause
effŏd-io, -ĕre, -fōdi, -fossum, I dig
 up
effŭg-io, -ĕre, -fūgi, I escape
effulg-eo, -ēre, -fulsi, I shine forth
effund-o, -ĕre, -fūdi, -fūsum, I shed
ego, *pron.*, I
ēgred-ior, -i, egressus sum, I go out
 ē nāve ēgredi, to disembark
ēgregius, *adj.*, excellent; extraordinary
ēic-io, -ĕre, -iēci, -iectum, I throw
 out
 se ēicĕre, to rush out
ēlāb-or, -i, elapsus sum, I slip away,
 escape
elephantus (2) *c.*, elephant
ēloquentia (1), eloquence
ēmitt-o, -ĕre, -mīsi, -missum, I send
 out
emo, emĕre, ēmi, emptum, I buy
enim, *conj.*, for
eo, *adv.*, to there, thither
ĕo, īre, ii *or* **īvi, ĭtum,** I go
 obviam īre *with dat.*, to go to meet
epistola (1), letter
equ-es, ĭtis, *m.*, cavalryman: *pl.*,
 cavalry
equitātus (4), cavalry
equus (2), horse
erro (1), I make a mistake, am mistaken
err-or, -ōris, *m.*, mistake, error
ērupti-o, -ōnis, *f.*, sortie
essedārius (2), charioteer
essedum (2), war-chariot
et *conj.*, and; also
 et ... et, both ... and
etiam, *adv.*, even; also
etsi, *conj.*, although
ēvād-o, -ĕre, -vāsi, -vāsum, I
 escape
ēvānesc-o, -ĕre, -vānui, I vanish,
 disappear
ēventus (4), result, outcome
ex, *see* **e**
excĭto (1), I rouse, stir up; excite

excut-io, -ĕre, -cussi, -cussum, I shake off

exemplum (2), example

ex-ĕo, -īre, -ii *or* **-īvi, -ĭtum,** I go out

exerc-eo, -ēre, -ui, -itum, I practise

exercitus (4), army

exhaur-io, -īre, -hausi, -haustum, I drain, drink; exhaust

exiguus, *adj.,* very small

exilium (2), exile

exinde, *adv.,* from then on

exitium (2), destruction

expedītus (2), light-armed soldier; unencumbered (*adj.*)

expell-o, -ĕre, -pŭli, -pulsum, I drive out

explōro (1), I explore; reconnoitre

expugno (1), I capture, take by storm

exsequi-ae, -ārum (1) *pl.,* funeral

exspecto (1), I await, wait for

exstingu-o, -ĕre, -stinxi, -stinctum, I put out, extinguish

exst-o, -āre, I stand out, project

externus, *adj.,* foreign, abroad

extra, *prep. with acc.,* outside

extrah-o, -ĕre, -traxi, -tractum, I draw out, withdraw

extrēmus, *adj.,* end of; farthest

fab-er, -ri (2), workman; engineer

fābula (1), story; a play

faciēs (5), face

facil-is, -e, *adj.,* easy

fac-io, -ĕre, fēci, factum, I make; do
  certiōrem facĕre, to inform
  iter facĕre, to travel

factum (2), deed

facult-as, -ātis, *f.,* chance, opportunity

fall-o, -ĕre, fefelli, falsum, I deceive, cheat

falso, *adv.,* falsely

fāma (1), fame, glory

fam-es, -is, *f.,* hunger, starvation

familia (1), household

fax, făcis, *f.,* torch

fēmina (1), woman

fera (1), wild beast

ferē, *adv.,* about, almost

fēri-ae, -ārum (1) *plur.,* holidays

fero, ferre, tuli, lātum, I bear; bring, carry

festus, *adj.,* sacred, festal
  dies festi, *pl.,* festivals

fidēl-is, -e, *adj.,* faithful

fides (5), faith

fīdus, *adj.,* faithful

fīlia (1), daughter

fīlius (2), son

fing-o, -ĕre, finxi, fictum, I invent

fīnio (4), I end, finish

fīn-is, -is, *m.,* end
  fīnes, *pl.,* boundaries, territories

fīnitimus (2), neighbour

fīnitimus, *adj.,* near-by, neighbouring

fīo, fīeri, factus sum, I am made; become; happen, take place

flamma (1), flame

fleo, flēre, flēvi, flētum, I weep

flōs, flōris, *m.,* flower

fluctus (4), wave

flūm-en, -ĭnis, *n.,* river
  secundo flūmĭne, downstream

flu-o, -ĕre, fluxi, fluxum, I flow

fluvius (2), river

fons, fontis, *m.,* well, spring; fountain

fŏrīs, *adv.,* out of doors

fortasse, *adv.,* perhaps

fortĕ, *adv.,* by chance

fort-is, -e, *adj.,* brave

fortūna (1), luck, chance

fŏrum (2), forum, market-place

fossa (1), ditch

fragmentum (2), fragment, broken piece

frang-o, -ĕre, frēgi, fractum, I break; wreck

frāt-er, -ris, *m.,* brother

frĕtum (2), strait, channel

frīg-us, -ŏris, *n.,* cold

frons, frontis, *f.,* front

frūmentum (2), corn

frustra, *adv.,* in vain

fuga (1), flight

fŭg-io, -ĕre, fūgi, I flee

fugo (1), I chase, put to flight

fulg-ens (*gen.* **-entis**), *adj.,* shining

fulg-eo, -ēre, fulsi, I shine

fulm-en, -ĭnis, *n.,* lightning

fūmus (2), smoke

funditus, *adv.,* utterly

fund-o, -ĕre, fūdi, fūsum, I pour

fur-or, -ōris, *m.,* fury; excitement

furtum (2), theft

gaudium (2), joy
gemma (1), jewel
gens, gentis, *f.,* people, race
gen-us, -ĕris, *n.,* sort, kind; race
geōmetria (1), geometry
ger-o, -ĕre, gessi, gestum, I wage;
  conduct; do
  res gestae, *f. pl.,* exploits, achieve-
  ments
gladiāt-or, -ōris, *m.* gladiator
gladius (2), sword
glōria (1), glory
gradus (4), step
grātia (1), thanks
  grātiam habēre, to feel thankful
  grātias agĕre, to give thanks
grātus, *adj.,* pleasing
grav-is, -e, *adj.,* heavy; serious; severe
gravit-as, -ātis, *f.,* weight
gubernāt-or, -ōris, *m.,* helmsman

habeo (2), I have; hold; consider
  ōrātiōnem habēre, to deliver a
  speech
  grātiam habēre, to feel thankful
habito (1), I dwell, live
haud, *adv.,* not
herba (1), herb
hīc, haec, hōc, this
hīc, *adv.,* here
hiemo (1), I spend the winter
hiems, hiĕmis, *f.,* winter
hinc, *adv.,* from here
hippopotamus (2), hippopotamus
histŏria (1), history
histri-o, -ōnis, *m.,* actor
hŏdie, *adv.,* today
hŏdiernus, *adj.,* of today
hŏm-o, -ĭnis, *m.,* man
hon-or, -ōris, *m.,* honour
hōra (1), hour
horrendus, *adj.,* terrifying, fearsome
hortor (1), I encourage, exhort
hortus (2), garden
hosp-es, -ĭtis, *m.,* guest; host
hostia (1), victim, offering
host-is, -is, *c.,* enemy
hūc, *adv.,* to here, hither
hūmānus, *adj.,* human
humerus (2), shoulder

iac-eo, -ēre, -ui, I lie; recline
iac-io, -ĕre, iēci, iactum, I throw
iacto (1), I toss
iam, *adv.,* now; already
ibi, *adv.,* there
īdem, eadem, ĭdem, same, the same
idōneus, *adj.,* suitable
igitur, *adv.,* therefore
ign-is, -is, *m.,* fire
ignōtus, *adj.,* unknown
ille, illa, illud, that; he, she, it, they
illūmino (1), I light, illuminate
imb-er, -ris, *m.,* rain, rain-storm
imitor (1), I imitate, copy
immōtus, *adj.,* motionless
impediment-a, -ōrum (2) *pl.,* baggage
impedio (4), I hinder
impedītus, *adj.,* not ready for battle;
  impenetrable
impell-o, -ĕre, -pŭli, -pulsum, I
  drive on, drive
imperāt-or, -ōris, *m.,* general; emperor
imperītus, *adj. with gen.,* inexperi-
  enced in
imperium (2), empire; rule; authority
impero (1), *with dat.,* I order
impetus (4), attack; violence
impl-eo, -ēre, -ēvi, -ētum, I fill
impōn-o, -ĕre, -posui, -positum, I
  place on; put in
importo (1), I import, bring in
imprŏbus, *adj.,* wicked
imprūd-ens (*gen.* **-entis**), *adj.,* off
  one's guard
īmus, *adj.,* lowest
in, *prep. with abl.,* in; on
in, *prep. with acc.,* into, to; against; on
  to; for
incend-o, -ĕre, -i, -censum, I burn
  (*trans.*)
incertus, *adj.,* uncertain, doubtful
incip-io, -ĕre, -cēpi, -ceptum, I begin
incĭto (1), I urge on
incognĭtus, *adj.,* unknown
incŏla (1), *c.,* inhabitant
incŏl-o, -ĕre, -ui, I inhabit, dwell in
incolum-is, -e, *adj.,* unharmed, safe
incursi-o, -ōnis, *f.,* invasion
inde, *adv.,* then, next; from there
indu-o, -ĕre, -i, -dūtum, I put on
  (*clothes*)

inerm-is, -e, *adj.,* unarmed
infēl-ix (*gen.* **-īcis**), *adj.,* unfortunate
infer-ior (*gen.* **-iōris**), *adj.,* lower
infero, inferre, intuli, inlātum, I inflict
infirmus, *adj.,* weak
infra, *adv.,* below
ingenium (2), ability, genius
ing-ens (*gen.* **-entis**), *adj.,* enormous, huge, very great
ingred-ior, -i, ingressus sum, I enter
inimīcus (2), (personal) enemy
inimīcus, *adj.,* hostile, unfriendly
initium (2), beginning
iniūria (1), wrong; injury
innoc-ens (*gen.* **-entis**), *adj.,* innocent
inŏpia (1), shortage, scarcity
inopīnātus, *adj.,* unexpected, sudden
inquam, I say, said
inquit: *pl.* **inquiunt,** he says, he said: they say
insānus, *adj.,* insane, mad
inscrīb-o, -ěre, -scripsi, -scriptum, I inscribe, write on
insign-ě, -is, *n.,* emblem
insign-is, -e, *adj.,* conspicuous
inspic-io, -ěre, -spexi, -spectum, I look into, examine
instru-o, -ěre, -struxi, -structum, I draw up; equip
insula (1), island; block of flats
intelleg-o, -ěre, I realise
inter, *prep. with acc.,* among; between
interdiu, *adv.,* by day
interdum, *adv.,* at times
interea, *adv.,* meanwhile
interfic-io, -ěre, -fēci, -fectum, I kill
interim, *adv.,* meanwhile
inter-ior (*gen.* **-iōris**), *adj.,* interior, inner
intermitt-o, -ěre, -mīsi, -missum, I leave between, allow to pass
interrŏgo (1), I question, ask
intersum, -esse, -fui, *with dat.,* I take part in
intra, *prep. with acc.,* within
intro (1), I enter
inundo (1), I flood (*trans.*)
inūtil-is, -e, *adj.,* useless
invěn-io, -īre, -vēni, -ventum, I find; invent

investīgo (1), I investigate
invictus, *adj.,* undaunted
invīto (1), I invite
invītus, *adj.,* unwilling
invŏco (1), I call upon, invoke
iŏcus (2), joke
ipse, ipsa, ipsum, himself, herself, *etc.*
īra (1), anger
īrātus, *adj.,* angry
is, ea, id, he, she, it; that
ita, *adv.,* so, in such a way
ita ut, so that
itaque, *adv.,* and so, therefore
iter, itiněris, *n.,* journey, march
iter facěre, to make a journey, travel
iterum, *adv.,* a second time, again
iub-eo, -ēre, iussi, iussum, I order
iūcundus, *adj.,* pleasant
iūd-ex, -ǐcis, *m.,* judge: *pl.,* jury
iūdicium (2), trial; judgement
iǔgum (2), yoke; ridge
iūmentum (2), baggage-animal
iung-o, -ěre, iunxi, iunctum, I join
iussum (2), order
iuven-is, -is, *m.,* young man

lab-or, -ōris, *m.,* labour, toil
labōro (1), I am in difficulties; work
lacess-o, -ěre, -īvi *or* **-ii, -ītum,** I provoke
lacrima (1), tear
laetus, *adj.,* glad, happy
lanio (1), I tear in pieces
lap-is, -ǐdis, *m.,* stone
lāte, *adv.,* far and wide
lātus, *adj.,* wide, broad
lǎt-us, -ěris, *n.,* side, flank
laudo (1), I praise
lectīca (1), litter
lect-or, -ōris, *c.,* reader
lectus (2), couch
lēgātus (2), legate, senior officer; envoy
legi-o, -ōnis, *f.,* legion
leg-o, -ěre, lēgi, lectum, I read
lēn-is, -e, *adj.,* gentle
leo, leōnis, *m.,* lion
lěv-is, -e, *adj.,* light; unimportant, trifling
lex, lēgis, *f.,* law

libenter, *adv.*, willingly
lĭb-er, -ri (2), book
līber-i, -ōrum (2) *pl.*, children
lībero (1), I free, set free
lībert-as, -ātis, *f.*, freedom, liberty
licet (2), *impers.*, it is allowed
ligneus, *adj.*, made of wood
lignum (2), wood
lingua (1), language; tongue
lint-er, -ris, *f.*, small boat
littera (1), letter (*of alphabet*)
litter-ae, -ārum (1), literature; letter
līt-us, -ŏris, *n.*, shore
lŏcus (2): *pl.* **lŏca,** *n.*, place
longē, *adv.*, by far; far
longinquus, *adj.*, distant
longius, *adv.*, farther; too far
longus, *adj.*, long
loqu-or, -i, locūtus sum, I speak, converse
lūdus (2), school; game
lūm-en, -ĭnis, *n.*, light
lūna (1), moon
lux, lūcis, *f.*, light
  lux prīma, dawn
luxuria (1), luxury
luxuriōsus, *adj.*, luxurious

māchĭna (1), machine, military engine
magicus, *adj.*, magical, magic
magist-er, -ri (2), master, teacher; captain
magistrātus (4), magistrate
magnificentia (1), magnificence
magnitūd-o, -ĭnis, *f.*, size
magnŏpere, *adv.*, greatly
magnus, *adj.*, large, great; loud
māiest-as, -ātis, *f.*, majesty, dignity
māiōr-es, -um, *c. pl.*, ancestors
mālo, malle, mālui, I prefer
malum (2), harm, evil
malus, *adj.*, bad
māne, *adv.*, in the morning, early
man-eo, -ēre, mansi, mansum, I stay, remain
manus (4), *f.*, hand
mare, maris, *n.*, sea
marīnus, *adj.*, of the sea, marine
marĭtĭmus, *adj.*, maritime, coastal
marmoreus, *adj.*, marble, of marble
māt-er, -ris, *f.*, mother
mātĕria (1), timber

mātrimōnium (2), marriage
mātrōna (1), matron, married woman
maxime, *adv.*, very much, most, especially
medicīna (1), medicine
medicīnus, *adj.*, of medicine
medicus (2), doctor
medius, *adj.*, the middle of; middle
membrum (2), limb, part (*of the body*)
memŏria (1), memory
mens, mentis, *f.*, mind
mensa (1), table
mens-is, -is, *m.*, month
mercāt-or, -ōris, *m.*, merchant
mercātūra (1), trade
merīdies (5) *m.*, south; midday
metus (4), fear
meus, *adj.*, my, mine
mīl-es, ĭtis, *m.*, soldier
mil-ia, -ium, *n. pl.*, thousands
mīlitār-is, -e, *adj.*, military
mille, *indec.*, a thousand
minist-er, -ri (2), servant
mĭnus, *adv.*, less
mīrābil-is, -e, *adj.*, marvellous
mīror, (1), I am amazed
mīrus, *adj.*, wonderful
mĭser, -a, -um, *adj.*, wretched, miserable
mitt-o, -ĕre, mīsi, missum, I send; launch, hurl
mōbil-is, -e, *adj.*, moveable
mŏdo, *adv.*, only
mŏdus (2), way, manner
moen-ia, -ium, *n. pl.*, walls
mōl-es, -is, *f.*, mole; causeway
molestus, *adj.*, tedious
mons, montis, *m.*, mountain
monstro (1), I show; describe
monumentum (2), monument, memorial
mŏra (1), delay
morbus (2), disease, sickness
mor-ior, -i, mortuus sum, I die
moror (1), I wait; delay
mors, mortis, *f.*, death
  mortem obīre, to meet one's death, die
mortuus, *adj.*, dead
mōs, mōris, *m.*, custom; fashion; *pl.*, character
mōtus (4), disturbance, rising

139

mŏv-eo, -ēre, mōvi, mōtum, I move

mox, *adv.*, soon; later

mulc-eo, -ēre, mulsi, mulsum, I lick

mult-i, -ae, -a, *adj.*, many

multitūd-o, -ĭnis, *f.*, number; great number

multo, *adv.*, much

multum, *adv.*, much

mundus (2), universe, world

mūnio (4), I fortify

mūniti-o, -ōnis, *f.*, fortification

mūrus (2), wall

mūto (1), I change (*trans.*)

nam, *conj.*, for

nancisc-or, -i, nactus sum, I obtain; meet with

narro (1), I relate, tell

nasc-or, -i, nātus sum, I am born

nāti-o, -ōnis, *f.*, tribe

nato (1), I swim

nātūra (1), nature

nauta (1) *m.*, sailor

nāvāl-is, -e, *adj.*, naval

nāvigāti-o, -ōnis, *f.*, sailing; voyage

nāvigo (1), I sail

nāv-is, -is, *f.*, ship

   nāvis longa, warship

   nāvis onerāria, transport; merchant ship

   nāvem conscendĕre, to board a ship

   nāvem solvĕre, to set sail

nē, *conj.*, lest

nec, *see* neque

necessārio, *adv.*, necessarily

necessārius, *adj.*, necessary

nĕfas, *indec.*, forbidden

negleg-o, -ĕre, -lexi, -lectum, I pass over; neglect

negōtium (2), business

nēmo (*acc.* **nēminem,** *gen.* **nullius**), no one

nēquāquam, *adv.*, by no means, not at all

neque *or* **nec,** *conj.*, nor, and not

   neque . . . neque, neither . . . nor

   neque iam, and no longer

nescio (4), I do not know

nig-er, -ra, -rum, *adj.*, black

nihil, *indec.*, nothing

nĭsi, *conj.*, unless; except

nix, nĭvis, *f.*, snow

nōbil-is, -e, *adj.*, high-born, noble

noceo (2) *with dat.*, I hurt, harm

nōdus (2), knot

nōlo, nōlle, nōlui, I am unwilling, do not wish

nōm-en, -ĭnis, *n.*, name

nōn, *adv.*, not

   nōn iam, no longer

   nōn sōlum . . . sed etiam, not only . . . but also

nōndum, *adv.*, not yet

nōnnull-i, -ae, -a, *adj.*, some

nōnnunquam, *adv.*, sometimes

nōnus, *adj.*, ninth

nōs, *pron.*, we, us

nost-er, -ra, -rum, *adj.*, our

nōtus, *adj.*, known, well known

nŏtus (2), south wind

nŏvem, nine

nŏvus, *adj.*, new; strange

nox, noctis, *f.*, night

nūb-es, -is, *f.*, cloud

nullus (*gen.* **nullius**), *adj.*, no; none

num, surely . . . not?

numero (1), I count

numerus (2), number

nunc, *adv.*, now

nunquam, *adv.*, never

nuntio (1), I announce, report

nuntius (2), messenger

nūper, *adv.*, lately, recently

ob, *prep. with acc.*, because of

ob-ĕo, -īre, -ii *or* **-īvi, -ĭtum,** I face, go to meet

   mortem obīre, to die

observo (1), I observe

obs-es, -ĭdis, *c.*, hostage

obtin-eo, -ēre, -ui, -tentum, I hold, retain

obviam, *with dat.*, to meet

   obviam īre, to go to meet

occīd-o, -ĕre, -cīdi, -cīsum, I kill

occulto (1), I hide

occupo (1), I seize, take possession of: *pass.*, I am occupied

octāvus, *adj.*, eighth

octo, *indec.*, eight

octōgēsimus, *adj.*, eightieth

octōginta, *indec.*, eighty

oculus (2), eye

officium (2), duty
    officium praestāre, to do one's duty
ōlim, *adv.*, once upon a time; once
omitt-o, -ĕre, -mīsi, -missum, I give up
omnīno, *adv.*, in all; at all
omn-is, -e, *adj.*, all; every
ŏn-us, -ĕris, *n.*, weight
ŏpes, ŏpum, *f. pl.*, resources
oppidum (2), town
opprim-o, -ĕre, -pressi, -pressum, I crush; weigh down
oppugno (1), I attack
ŏp-us, -ĕris, *n.*, work
ōra (1), shore, coast
    ōra marĭtĭma, seashore
ōrāculum (2), oracle
ōrāti-o, -ōnis, *f.*, a speech
    ōrātiōnem habēre, to deliver a speech
ōrāt-or, -ōris, *m.*, orator
orbis terrārum, *m.*, the world
ord-o, -ĭnis, *m.*, line, rank
oriens, orientis, *m.*, the East
orientāl-is, -e, *adj.*, eastern, in the east
orīg-o, -ĭnis, *f.*, origin
orior, orīri, ortus sum, I arise, rise
orno (1), I adorn, decorate
ōro (1), I beg
ōs, ōris, *n.*, face; mouth
ostend-o, -ĕre, -i, ostentum, I show, reveal
ostium (2), entrance, mouth
ōtiōsus, *adj.*, leisurely

pābulāt-or, -ōris, *m.*, forager
pābulor (1), I forage, get food
pāco (1), I pacify
paene, *adv.*, almost
pal-us, -ūdis, *f.*, marsh
pān-is, -is, *m.*, bread
pār (*gen.* **păris**), *adj.*, equal
par-ens, -entis, *c.*, parent
pāreo (2) *with dat.*, I obey
paro (1), I prepare
pars, partis, *f.*, part; side; direction
parvus, *adj.*, small
passus (4), pace
    passūs mille, 1,000 paces, one mile
păt-er, -ris, *m.*, father
patienter, *adv.*, patiently

pat-ior, -i, passus sum, I endure, suffer
patria (1), native land, country
patruus (2), uncle
pauc-i, ae, -a, *adj.*, few
paulātim, *adj.*, gradually
paulisper, *adv.*, for a short time
paulum, *adv.*, a little
paup-er (*gen.* **-ĕris**), *adj.*, poor
pax, pācis, *f.*, peace
pecco (1), I sin, do wrong
pect-us, -ŏris, *n.*, breast
pecūnia (1), money
pec-us, -ŏris, *n.*, herd; cattle
ped-es, -ĭtis, *m.*, infantryman: *pl.*, infantry
pedest-er, -ris, -e, *adj.*, infantry
pell-is, -is, *f.*, skin, hide
pell-o, -ĕre, pepuli, pulsum, I drive
pend-o, -ĕre, pependi, pensum, I pay
per, *prep. with acc.*, during; through; at the hands of
percut-io, -ĕre, percussi, percussum, I strike; pierce
perdūc-o, -ĕre, -duxi, -ductum, I bring across
per-ĕo, -īre, -ii *or* **-īvi, -ĭtum,** I perish
perfic-io, -ĕre, -fēci, -fectum, I complete
perfĭdia (1), treachery
perfŭga (1) *m.*, deserter
perĭculōsus, *adj.*, dangerous
perĭculum (2), danger
perĭtus, *adj. with gen.*, skilled (in)
permitt-o, -ĕre, -mīsi, -missum, I entrust
perrump-o, -ĕre, -rūpi, -ruptum, I break through
persequ-or, -i, persecūtus sum, I persecute
perspic-io, -ĕre, -spexi, -spectum, I examine, study
persuād-eo, -ēre, -suāsi, -suāsum, *with dat.*, I persuade
perterreo (2), I frighten
perturbāti-o, -ōnis, *f.*, confusion, consternation
perturbo (1), I confuse, frighten
pervĕn-io, -īre, -vēni, -ventum, I reach, arrive at

pēs, pĕdis, *m.,* foot
  pedibus, on foot
pet-o, -ĕre, -īvi *or* **-ii, -ītum,** I seek;
  make for
phal-anx, -angis, *f.,* the phalanx
philosophia (1), philosophy
philosophus (2), philosopher
ping-o, -ĕre, pinxi, pictum, I paint
placeo (2) *with dat.,* I please
plāco (1), I appease, pacify
plānities (5), plain
plānus, *adj.,* level
plebs, plēbis, *f.,* the common people
plēnus, *adj. with abl.,* full (of)
plērumque, *adv.,* generally, usually
poena (1), penalty, punishment
poēta (1), *m.,* poet
pond-us, -ĕris, *n.,* weight
pōn-o, -ĕre, posui, positum, I place;
  set up
pons, pontis, *m.,* bridge
populus (2), a people; nation
porta (1), gate; door
porto (1), I carry
portus (4), harbour
posc-o, -ĕre, poposci, I demand
possum, posse, potui, I am able, can
post, *prep. with acc.,* after: behind
postea *or* **post,** *adv.,* later, afterwards
posterus, *adj.,* next
postrēmo, *adv.,* finally
postrīdie, *adv.,* on the next day
pŏt-ens (*gen.* **-entis**), *adj.,* powerful
potest-as, -ātis, *f.,* power
pot-ior, -īri, -ītus sum, *with abl.,* I
  gain, get possession of
potius, *adv.,* rather
praebeo (2), I show (*myself*); provide
praec-eps (*gen.* **-ĭpitis**), *adj.,* headlong
praecīd-o, -ĕre, -cīdi, -cīsum, I cut,
  cut short
praedīc-o, -ĕre, -dixi, -dictum, I
  predict, foretell
praed-o, -ōnis, *m.,* pirate
praedor (1), I plunder
praefic-io, -ĕre, -fēci, -fectum, I put
  in command
praemitt-o, -ĕre, -mīsi, -missum,
  I send ahead
praemium (2), reward
praesertim, *adv.,* especially
praes-ens (*gen.* **-entis**), *adj.,* present

praesidium (2), garrison
praest-o, -āre, praestiti, I show (*a
  quality*)
  officium praestāre, to do one's
  duty
praesum, -esse, -fui, *with dat.,* I am
  in charge of; rule over
praeter, *prep. with acc.,* except
praeterea, *adv.,* besides, in addition
praet-or, -ōris, *m.,* praetor
prĕces, *f. pl.,* prayers
precor (1), I pray
prem-o, -ĕre, pressi, pressum, I
  press, oppress
pretium (2), price
prīdie, *adv.,* the day before
prīmo, *adv.,* at first
prīmum, *adv.,* first
prīmus, *adj.,* first
  lux prīma, dawn
princ-eps, -ĭpis, *m.,* chief; emperor;
  chieftain, chief man
prīvātus, *adj.,* private
prō, *prep. with abl.,* for, in return for; in
  front of
prōcēd-o, -ĕre, -cessi, -cessum, I go
  forward, advance
procul, *adv.,* far; at a distance
prōcūrāt-or, -ōris, *m.,* governor
prōcurr-o, -ĕre, -curri, -cursum, I
  run forward
prōd-o, -ĕre, -idi, -itum, I hand over,
  betray
prōdūc-o, -ĕre, -duxi, -ductum, I
  bring forward; prolong
proelium (2), battle
proficisc-or, -i, profectus sum, I set
  out
prōgred-ior, -i, -gressus sum, I
  advance
prohibeo (2) *with infin.,* I prevent;
  hinder
prōic-io, -ĕre, -iēci, -iectum, I
  throw away
prōmitt-o, -ĕre, -mīsi, -missum, I
  promise
prŏpe, *prep. with acc.,* near
prŏpe, *adv.,* almost
prŏpero (1), I hasten
propter, *prep. with acc.,* on account of
prōra (1), prow, bow
prōtinus, *adv.,* at once

prōvincia (1), province
proximus, *adj.,* next; nearest
publicus, *adj.,* public
  rēs publica, the Roman state
puella (1), girl
puer, -i (2), boy
pūgi-o, -ōnis, *m.,* dagger
pugna (1), fight, battle, fighting
pugno (1), I fight
pulch-er, -ra, -rum, *adj.,* beautiful,
  handsome
pulv-is, -ĕris, *m.,* dust
pūnio (4), I punish
pupp-is, -is, *f.,* stern
pūrus, *adj.,* pure
puto (1), I think

quadrāginta, *indec.,* forty
quaer-o, -ĕre, -sīvi, -sītum, I seek,
  look for
quaest-or, -ōris, *m.,* quaestor
quāl-is, -e, *adj.,* of what kind? what
  kind of?
quam, *adv.,* than
  quam prīmum, as soon as possible
quamdiu, *adv.,* as long as
quamquam, *conj.,* although
quantus, *adj.,* how great?
quartus, *adj.,* fourth
quattuor, *indec.,* four
quattuordecim, *indec.,* fourteen
-que, *conj.,* and
qui, quae, quod, *rel. pron.,* who, which,
  that
qui, quae, quod, *interrog. adj.,* what?
  which?
quīdam, quaedam, quoddam, *adj.,*
  a certain; a sort of
quĭdem, *adv.,* indeed
qui-es, -ētis, *f.,* rest
quindecim, *indec.,* fifteen
quingent-i, -ae, -a, *adj.,* five hundred
quinquāgēsimus, *adj.,* fiftieth
quinquāginta, *indec.,* fifty
quinque, *indec.,* five
quintus, *adj.,* fifth
quis, quid (*after* **si** *or* **ne**), *pron.,* anyone, anything
quis, quid, *interrog. pron.,* who? what?
quisquam, quicquam, *pron.,* anyone,
  anything
quo, *adv.,* whither, to where

quoad, *adv.,* until
quod, *conj.,* because
quōmodo, *adv.,* how?
quondam, *adv.,* once
quŏque, *adv.,* also
quotiens, *adv.,* whenever

raeda (1), carriage
rāmus (2), branch
rapidus, *adj.,* swift
rāro, *adv.,* rarely
rārus, *adj.,* rare: *pl.* in small groups
rebelli-o, -ōnis, *f.,* renewal of war,
  rebellion
rec-ens (*gen.* **-entis**), *adj.,* recent
recip-io, -ĕre, -cēpi, -ceptum, I
  recover (*trans.*)
  sē recipĕre, to retreat; recover
rectus, *adj.,* direct, straight
recupero (1), I get back, recover
redd-o, -ĕre, -didi, -ditum, I give
  back, restore
red-ĕo, -īre, -ii, *or* **-īvi, -ĭtum,** I
  return, go back
redūc-o, -ĕre, -duxi, -ductum, I
  bring back, lead back
refic-io, -ĕre, -fēci, -fectum, I repair
  sē reficĕre, to refresh oneself
rēgia (1), palace
rēgīna (1), queen
regi-o, -ōnis, *f.,* region, district
rēgius, *adj.,* royal
regno (1), I rule, reign
regnum (2), kingdom
reg-o, -ĕre, rexi, rectum, I govern;
  control
regred-ior, -i, -gressus sum, I
  return
relinqu-o, -ĕre, -līqui, -lictum, I
  leave; abandon, give up
relĭquus, *adj.,* remaining, left; the rest
  of
  relĭqui, *pl.,* the others, the rest (of)
remĕdium (2), remedy
remŏv-eo, -ēre, -mōvi, -mōtum, I
  draw away, remove
repell-o, -ĕre, reppŭli, repulsum, I
  drive back
repente, *adv.,* suddenly
repentīnus, *adj.,* sudden
reper-io, -īre, reppĕri, repertum, I
  find

reporto (1), I bring back
  victōriam reportāre, to win a
    victory
rēs (5), thing
  res publica, the Roman state
  res gestae, *f. pl.,* exploits
  rē vēra, really, actually
resist-o, -ĕre, restiti, *with dat.,* I resist
respond-eo, -ēre, -i, -sponsum, I
    reply, answer
responsum (2), answer
revŏco (1), I recall
rex, rēgis, *m.,* king
rhēt-or, -ŏris, *m.,* teacher of rhetoric
rīpa (1), river bank
rixa (1), quarrel
rŏgo (1), I ask for; ask
rōs, rōris, *m.,* dew
rōstrum (2), beak (*of ship*); *plur.,*
    platform
rursus, *adv.,* again

sac-er, -ra, -rum, *adj.,* sacred
sacerd-ōs, -ōtis, *c.,* priest
sacrifico (1), I sacrifice
saeculum (2), century
saepe, *adv.,* often
saevus *adj.,* fierce, cruel
sagitta (1), arrow
saltāt-or, -ōris, *m.,* dancer
salto (1), I dance
saltus (4), pass
sal-us, -ūtis, *f.,* safety
salūto (1), I greet; salute
sangu-is, -ĭnis, *m.,* blood
sāno (1), I heal, cure
sapi-ens (*gen.* **-entis**), *adj.,* wise
sapientia (1), wisdom
satis, *adv.,* enough
saxum (2), stone, rock
scaena (1), stage
scapha (1), skiff, small boat
scelerātus, *adj.,* criminal
scelestus, *adj.,* criminal, wicked
scel-us, -ĕris, *n.,* crime
schŏla grammatica (1), grammar
    school
scientia (1), knowledge
scio (4), I know; know how (to)
scrīb-o, -ĕre, scripsi, scriptum, I
    write
script-or, -ōris, *m.,* writer

scūtum (2), shield
sē, *pron.,* himself, herself, itself, them-
    selves
secundus, *adj.,* second; favourable
  secundo flūmine, downstream
sed, *conj.,* but
sed-eo, -ēre, sēdi, sessum, I sit
sēd-es, -is, *f.,* seat; foundation
seminūdus, *adj.,* half naked
semper, *adv.,* always
senāt-or, -ōris, *m.,* senator
senātus (4), the Senate
senesc-o, -ĕre, senui, I grow old
sententia (1), opinion
  sententiam dīcĕre, to state an
    opinion
sent-io, -īre, sensi, sensum, I feel,
    realise
sepel-io, -īre, -īvi, sepultum, I bury
septem, *indec.,* seven
septendecim, *indec.,* seventeen
septimus, *adj.,* seventh
septingent-i, -ae, -a, *adj.,* seven
    hundred
septuāgēsimus, *adj.,* seventieth
septuāginta, *indec.,* seventy
sepulcrum (2), tomb
sequ-or, -i, secūtus sum, I follow;
    pursue
serm-o, -ōnis, *m.,* talk, conversation
serp-ens, -entis, *f.,* serpent
servit-us, -ūtis, *f.,* slavery
servo (1), I keep; save; watch
servus (2), slave
sex, *indec.,* six
sexāginta, *indec.,* sixty
si, *conj.,* if
sīc, *adv.,* thus, in this way
sīcut, *adv.,* just as; like
signum (2), signal; sign; standard
silentium (2), silence
silva (1), wood
silvestr-is, -e, *adj.,* wooded
simil-is, -e, *adj. with dat.,* similar, like
simul, *adv.,* at the same time
simul atque, as soon as
simulācrum (2), image
sine, *prep. with abl.,* without
sinist-er, -ra, -rum, *adj.,* left, on the
    left
sin-o, -ĕre, sīvi, sĭtum, I allow
sĭtus (4), site

sĭtus, *adj.*, situated
sīve . . . sīve, whether . . or
socius (2), ally
sōl, sōlis, *m.*, sun
sŏl-eo, -ēre, solitus sum, I am accustomed
sollicito (1), I stir up
sōlum, *adv.*, only
sōlus (*gen.* sōlius), *adj.*, alone; only
solv-o, -ĕre, -i, solūtum, I loosen
   nāvem solvĕre, to set sail
somnium (2), dream
somnus (2), sleep
sparg-o, -ĕre, sparsi, sparsum, I scatter
spatium (2), space, area; interval
species (5), appearance
spectāculum (2), sight, spectacle; show
spectātor, -ōris, *m.*, spectator
specto (1), I look at, look
speculum (2), mirror
spēlunca (1), cave
spēro (1), I hope
spēs (5), hope
spīna (1), thorn
splend-or, -ōris, *m.*, splendour
statim, *adv.*, at once
stati-o, -ōnis, *f.*, picket, guard-post
statua (1), statue
statu-o, -ĕre, -i, statūtum, I decide
statūra (1), stature, height
stella (1), star
stilus (2), pen
sto, stāre, stĕti, stătum, I stand
strepitus (4), noise, din
studium (2), enthusiasm; desire; study
stultitia (1), folly
stultus, *adj.*, foolish
suād-eo, -ēre, suāsi, suāsum, *with dat.*, I advise
sub, *prep. with abl.*, under
subdūc-o, -ĕre, -duxi, -ductum, I draw up (*of ships*)
subito, *adv.*, suddenly
subitus, *adj.*, sudden
submitt-o, -ĕre, -mīsi, -missum, I send to the help
subsequ-or, -i, -secūtus sum, I follow up
subsidium (2), reinforcement, support

succēd-o, -ĕre, -cessi, -cessum, *with in and acc.*, I succeed to, take place of
sud-is, -is, *f.*, stake, pile
sulphureus, *adj.*, of sulphur
sum, esse, fui, I am
summa (1), total
   summa imperii, chief command
summus, *adj.*, utmost, very great; highest; top of
sūm-o, -ĕre, sumpsi, sumptum, I take; take up
super, *prep. with acc.*, above, over; upon
superbus, *adj.*, proud
super-ior (*gen.* -iōris), *adj.*, upper; previous; higher; superior
supero (1), I overcome; surpass, excel
supersum, -esse, -fui, I am left
supplicium (2), punishment
supra, *adv. or prep. with acc.*, above
surg-o, -ĕre, surrexi, surrectum, I rise
suscip-io, -ĕre, -cēpi, -ceptum, I undertake
sustin-eo, -ēre, -ui, sustentum, I withstand, resist; support
suus, *adj.*, his, her, its, their

taberna (1), shop
tabernāculum (2), tent
tabula (1), tablet
taceo (2), I am silent
talentum (2), talent
tāl-is, -e, *adj.*, such
tam, *adv.*, so
tamen, *adv.*, however, yet
tandem, *adv.*, at last
tantus, *adj.*, so great, such
tectum, (2), roof
teg-o, -ĕre, texi, tectum, I cover
tēlum (2), weapon
tempest-ās, -ātis, *f.*, storm; weather
templum (2), temple
temp-us, -ŏris, *n.*, time
tenebr-ae, -ārum (1), *pl.*, darkness
ten-eo, -ēre, -ui, tentum, I hold, keep
tenu-is, -e, *adj.*, thin
tergum (2), back, rear
   tergum vertĕre, to turn the back, flee
terra (1), earth; land; ground
   orbis terrārum, the world

terreo (2), I frighten
tertius, *adj.,* third
test-is, -is, *c.,* witness
theātrāl-is, -e, *adj.,* of the theatre, theatrical
theātrum (2), theatre
thēsaurus (2), treasure
timeo (2), I fear, am afraid
tim-or, -ōris, *m.,* fear
titulus (2), title
toll-o, -ĕre, sustuli, sublātum, I raise
tormentum (2), catapult: *pl.* artillery
torridus, *adj.,* scorched
tŏt, *indec. adj.,* so many
tōtus (*gen.* **tōtius**), *adj.,* whole of; whole
trād-o, -ĕre, -didi, -ditum, I hand over, surrender; hand down
tragicus, *adj.,* tragic
trah-o, -ĕre, traxi, tractum, I pull, drag
trāic-io, -ĕre, -iēci, -iectum, I lead across
trāiectus (4), a crossing
tranquillit-as, -ātis, *f.,* calm
trans, *prep. with acc.,* across
trans-ĕo, -īre, -ii *or* **-īvi, -ĭtum,** I cross
transfīg-o, -ĕre, -fixi, -fixum, I pierce
transgred-ior, -i, -gressus sum, I cross
transporto (1), I transport, carry
trem-or, -ōris, *m.,* tremor, shaking
tres (*gen.* **trium**), *adj.,* three
tribūnus (2), tribune, junior officer
trīginta, *indec.,* thirty
trist-is, -e, *adj.,* sad
triumphāl-is, -e, *adj.,* triumphal
triumphus (2), triumph
tū, *pron.,* you (*sing.*), thou
tum, *adv.,* then
tumultus (4), tumult, uproar, riot
tumulus (2), tomb, funeral mound
turba (1), crowd
turbo (1), I stir up
turma (1), squadron
turr-is, -is, *f.,* tower
tūtus, *adj.,* safe
tuus, *adj.,* your, thy
tyrannus (2), tyrant

ubi, *conj.,* where; when
ubīque, *adv.,* everywhere
ullus (*gen.* **ullius**), *adj.,* any
ultimus, *adj.,* farthest
umbra (1), shade
umbrōsus, *adj.,* shady
ūna, *adv.,* together
unda (1), wave
unde, *adv.,* from where
undēvīcēsimus, *adj.,* nineteenth
undíque, *adv.,* on *or* from all sides
ūniversi, *pl. adj.,* all together
unquam, *adv.,* ever
ūnus (*gen.* **ūnius**), *adj.,* one
urbs, urbis, *f.,* city
usque ad, *with acc.,* right up to
ūsus (4), use
ut, *with indic.,* as; when
ut, *with subj.,* in order that, that; so that
uterque, utraque, utrumque, *adj.,* each, both
ūtil-is, -e, *adj.,* useful
ūtor, ūti, ūsus sum, *with abl.,* I use
utrum … an, whether … or
ux-or, -ōris, *f.,* wife

vadum (2), shallow place, ford
vagor (1), I stray, wander
valē, *imperative,* good-bye
validus, *adj.,* strong
vallum (2), rampart
vānus, *adj.,* vain
varius, *adj.,* various, different
vasto (1), I lay waste
vastus, *adj.,* vast
vectīg-al, -ālis, *n.,* tax, tribute
vehiculum (2), vehicle
veho, vehĕre, vexi, vectum, I convey: *pass.* I ride
vel, *conj.,* or
vel … vel, either … or
vēlum (2), sail
velut, *adv.,* as if; just like
venēnum (2), poison
vĕn-io, -īre, vēni, ventum, I come
ventus (2), wind
verbero (1), I whip, beat
verbum (2), word
vereor (2), I fear
vēro, *adv.,* however
versus (4), verse

vert-o, -ĕre, -i, versum, I turn
  tergum vertĕre, to flee
vĕrus, *adj.*, true
  rē vēra, really, actually
vesperi, *adv.*, in the evening
vest-er, -ra, -rum, *adj.*, your
vestīgium (2), trace; track
vest-is, -is, *f.*, dress
vet-o, -āre, -ui, -itum, I forbid
vexo (1), I distress, worry
via (1), road, way
viāt-or, -ōris, *m.*, traveller
vīcīnus (2), a neighbour
vīcīnus, *adj.*, nearby, neighbouring
vict-or, -ōris, *m.*, conqueror, victor:
  as adj., victorious
victōria (1), victory
  victōriam reportāre, to win a
  victory
vĭd-eo, -ēre, vīdi, vīsum, I see
vĭd-eor, -ēri, vīsus sum, I seem; am
  seen
vigeo (2), I thrive
vigilia (1), watch
vīginti, *indec.*, twenty
villa (1), country house

vinc-o, -ĕre, vīci victum, I conquer,
  overcome
vinculum (2), chain; fastening
vīnum (2), wine
violo (1), I violate
vir, viri (2), man; husband
virg-o, -ĭnis, *f.*, maiden, virgin
virt-us, ūtis, *f.*, courage, virtue
vīs (*acc.* **vim,** *abl.* **vi**),*f.*, force, violence
  vīres, *pl.*, strength
vīta (1), life
vitium (2), vice
vīto (1), I avoid
vīv-o, -ĕre, vixi, victum, I live, am
  alive
vīvus, *adj.*, alive
vix, *adv.*, scarcely
vŏco (1), I call; summon
vŏlo (1), I fly
vŏlo, velle, vŏlui, I wish, am willing
volupt-as, -ātis, *f.*, pleasure
vōs, *pron.*, you, *pl.*
vōx, vōcis, *f.*, voice
vulnero (1), I wound
vuln-us, -ĕris, *n.*, wound
vultus (4), face, countenance

VOCABULARY OF PROPER NAMES

NOTE: 1. When the English name is the same as the Latin name, it is not repeated.
2. A capital letter in brackets after a Latin word shows on which of the maps the place can be found.

Achill-ēs, -is, *m.*	Trojan War hero, son of Peleus and Thetis
Acropolis	the citadel of Athens
Actiacus, *adj.* (J)	of Actium, scene of naval battle between Antony and Octavian, 31 B.C.
Aegyptius (2)	an Egyptian
Aegyptius, *adj.*	Egyptian
Aegyptus (2) *f.* (J)	Egypt
Aenē-as, -ae, *m.*	a Trojan, son of Venus and Anchises, ancestor of the Romans
Aeschylus (2)	first great tragic poet of Greece
Aesculāpius (2)	Asclepius, god of medicine
Aethiŏpia (1) (J)	country in Africa, south of Egypt
Afr-ī, -ōrum (2)	Africans
Africa (1) (H)	Africa
Alcibiad-ēs, -is, *m.*	Athenian statesman and general
Alexander Magnus	Alexander the Great, conqueror of the then known world, died 323 B.C.
Alexandria (1) (J)	city of Egypt, founded by Alexander
Alexandrīnus, *adj.*	of Alexandria
Amphipol-is, -is, *f.* (K)	Greek city on borders of Thrace
Amphitheātrum Flāvium (2)	the Flavian Amphitheatre or Colosseum at Rome
Androcl-ēs, -is, *m.*	a Greek slave
Anglicē, *adv.*	in English
Anglicus, *adj.*	English
Antipat-er, -ri, (2)	oldest of Alexander's generals and his successor
Antipatris (*acc.* **Antipatrida**) (K)	city of Palestine
Antōnius Fēlix	*see* Felix
Antonius M.	Mark Antony, opponent of Augustus, defeated at Actium, 31 B.C.
Apoll-o, -ĭnis, *m.*	Greek god of the arts, etc., and of the oracle at Delphi
Appia Via (1)	the Appian Way, leading south from Rome
Arabia (1) (J)	Arabia
Ariobarzan-ēs, -is, *m.*	Persian general
Arria (1)	wife of Paetus, a Roman senator
Arx, Arcis, *f.* (F)	citadel of Rome, on Capitoline hill
Asia (1) (J)	Asia Minor *or* the continent of Asia
Athēn-ae, -ārum, *f. pl.* (K)	Athens
Athēniens-is, -is, *c.*	an Athenian
Augustus (2)	the emperor Augustus

Augustus (2)	month of August, named after the emperor
Augustus (2)	a general title assumed by Roman emperors
Aurōra (1)	goddess of the dawn
Babyl-ōn, -ōnis (*acc.* **Babylōna**), *f.* (J)	ancient capital of the Babylonian empire
Babylōnia (1) (J)	ancient kingdom between rivers Tigris and Euphrates
Bacchus (2)	god of wine
Bactria (1) (J)	country north-east of Persia
Bessus (2)	governor of Bactria
Betis	governor of Gaza
Britannia (1) (H)	Britain
Britannus (2)	a Briton
Brutus M. (2)	one of the murderers of Julius Caesar
Byzantium (2) (K)	Greek city on the Bosporus
Caecīna Paetus	*see* Paetus
Caes-ar, -aris, *m.*	Julius Caesar, conqueror of Gaul
Caes-ar, -aris	adopted by later emperors as an imperial title
Caesarēa (1) (K)	city of Palestine
Campānia (1) (H)	district of Italy, south of Rome
Cantium (2) (H)	district in south-east Britain
Capēna porta	southern gate of Rome
Capitolīnus	*see* Iuppiter
Capitōlium (2) (F)	the Capitol hill and citadel of Rome
Carthāginiens-is, -is, *c.* (H)	a Carthaginian, citizen of Carthage
Cassivellaunus (2)	British chieftain, defeated by Caesar
Cast-or, -ōris, *m.*	twin brother of Pollux; both patron deities of sailors
Chaeronēa (1)	town of Boeotia, north of Athens
Christiānus (2)	a Christian
Christiānus, *adj.*	Christian
Christus	Christ
Cicer-o, -ōnis, *m.*	famous Roman orator
Cilicia (1) (K)	district of Asia Minor
Clauda (1) (K)	small island off Crete
Claudius (2)	the emperor Claudius
Claudius Lysias	*see* Lysias
Cleopātra (1)	Egyptian queen and wife of Mark Antony
Clitus (2)	friend of Alexander the Great
Colossēum (2)	great amphitheatre at Rome, scene of the gladiatorial shows
Constantīnōpolis	Constantinople, originally Byzantium, renamed after emperor Constantine in A.D. 330
Constantīnus (2)	Constantine, Roman emperor, died A.D. 337
Cornēlia (1)	daughter of Scipio Africanus and mother of Tiberius and Gaius Gracchus
Cornēlius Tacitus	*see* Tacitus
Crēta (1) (K)	island south east of Greece
Cūria (1) (G)	the Senate House at Rome

Cydnus (2) (J)	river of Cilicia
Cyprus (2) *f.* (J)	island in eastern Mediterranean
Damascus (2) *f.* (K)	ancient city of Syria
Darīus (2)	king of Perisa, defeated by Alexander
Dēmosthen-ēs, -is, *m.*	famous Athenian orator
Diāna (1)	goddess of the moon and hunting
Dūrus, Q. Labĕrius	one of Caesar's officers, killed in Britain
Eborācum (2) (H)	York, city of northern Britain
Ecbătăn-a, -ōrum (2) *pl.* (J)	capital of Media
Elizabētha (1)	Elizabeth
Endymi-ōn, -ōnis, *m.*	beloved of Diana and carried by her to the moon
Etruscus (2)	an Etruscan
Euphrāt-ēs, -is, *m.* (J)	great river of Mesopotamia
Euraquil-o, -ōnis, *m.*	north-easterly storm wind
Eurīpid-ēs, -is, *m.*	Athenian tragedian of 5th century B.C.
Eurōpa (1)	Europe
Fēl-ix -īcis, Antōnius	governor of Judaea A.D. 53–60
Festus, Porcius	successor of Felix in Judaea
Flāvius	*see* Iosephus
Fŏrum Appii (K)	on the Appian Way, south of Rome
Fŏrum Rōmānum (2) (G)	the old Forum or marketplace of Rome
Gaius Gracchus	son of Sempronius Gracchus and Cornelia
Galēnus (2)	famous doctor of 2nd century A.D.
Gallia (1) (H)	Gaul
Gallicus, *adj.*	Gallic, of Gaul; French
Gallus (2)	a Gaul
Gang-es, -is, *m.*	river of India
Gaugamēla (1) (J)	town beyond the Tigris, where Alexander defeated Darius
Gaza (1) (J)	town of southern Palestine
Germānia (1) (H)	Germany
Germānus (2)	a German
Germānus, *adj.*	of Germany, German
Gordium (2) (J)	town of Phrygia
Gordius (2)	ancient king of Phrygia
Graecē, *adv.*	in Greek
Graecia (1) (K)	Greece
Graecus (2)	a Greek
Graecus, *adj.*	of Greece, Greek
Granīcus (2) (K)	river of Bithynia, where Alexander defeated the Persians
Hadriānus (2)	Hadrian, Roman emperor A.D. 117–138
Hamm-on, -ōnis, *m.*	god worshipped in Libya whose temple had a famous oracle
Hebrāicus, *adj.*	Hebrew
Hect-or, -ŏris, *m.*	Trojan hero, killed by Achilles

Helĕna (1)	Helen, wife of Menelaus, carried off to Troy by Paris
Hellēspontus (2)	the Hellespont, a narrow strait between Europe and Asia
Hercul-ēs, -is, *m.*	Greek hero, famous for his twelve labours
Hērōd-ēs, -is, *m.*	Herod the Great, king of Judaea 37–4 B.C.
Hērŏdŏtus (2)	5th century Greek historian
Hierosŏlym-a, -ōrum, *n. pl.* (K)	Jerusalem
Hippocrat-ēs, -is, *m.*	Greek doctor born 460 B.C.
Hīspānia (1) (H)	Spain
Hīspānus (2)	a Spaniard
Hīspānus, *adj.*	of Spain, Spanish
Homērus (2)	Homer, father of Greek poetry, author of *Iliad* and *Odyssey*
Hyphăs-is, -is, *m.* (J)	river of India
Iānus (2)	Janus; a Roman god, shown with two faces
Iēsus (2)	Jesus
Īli-as, -ădis, *f.*	the Iliad
Ind-i, -ōrum, *m. pl.*	the Indians
India (1) (J)	India
Indus (2) (J)	river of India
Iōsēphus (2), **Flāvius**	Josephus, Jewish historian of the Jewish War of A.D. 70
Issus (2) *f.* (J)	town of Cilicia, where Darius was defeated by Alexander
Ītălia (1) (H)	Italy
Ītalicus, *adj.*	of Italy, Italian
Ītalus, *adj.*	of Italy, Italian
Ithăca (1) (K)	island off west coast of Greece, home of Ulysses
Iūdaea (1) (K)	Judaea
Iūdaeus, *adj.*	Jewish
Iūdaeus (2)	a Jew
Iūlius (2)	Roman centurion
Iūn-o, -ōnis, *f.*	Juno, wife of Jupiter
Iuppiter, Iŏvis, *m.*	Jupiter, chief of the gods
Iuppiter Capitolīnus	Capitoline Jupiter, whose temple was on the Capitoline Hill at Rome
Labĕrius	*see* Durus
Lacedaemŏnius (2)	a Spartan, inhabitant of Lacedaemon
Latīnē, *adv.*	in Latin
Latīnus, *adj.*	Latin
Līvius, Titus (2)	Livy, a Roman historian
Lūc-as, -ae, *m.*	St. Luke
Luciānus (2)	Lucian; Greek writer of the 2nd century A.D.
Lugotor-ix, -igis, *m.*	a leader of the Britons
Lycia (1) (K)	district of Asia Minor
Lȳdia (1) (J)	kingdom of western Asia Minor
Lysias, Claudius	Roman in command of Jerusalem garrison

152

Macĕdŏn-es, -um, *pl.*	the Macedonians
Macedŏnia (1) (J)	kingdom of northern Greece
Marcus Aurēlius	Roman emperor A.D. 161–180
Mars, Martis, *m.*	Roman god of war
Maxentius (2)	rival of Constantine, defeated at the Milvian bridge, A.D. 317
Mĕlĭta (1) (K)	Malta
Memn-on, -ŏnis, *m.*	son of Aurora, goddess of Dawn
Memph-is, -is, *f.* (J)	Egyptian city, capital of the Pharaohs
Milvius pons	bridge over the Tiber at Rome
Minerva (1)	goddess of wisdom and the arts
Mons Palātīnus (F)	the Palatine, largest of the hills of Rome
Mŏrĭn-i, -ōrum, *m.* (H)	a Belgian tribe
Myra (1) (K)	town of Lycia
Nearchus (2)	an admiral of Alexander
Neptūnus (2)	Neptune, god of the sea
Nēr-o, -ōnis, *m.*	Roman emperor A.D. 54–68
Nīlus (2) (J)	the river Nile
Nŏtus (2)	the south wind
Ocĕănus (2) (H)	the Ocean, great sea surrounding the world; also the Atlantic
Octāviānus M. (2)	Octavian; heir of Julius Caesar; later the emperor Augustus
Odyssēa (1)	the Odyssey of Homer
Olympia (1) (K)	in southern Greece, where Olympic Games were held
Olympus (2) (K)	mountain in northern Greece, supposed dwelling of the gods
Paetus, Caecīna	husband of Arria, condemned to death by emperor Claudius, A.D. 42
Palātīnus	*see* Mons Palatinus
Palātium (2)	palace of the Roman emperor on the Palatine Hill
Parmĕni-o, -ōnis, *m.*	a general of Alexander
Parthĕn-on, -ōnis, *m.*	famous temple on Acropolis at Athens
Patăli-i, -ōrum, *m. pl.* (J)	a people near mouth of River Indus
Paulus (2)	the Apostle Paul
Perdicc-as, -ae, *m.*	a general of Alexander
Pers-ae, -ārum, *m. pl.*	the Persians
Persēpŏl-is, -is, *f.* (J)	city of Persia, containing the royal palace
Persĭcus, *adj.*	Persian, of Persia
Phārus (2) *f.*	island near Alexandria
Phīdi-as, -ae, *m.*	famous Greek sculptor of 5th century B.C.
Philippus (2)	Philip, king of Macedon, father of Alexander the Great
Philippus (2)	a doctor with Alexander's army
Phoenicē (K)	a town in Crete
Phoenīc-ēs, -um, *m. pl.*	the Phoenicians

Phoenīcia (1) (J)	a district of Syria
Phrygia (1) (J)	a district of Asia Minor
Pindărus (2)	Pindar, Greek poet of 5th century B.C.
Plīnius (2)	Roman author of about A.D. 100
Poll-ux, -ūcis, *m.*	*see* Castor
Pompēiān-i, -ōrum, *m. pl.*	inhabitants of Pompeii
Pompēi-i, -ōrum, *m. pl.* (H)	city of Campania, destroyed by the eruption of Vesuvius in A.D. 79
Pompēius, Cnaeus	Pompey, famous Roman general and opponent of Julius Caesar
Pontifex Maximus	president of the Roman college of priests
Pontius Pīlātus (2)	Pilate; Roman governor of Judaea who condemned Christ to death
Porcius	*see* Festus
Pōrus (2)	an Indian king
Prĭămus (2)	Priam, king of Troy
Ptolemaeus (2)	Ptolemy, a king of Egypt
Publius (2)	a Roman governor of Malta
Putĕŏl-i, -ōrum, *m. pl.* (K)	town on coast of Campania
Rēgia (1) (G)	residence of the Pontifex Maximus
Rhēgium (2) (K)	city in south-west Italy
Rhĕnus (2) (H)	the river Rhine
Rhŏdus (2) *f.* (J)	Rhodes, island near coast of Asia Minor
Rōma (1) (H)	Rome
Rōmānus (2)	a Roman
Rōmānus, *adj.*	Roman, of Rome
Rōstr-a, -orum, *n. pl.* (G)	speakers' platform in the Forum
Rubico, -ōnis, *m.*	the Rubicon; a stream forming part of N. boundary of Italy (position not known)
Sard-ēs, -ium, *f.* (J)	Sardis, ancient capital of Lydia
Scīpio Africānus	adopted grandson of Publius Cornelius Scipio Africanus, father of Cornelia
Semprōnius Gracchus	father of the Gracchi
Septemb-er, -ris	the month of September
Sērēs, *pl.*	the Chinese
Sicilia (1) (K)	Sicily
Sĭd-on, -ōnis, *f.* (K)	city and port of Phoenicia
Sōcrat-ēs, -is, *m.*	famous Greek philosopher
Sŏphŏcl-ēs, -is, *m.*	Greek tragedian
Sūs-a, -ōrum, *n. pl.* (J)	capital of Persia
Syracūs-ae, -ārum, *f. pl.* (K)	Syracuse, city of Sicily
Syria (1) (J)	country between Mediterranean and river Euphrates
Syrus (2)	native of Syria, a Syrian
Syrt-is, -is, *f.* (K)	sand bank off coast of N. Africa
Tacitus, Cornēlius	Roman historian of about A.D. 100
Tămĕs-is, -is, *m.* (H)	the river Thames

Tarsus (2) *f.* (J)	capital of Cilicia, birthplace of St. Paul
Tēlemachus (2)	an eastern Christian
Thēb-ae, -ārum, *f. pl.* (J)	Thebes, capital of Boeotia
Thēbān-i, -ōrum, *m. pl.*	the Thebans, citizens of Thebes
Thrācia (1) (J)	Thrace, district east of Macedonia
Thūcȳdid-ēs, -is, *m.*	Greek historian
Tiberius Gracchus	son of Sempronius Gracchus and Cornelia
Tigr-is, -idis, *m.* (J)	river of Mesopotamia
Timŏtheus (2)	Timothy, companion of St. Paul
Tītus (2)	destroyer of Jerusalem in A.D. 70; later emperor
Tĭtus Līvius	*see* Livius
Trebōnius, Caius	a general of Caesar in Gaul
Trēs Tabernae (K)	Three Taverns, a stopping place on the Appian Way
Trōia (1) (J)	Troy
Trōiānus, *adj.*	Trojan, of Troy
Turcus (2)	a Turk
Tyri-i, -ōrum, *m. pl.*	Tyrians, people of Tyre
Tyrus (2) *f.* (J)	Tyre, chief town of Phoenicia
Ulix-ēs, -is, *m.*	Ulysses or Odysseus, a Greek hero famous for his cunning
Vĕn-us, -ĕris, *f.*	goddess of love
Vergĭlius (2)	Vergil, greatest of Roman poets; author of the *Aeneid*
Vespasiānus (2)	Vespasian, Roman emperor A.D. 69–79
Vesta (1) (G)	goddess of the hearth: in her temple burned an undying fire
Vestāl-is, -is, *f.*	a Vestal Virgin, priestess of the goddess Vesta
Vĕsŭvius (2) (H)	volcano in Campania
Via Sacra (G)	street in Rome leading from the Forum to the Capitol
Volusēnus, Caius	an officer in Caesar's army

English-Latin Exercises

The following exercises are revision of the accidence and elementary syntax in Part One. These are followed by Exercises 61 to 120 which keep step with the syntax used in the translation passages. The English–Latin Vocabulary in this volume contains all the words.

Revision of I–IV

1

1 We decide.   **2** They jump down.   **3** You (*s.*) are sacrificing.   **4** He does not remain.   **5** You (*pl.*) praise.   **6** They are running.   **7** He is reporting.   **8** We do not see.   **9** They fortify.   **10** You (*s.*) are guarding.   **11** They are not hurting.   **12** You (*s.*) are learning.

2

1 in the land.   **2** from Asia.   **3** on the river-bank.   **4** into Britain. **5** out of the cave.   **6** into the country-house.   **7** in the ditch.   **8** out of the gate.   **9** into Greece.   **10** from Italy.   **11** into the province.   **12** on the water.

3

1 The wood has wild beasts.   **2** You frighten the girl, Cornelia.   **3** We give money to the sailors.   **4** The forces are winning a victory.   **5** I see the streets of Rome.   **6** They overcome the Persians with spears.   **7** The girl tells stories.   **8** They destroy the gates with catapults.   **9** The queen's daughter is weeping.   **10** The queen is sleeping, Arria.   **11** You hand over the jewels to the queen.   **12** The women are standing in the road.

4

1 We look at the statues in the streets of Troy.   **2** The girls fall out of the cave into the water.   **3** By (our) eloquence we overcome the inhabitants' anger.   **4** You promise the forces victory, goddess.   **5** The Persians are leading (their) forces into the islands of Greece.   **6** In the cave we do not see the moon and the stars.   **7** Wild beasts kill cows but eagles do not attack farmers.   **8** The poet's eloquence wins (him) fame and money.   **9** The forces are marching out of Gaul into Italy.   **10** With (our) spears we slaughter the farmers' cows.

Revision of V–VII

1

1 He was fortifying.   **2** He is warning.   **3** You (*pl.*) were leading.   **4**

They used to help.   **5** I was fearing.   **6** We were jumping down.   **7**
You (*s.*) used to sit.   **8** They are coming.   **9** He was inviting.   **10** I
used to send.   **11** You (*pl.*) are writing.   **12** We were guarding.

2

1 He is sending food to the farm.   **2** They used to give books to the boys.
3 They run to the walls.   **4** He is coming to the temple.   **5** He shows
the sword to (his) son.   **6** They were leading (their) forces to the town.

3

1 We order the forces to halt.   **2** (My) friends decide to remain.   **3** The
boy is afraid to jump down.   **4** He allows (his) pupils to depart.   **5**
They were compelling the people to obey.   **6** I forbid the children to
swim.   **7** He decides to sleep.   **8** He orders the slaves to work.   **9**
They are afraid to open the gates.   **10** The boys were learning to read.

4

1 The gods were ordering the Romans to build temples in the market-
place.   **2** The master compels the boys and girls to read Vergil.   **3** They
were leading the waggons to the river and were collecting water.   **4** He
orders the people to guard the town with a wall and ditch.   **5** I give the
book to the boy and walk to the garden.   **6** The Romans were deciding
to send workmen to the province.   **7** They come out of the town and
hand over (their) weapons to Alexander.   **8** He is building temples on
the Capitol and adorning (them) with statues.

Revision of VIII–X

1

1 They gave.   **2** We were arriving.   **3** I did not buy.   **4** He has
slept.   **5** We saw.   **6** You (*s.*) have opened.   **7** You (*pl.*) are falling.
8 She was weeping.   **9** They do not write.   **10** We did not fear.   **11**
They used to fight.   **12** We departed.

2

1 of the foolish sailor.   **2** We have many gifts.   **3** O good boy.   **4** to
the wicked woman.   **5** The cowardly farmers are running.   **6** I see a
skilled workman.   **7** of our camp.   **8** in the great ditch.   **9** The
angry teacher is shouting.   **10** O beautiful girls.   **11** He praises dead
poets.   **12** into the wide field.   **13** by long stories.   **14** The wretched
prisoner was weeping.   **15** to two-hundred children.   **16** The high
rocks are falling.

3

1 Darius was a Persian.   **2** I am a pupil.   **3** The boy was not good.
4 Crassus, you will be a poet.   **5** She will be queen.   **6** The workman
is skilled.   **7** We are not sailors.   **8** There is a wild beast in the wood.

9 Troy had walls.　**10** There will be many years.　**11** You are safe, Cornelia.　**12** The Persian has a long sword.　**13** They will be foolish. **14** I was not sick.　**15** There wasn't a doctor in the town.　**16** Girls, you will be beautiful.

4

1 'I have decided,' he said, 'to be your teacher.'　**2** The good workman was not afraid to work in the high cave.　**3** He is learned, for (*nam*) he has read two-hundred books.　**4** 'Alexander the Great,' they say, 'led (his) forces to India.'　**5** There are wicked slaves on the farm of Crassus. **6** 'The poor people haven't (any) food,' shouted the doctor.　**7** 'We have ordered our sailors,' he said, 'to sail to Britain.'　**8** Crassus is a good farmer. He works in the fields and looks after the cows.

Revision of XI–XX

I

1 by a cruel defeat.　**2** of all the kings.　**3** a bold plan (*acc*).　**4** serious wounds (*nom*).　**5** O rich Roman.　**6** a large fire (*acc*).　**7** by an easy road.　**8** many citizens (*acc*).　**9** to the faithful guards.　**10** in my ship.　**11** a fierce animal (*acc*).　**12** of our mothers.　**13** of the innocent girl.　**14** a difficult example (*nom*).　**15** with equal love.　**16** to the tenth legion.　**17** a huge cave (*acc*).　**18** of the wise consuls.　**19** O great Caesar.　**20** cruel words (*nom*).

2

1 He gave the bread to me.　**2** I saw her in the city.　**3** I like you, Crassus.　**4** I announced the defeat to him.　**5** He sent us out of prison. **6** I showed the wound to them.　**7** We fear you, Romans.　**8** I didn't buy it.　**9** He gave us money.　**10** I dedicate it to you, citizens.

3

1 By a wise plan they overcame the huge forces of the enemy.　**2** We gave him bread, and he sent it to his poor friend.　**3** I am a good citizen; you are a traitor, Crassus.　**4** There are several Christians in the prison, because they do not sacrifice to the gods of the Romans.　**5** Fierce animals live in the huge forest.　**6** We defended you, Romans; but you allowed the enemy to defeat us.　**7** There are high trees in our part of the island. We have never climbed them.　**8** In our city we are judges, you are generals.　**9** Many citizens blame the cruel deed of the wicked consuls.　**10** The helmsman has a ship. He sails in it to the shores of Greece.

Revision of XXI–XXIII

I

1 We will give.　**2** He has given.　**3** They give.　**4** You (*s.*) will give. **5** I used to give.　**6** You (*pl.*) had given.　**7** He is giving.　**8** You

159

(*pl.*) gave.   **9** They will have given.   **10** We do not give.   **11** They will give.   **12** You (*s.*) were giving.   **13** I shall give.   **14** He did not give.   **15** We are giving.   **16** You (*pl.*) will have given.   **17** You (*s.*) do not give.   **18** We have given.   **19** They gave.   **20** You (*pl.*) give. **21** I was giving.   **22** He had given.   **23** You (*pl.*) did not give.   **24** You (*s.*) shall give.   **25** They are giving.   **26** I had given.   **27** She will have given.   **28** We gave.   **29** You (*s.*) have given.   **30** We used to give.   **31** They do not give.   **32** I did not give.   **33** He was giving. **34** You (*pl.*) are giving.   **35** You (*s.*) will have given.   **36** We had given. **37** You (*pl.*) will give.   **38** I gave.   **39** She gives.   **40** They shall give.

For further practice substitute for 'give' the verbs 'remain', 'say', 'come' or any desired alternation of the four verbs.

2

1 The man who came had been a farmer.   **2** The girl whom you sent will help us.   **3** The spear with which he killed them was long.   **4** The buildings which we saw had been a citadel.   **5** The boy whose mother I like is not strong.   **6** The girl to whom we gave money did not help us. **7** The weapons with which they attacked us wounded many.   **8** The towers whose walls I see are high.   **9** The soldiers who are fighting had been centurions.   **10** The citizens to whom we showed the plan praised it.

3

1 What you said was foolish. We do not like it.   **2** The caves you saw are in the high mountain. We will find them.   **3** He ordered the children to read the books which the master had sent.   **4** The poor man came into the farm. When we saw him we gave him bread.   **5** The king you announced the victory to will have heard it before (*antea*).   **6** I will burn your books. What you wrote was wicked.   **7** The traitor you killed had been general of our forces.   **8** He told a strange story. When I heard it I was silent.

Revision of XXIV–XXXI

I

Give the positive, comparative and superlative of the adjectives meaning: high, good, faithful, beautiful, difficult, many, fierce, learned, sick, great.

2

1 by a more serious wound.   **2** a very good harbour (*nom*).   **3** to the longer paces.   **4** a stronger poison (*acc*).   **5** of the very difficult letters. **6** crueller boys (*acc*).   **7** greater examples (*nom*).   **8** of the more beautiful days.   **9** to the bravest soldier.   **10** with greater hope.   **11** to the more faithful magistrate.   **12** the safest ships (*acc*). **13** a fiercer animal (*nom*).   **14** by a very easy victory.   **15** a higher step (*acc*).   **16** to the very sick soldiers.   **17** with more words.   **18** O most learned

160

magistrate.   **19** more beautiful buildings (*acc*).   **20** of the very bold plans.   **21** by a better deed.   **22** very sick girls (*nom*).   **23** of the more cowardly armies.   **24** very many farmers (*acc*).   **25** a more ancient temple (*nom*).   **26** a most innocent girl (*acc*).

3

1 They are going.   **2** I will go away.   **3** He was going round.   **4** We have crossed.   **5** You (*s.*) return.   **6** You (*pl.*) had gone.   **7** They returned.   **8** He does not go away.   **9** They will cross.   **10** They will have gone.   **11** We will return.   **12** I was going away.   **13** You (*pl.*) did not cross.   **14** He had returned.   **15** You (*s.*) were going.   **16** We cross.   **17** I will have gone round.   **18** You (*pl.*) will return.   **19** You (*s.*) are not going away.   **20** He has not gone.

4

1 We all blame boys who praise themselves.   **2** The Persians led very large forces into all the islands.   **3** 'We shall defend ourselves,' they said, 'in the very high citadel.'   **4** The girls used to look at themselves in a huge mirror.   **5** The foolish king is sacrificing very many animals to himself!   **6** You, who give the greater part of the gold to yourselves, are not worthy of glory.   **7** After the more serious punishment the poor slave killed himself.   **8** I despise myself because I did not punish the very cowardly soldiers who handed themselves over to the enemy.

Revision of XXXII–XL

1

1 They were betrayed.   **2** You (*s.*) are being corrupted.   **3** She was forbidden.   **4** They are being guarded.   **5** The animals have been sacrificed.   **6** It was destroyed.   **7** We are not being prevented.   **8** The children were blamed.   **9** I am listened to.   **10** The ship has been launched.   **11** You (*pl.*) are invited.   **12** The camp was built.   **13** You have been deceived, girl.   **14** We are being betrayed.   **15** The enemy were defeated.

2

1 of this poet.   **2** that mirror (*nom*).   **3** to these brothers.   **4** to this woman.   **5** those ships (*nom*).   **6** by this defeat.   **7** these plans (*acc*).   **8** of that ship.   **9** by those storms.   **10** to that queen.   **11** this city (*acc*).   **12** of these legions.

3

1 On the sixth night we were attacked by the enemy.   **2** These men have decided to defend themselves for three hours.   **3** In winter rocks are rolled down by the very fierce storms.   **4** In a hundred days they will go out of the very strong prison.   **5** He said these things on that day because he was frightened by the magistrates.   **6** He was wounded by a rock but the wound was cured by a very good doctor.   7 He stayed for ten days and returned to the camp in two days.   8 Next day they were invited to dinner by Claudia and Crassus.   9 I like these women who looked after the sick for many months.   10 This girl bought a mirror and looked at herself in it.   11 The signal you see was given to the tenth legion by Caesar.   12 Where is that brave soldier who was not afraid to hand himself over to punishment and death?

Revision of XLI–L

1

1 You (*s.*) wish.   2 We shall be willing.   3 They have wished.   4 I had wished.   5 He is willing.   6 You (*pl.*) were wishing.   7 She will wish.   8 We are unwilling.   9 You (*s.*) were unwilling.   10 You (*pl.*) will be unwilling.   11 They will have been unwilling.   12 He is unwilling.   13 I had been unwilling.   14 They do not prefer.   15 You (*s.*) will prefer.   16 We were preferring.   17 He bears.   18 I will have borne.   19 You (*pl.*) will bear.   20 They were bearing.   21 You (*pl.*) have borne.   22 You (*s.*) are bearing.   23 We had borne.   24 They will be able.   25 He has been able.   26 I was able.   27 You (*s.*) are not able.   28 I will be able.   29 He had been able.   30 We are able.

2

1 You (*s.*) will be saved.   2 She was saved.   3 They are being saved.   4 You (*pl.*) were being saved.   5 It had been saved.   6 We shall be saved.   7 He has been saved.   8 I am being saved.   9 They will have been saved.   10 We were being saved.   11 You (*pl.*) will be saved.   12 She had been saved.   13 It was saved.   14 You (*s.*) are being saved.   15 We had been saved.   16 I was being saved.   17 They will be saved.   18 He is not being saved.   19 You (*pl.*) have been saved.   20 You (*s.*) will have been saved.

For further practice substitute for the verb 'save' the verbs 'see', 'send', 'punish', 'bear' (*fero*) or any desired alternation.

3

1 They fought more boldly.   2 We arrived safely.   3 We shall conquer very easily.   4 I foolishly blamed them.   5 He betrayed us innocently.   6 He ran well.   7 He was seriously wounded.   8 He punished them too cruelly.   9 He writes most learnedly.   10 He defended us faithfully.   11 He swims very beautifully.   12 They praised him greatly.   13 He gladly gave it to me.   14 They attacked more fiercely.   15 First he handed over the letter.   16 They most wickedly slaughtered the prisoners.   17 He wisely stayed in camp.   18 They conspired wickedly.   19 They will fight better.   20 They were punished equally.

4

1 Come here, boy. The master will arrive in two hours. 2 Farmers, slaughter the wild beasts which are killing your cows. 3 Read this book, Crassus. You will be punished by the master. 4 Be glad, citizens. We will defend ourselves easily. 5 Order the children to work well, master. 6 Stay here for twenty days, soldiers. You cannot save yourselves. 7 Sleep in this cave, girl. You will be safe. 8 Do this at once, consul. Our camp has been stormed by the enemy.

Revision of LI–LX

1

1 They are capturing. 2 You (*s.*) escaped. 3 He will become king. 4 We will do this. 5 She has become foolish. 6 They had fled. 7 You (*pl.*) were making. 8 He is becoming angry. 9 It was done. 10 You (*pl.*) will escape. 11 I fled. 12 You (*s.*) are undertaking. 13 We were being made. 14 It has become. 15 We had captured. 16 She had become. 17 They will have made. 18 I was escaping. 19 You (*pl.*) do not capture. 20 You (*s.*) will not undertake.

2

1 of one legion. 2 by hope alone. 3 to the whole Senate. 4 I see neither consul. 5 of any soldier. 6 No ship will sail. 7 to Cornelia alone. 8 of the whole people. 9 to any teacher. 10 by one law.

3

1 They advanced. 2 You (*s.*) are amazed. 3 It had arisen. 4 We will delay. 5 You (*pl.*) were dying. 6 They will have encouraged. 7 You (*s.*) will follow. 8 We are foraging. 9 She imitated. 10 You (*pl.*) had obtained. 11 We were plundering. 12 He prayed. 13 She had set out. 14 I shall not speak. 15 You (*pl.*) will threaten. 16 It tried. 17 You (*s.*) are advancing. 18 I will have used. 19 They do not use. 20 He was setting out.

4

1 by two ships. 2 seventeen sailors (*acc*). 3 of one hundred prisoners. 4 to eight hundred soldiers. 5 with one thousand trees. 6 thirty-three rocks (*nom*). 7 569 pupils (*acc.*) 8 of the twelfth legion. 9 to the twentieth reader. 10 of three provinces. 11 the hundredth winter (*nom*). 12 five hundred cavalry (*acc*). 13 to sixty-eight boys. 14 on the sixteenth step. 15 451 ships (*nom*). 16 of twelve harbours. 17 to the third part. 18 two hundred statues (*acc*). 19 in the thirtieth year. 20 forty-five books (*nom*).

5

1 We will advance ten miles into the very high mountains. 2 Try to read the book I gave you, boy. 3 In fourteen days you will become king

of the whole island.   4 They were seriously wounded by the Gauls and wished to set out for the city.   5 Speak more boldly, consuls. The soldiers are unwilling to defend themselves.   6 How many miles will we march? We prefer to forage in this wood.   7 What you said was very fierce, Crassus. You threatened death to the very cowardly traitors. 8 Send 3,000 cavalry at once. We are being surrounded by the enemy. 9 Imitate your mother, girls. Listen to her wise words.   10 Return soon, slave. Bring me the money that was hidden on the high citadel. 11 Advance, Caesar! You will be welcomed by all the soldiers.   12 In the second year of that war the Romans were defeated. Neither consul could save himself.

1 I will wait (for) three months.   **2** We sailed to Troy from Greece.
3 The consul is not in Rome.   **4** The tree is thirty feet high.   **5** They
set us free on the sixth day.   **6** They chased the master to Veii.   **7**
London (=*Londinium*) is not in Greece.   **8** We marched for three miles.
9 Within two hours the city will have been captured.   **10** I will go from
Gaul to Syracuse in ten days.

1 They march twenty-five miles at a very great speed.   **2** In eight years
we will be able to disband all our armies.   **3** Some want to stay at home,
others to go to the country.   **4** The field is 200 paces long, 160 paces
wide.   **5** We don't want to delay here for eight hours.

1 I have stood here for two hours.   **2** We saw a line of prisoners two miles
long.   **3** This river flows about 200 miles from the mountains to the sea.
4 In the third month after the battle the triumph took place (=*fio*) at
Rome.   **5** Many years ago (=*abhinc* with *acc*) there were not large cities
in Britain.

64

1 I climb twenty steps from the street to my house.   **2** In seven days the
citizens of the whole province will meet.   **3** I want to stay here for a week
(=seven days) but business (=*negotia n. pl.*) compels me to return to Rome.
4 The ship is 30 feet long and seven feet wide.   **5** This building can hold
2,000 people (=men).

1 The sun is much fiercer in Italy than in Britain.   **2** Our language has
twenty-six letters.   **3** He used a spear seven feet long.   **4** We will try
to hide the money under the rocks.   **5** The fame of the Roman Empire
lived for very many years.

1 Why does he wish to come?   **2** Did you see her?   **3** What did he say?
4 How big is your city?   **5** Do you teach arithmetic or geometry?   **6**
When did the Romans go to their country-houses?   **7** Did he not try to
save you?   **8** How many slaves are working here?   **9** Surely he didn't
destroy the whole city?   **10** In what part of the city do you live?

1 Where did you find these very beautiful jewels?   **2** Is your friend dead
or is he still alive?   **3** What was inscribed on Cornelia's statue?   **4**
Surely he didn't punish the very faithful slave?   **5** Was Cornelia a good
example to other mothers?

1 Why are you weeping, boy? Is your father sick? 2 What woman followed Paetus to Rome? 3 Did Arria or Paetus die first? 4 How did Arria save her husband's life? 5 Surely you did not conspire against the emperor, Paetus?

69

1 Did you sail seventy miles to the south? 2 Didn't two gods come here? 3 For how many days were they tossed by the storm? 4 Do you believe Lucian's True Story? 5 How big was the ship in which Lucian sailed?

70

1 What did Lucian see in the huge mirror? 2 Who was king of the Moon? Was he god or man? 3 Could Lucian and his companions see the Earth? 4 Surely they did not vanish into smoke? 5 Don't you want to travel to the Moon?

71

1 Don't frighten the children, master. 2 Don't be afraid of the cows, children. 3 Don't despair, soldiers. 4 Do not walk in the woods. 5 Don't obey the wicked master. 6 Don't kill the poor prisoners. 7 Do not order men to travel to the moon. 8 Don't use that sword. 9 Don't go away. You'll see her soon. 10 Don't shout, boy. I can hear you easily.

72

1 Don't despise these stories, reader. 2 Have you never seen dew, children? 3 Who was the son of Aurora? Did she love him? 4 Don't be afraid of the lightning, girls. 5 How did the Greeks overcome their fear of nature?

73

1 Have you not read the works of Homer? 2 Don't try to avoid work, pupils. 3 How many works did Homer write? Do you like them? 4 Don't imitate the deeds of wicked men. 5 When did you begin to read Vergil?

74

1 Don't tell the story always in the same way. 2 Can you find a poet equal to Aeschylus? 3 How many dancers were there in the Greek chorus? 4 Don't try to despise the works of Aeschylus. 5 Was Sophocles or Euripides a better poet?

75

1 Do you prefer to read Livy or Tacitus? 2 Don't hide the emperors'

vices, Tacitus.　**3** Don't you want to read Herodotus? Bring me the book.
4 About what war did Thucydides write?　**5** Don't drive the general
into exile, citzens.

76

1 He is coming to help his friends.　**2** They fought to save their city.
3 He fled lest he might be captured.　**4** He is working that he may not
be poor.　**5** He has built a temple to adorn the citadel.　**6** Work well
lest the master punish you.　**7** The statue is so beautiful that everyone
praises it.　**8** They were so wise that they knew everything.　**9** The
wall was so strong that we did not attack it.　**10** He is so cowardly that
we despise him.

77

1 He was so foolish that no one listened to him.　**2** I will send men to
dig up the ancient tombs.　**3** He was silent to avoid being punished.　**4**
The boy talked so much (=*adeo*) that his father became angry.　**5** They
dug a long ditch to find the site of Troy.

78

1 She is so pure that she does not deserve (=is not worthy of) punishment.
2 They sacrificed many victims to appease the gods.　**3** The doctor went
round the tents to cure the sick.　**4** He was so (=*adeo*) afflicted by disease
that he wished to die.　**5** He went away from Rome that he might not
become sick.

79

1 The boy was so foolish that he neglected the study of philosophy.　**2**
Men were sent to take (=*duco*) Socrates to prison.　**3** I accuse Socrates
so that our young men may not be corrupted.　**4** Socrates fought very
bravely to save the life of his friend.　**5** The philosopher was so learned
that we listened to him willingly.

80

1 He was so wicked that no one believed him.　**2** We resisted the Romans
to recover our liberty.　**3** He was so bold that he dared to deceive the
magistrates.　**4** He took poison to avoid being captured.　**5** So great is
his eloquence that he can plead a case himself.

81

1 The soldiers having been captured were killed.　**2** We saw him writing
a letter.　**3** The prisoner (when) about to run out of the camp was seen
by the guards.　**4** The girl having followed the slave was led to the farm.
5 The walls of the captured city were destroyed.
　　　(replace 'when', 'since' 'while' clauses by participles)
6 While they were sleeping the soldiers were captured.　**7** Since he had

been wounded he returned to the camp. **8** When the city was built it was well fortified. **9** When she was about to depart the queen spoke to me. **10** Since he had set out early he arrived first.

82

1 While staying in Britain we saw our friend. **2** The girl having been punished by the master shed tears. **3** Having spoken for a long time the orator was tired (= *defessus*). **4** I saw the queen when she was about to enter the city. **5** I will punish the guard who is sleeping.

83

1 The war having been finished, the soldiers departed. **2** The goddess having been seen, the girls were frightened. **3** A couch having been placed, we sat in the garden. **4** Having bought a book (= a book having been bought) he wished to learn Latin. **5** Having found the money he was able to buy food. **6** The gold having been found was placed in the temple. **7** Having prepared a great army Xerxes attacked Greece. **8** While the boy was reading, the girl was sleeping. **9** While you were sitting, we were standing. **10** While the citizens were sleeping the enemy captured them.

11 Since their general had been killed, the soldiers were unwilling to fight. **12** You saw me while I was sitting in the garden. **13** After preparing the dinner the slaves were able to sleep. **14** Because the walls had been well built we did not attack them. **15** When the soldiers had been ordered to advance Caesar set out from the camp.

84

1 Since the walls were guarded we did not fear the enemy. **2** Having collected the money he decided to buy a waggon. **3** When the signal was given they marched against the enemy. **4** While Caesar was fighting in Gaul the Senate were accusing him. **6** Having undertaken the work (*opus*) he began to build the temple.

85

1 Since the walls were bravely defended, we could not capture the city. **2** The camp, surrounded by a high rampart, seemed to be safe. **3** When the Temple was burned, the Jews tried to escape. **4** While the Romans were hurling stones, The Jews were defending the walls. **5** The image having been dedicated was placed (= *pono*) in the temple of Jupiter.

86

1 Who ordered the gladiators to fight? **2** When he had risen from his seat he welcomed his friends. **3** I will ask the boys not to chase the dog. **4** Since you wish to go, I shall not prevent you. **5** Why did they forbid the centurion to punish the soldiers? **6** When I was going home, I saw many people in the market-place. **7** I told (= ordered) them not to despise the poor (= poor men).   **8** When he comes here, he will be greeted by all the citizens.   **9** They are asking us to come to see the games.   **10** When he killed the prisoner, he was punished by his general.

<h2 style="text-align:center">87</h2>

1 I will order the jury to condemn the wicked girl.   **2** When I celebrate games, I always import many animals.   **3** We told (= ordered) the girls not to jump down from the high cave.   **4** When he jumped down into the river, he swam to the other bank.   **5** When he fell into the water, he was saved by his friend.

<h2 style="text-align:center">88</h2>

1 I will order the cruel teacher not to hurt the boys.   **2** Since you have decided to help us, I will not harm you.   **3** Why did he ask us to examine these books?   **4** When he had examined the wound, he told the girl to go to a doctor.   **5** Although the lion frightens him, he prefers to stay rather than to flee.

<h2 style="text-align:center">89</h2>

1 Since you feel grateful to me, give me money to buy food.   **1** I will ask the farmer to feed my animals daily.   **3** When I was examining this book, I found in it many strange stories.   **4** Why did you forbid the girl to go to meet Crassus?   **5** When the lion licked Androcles, the Romans were amazed.

<h2 style="text-align:center">90</h2>

1 He warned the citizens to fortify the town well.   **2** When the city (of) Rome was being founded, Remus, brother of Romulus, was killed.   **3** The Romans ordered all the peoples to worship Caesar.   **4** Since you don't want to go to the baths, stay at home.   **5** When you see the enemy, warn the citizens to prepare arms.

<h2 style="text-align:center">91</h2>

1 They say that Alexander will defeat the Persians.   **2** I hear that Thebes has been destroyed.   **3** We think that they have departed.   **4** He says that his neighbours are angry.   **5** I know that she is going home. **6** He said that the king was calling together the soldiers.   **7** I did not think that the prisoners would be killed.   **8** How did he know that the city was being attacked?   **9** He said that we had won great fame.   **10** I did not believe that he would read the book.   **11** Crassus says that he (Crassus) has been blamed.   **12** Crassus says that he (someone else) has been blamed.   **13** The girl said that she (the girl) would come.   **14** The girl said that she (another girl) would come.   **15** I hope to find (= that I will find) the money.   **16** He promised to give (= that he would give) me the book.   **17** The master threatened to punish (= that he would punish) the pupils.   **18** He promised to look after the sick children.   **19** The general said that not he, but the soldiers had saved the camp.

20 He said he had decided to set out and would follow us soon.

92

1 He said that reinforcements would arrive in three days. **2** We heard that Alexander had advanced into Asia. **3** I hope to spend the winter with you at Rome. **4** Alexander said he wished to sacrifice to Priam. **5** He promised to come and I hope to see him.

93

1 He says that he will soon get possession of the camp. **2** I hope to find men skilled in medicine. **3** Don't throw away the money. I hope to buy many books. **4** Why did you say that Alexander had loosened the knots? **5** Messengers reported that the city had been taken by storm.

94

1 He said that the catapults were breaching the wall. **2** When I said that help would arrive, he promised not to despair. **3** He says that the theatre can hold 10,000 people. **4** The Macedonians heard that Alexander had been seriously wounded. **5** They say that they (other people) are building very many ships.

95

1 He said he would cover the land with trees. **2** I hear that Alexander did not accept the money sent by Darius. **3** Messengers announced that the cavalry were approaching. **4** They heard that the camp had been surrounded by the Macedonians. **5** I hope you will change this money. I can't use it any longer.

96

1 If you come down to the river, I will show you the bridge. **2** If he had escaped, I would have been glad. **3** If you saw the Capitol, you saw the temple of Jupiter. **4** If I were to try to do this, I would be punished. **5** If he had drawn up his forces, he would have won a victory. **6** If you are obeying your father, you are a good son. **7** If the traitor had opened the gate, the enemy would have entered the city. **8** If you read these books, you will become very wise. **9** If you were building this wall, you would make it much (= *multo*) higher. **10** If the master were to hurt the boy, he would be blamed by the father. **11** If you do not come at once, I shall be angry. **12** If Caesar had not sent help, the Romans would have been defeated.

97

1 If you run into the wood, you will see many wild beasts. **2** If they had rolled down stones, they would have prevented the Macedonians from advancing (*infinitive*). **3** If he were to snatch up a sword, I would run away (=*fugio*).   **4** If you put out the fire, you saved the city.   **5** If we had not urged them to fight (LXXXVI, para. 3), they would have asked for peace.

<h2 style="text-align:center">98</h2>

1 I will ask him what he is doing.   **2** I knew why he was saying this.   **3** He does not know who gave me the money.   **4** They found out (to) where we had gone.   **5** They heard how the city had been captured.   **6** He will report where the army has halted.

7 They reported what had happened in Greece.   **8** I will soon hear why they were unwilling to depart.   **9** He found out who was plotting against the Roman state.   **10** Have you asked them what sort of books they are reading?   **11** I don't know if we will ever persuade them.   **12** They knew well what the girl would say.

<h2 style="text-align:center">99</h2>

1 Ask them why they slaughtered the prisoners.   **2** I soon found out why he formed this plan.   **3** Tell me who allows you to do this.   **4** I didn't know how they were putting the fire out.   **5** I will ask him when Caesar will arrive.

<h2 style="text-align:center">100</h2>

1 Can you tell me who stated this?   **2** He asked them why they had plundered the city.   **3** I didn't know why she was putting on that dress. **4** We will find out what is causing the disease.   **5** I asked him who would lead the army.

<h2 style="text-align:center">101</h2>

(Note: sentences in **101** to **110** are mainly revision)
1 When they had come together, they tried to arrest the traitors.   **2** Do you think that the enemy will plunder our city?   **3** I begged the children not to stand in the road.   **4** I decided to ask why they were making this uproar.   **5** Having arrested Paul the Romans returned to the tower.   **6** He attacked the soldiers while they were standing in the water.

<h2 style="text-align:center">102</h2>

1 If the sun shines forth, it will show us the road.   **2** When will you find out how the girl was wounded?   **3** He was so foolish that he did not obey the master's advice.   **4** When you hand over the money, you will be released from prison.   **5** Saul persecuted the Christians to please the Jews.   **6** I will beg the teacher not to beat the boys.

<h2 style="text-align:center">103</h2>

1 He promised not to violate the city's laws.   **2** If you had brought him forward, we would not have condemned him.   **3** Don't bring back the teacher by whom my son was beaten.   **4** When I was standing in the market-place, I looked at the very beautiful temples.   **5** Having plundered the camp the soldiers found arms and money.   **6** I will ask him why he is whipping this innocent boy.

104

1 If we were to recall Caesar, we would win a great victory.   **2** My friends are begging me to appeal to Caesar.   **3** He was so innocent that no judge could condemn him.   **4** Having persecuted the innocent men he was whipped by the citizens.   **5** He reported that all the cavalry had been recalled.   **6** Can you tell me (=say to me) when Caesar recalled the tenth legion?

105

1 We will board the ship to sail to Greece.   **2** The helmsman having been warned decided to remain in harbour.   **3** The helmsman having been warned, the captain was unwilling to set out.   **4** When they had refreshed themselves, they set out from Rome into Gaul.   **5** Sailors tell me that Britain faces Gaul.   **6** I warned you not to board ship in winter.

106

1 This book will be of great use to me.   **2** One thousand soldiers were sent to protect the citizens.   **3** This sword was given me as a gift.   **4** We will leave the cavalry to support the legions.   **5** If they lower the sails the ship will not be able to sail.   **6** We asked him why he had thrown the money away.   **7** I think the south wind will blow for several hours. **8** When things seem difficult, Caesar always comes to help us.   **9** Don't ask them to save you. We will be your safety.   **10** When the sails had been lowered, the ship was carried away by the storm.

107

1 He drove the ship onto the shore to save the sailors.   **2** He took up the bread and ate it.   **3** When they were sailing near the shore, a great storm arose.   **4** I don't know who they saw in that city.   **5** If the women had been saved, they would have given thanks to the gods.   **6** Do you not think they realised this?

108

1 Stay in the ship, sailors. Do not try to escape.   **2** The centurion was so kind that he allowed Paul to see his friends.   **3** Having collected wood the sailors began to make a fire.   **4** I hope to arrive soon.   He says he will help me.   **5** Do you know how big the serpent is?   **6** If the ship were to be damaged, we would not be able to return home.

109

1 They prayed to the gods that they might not be killed.   **2** I see the ship approaching and entering harbour.   **3** He warned the slaves not to try to escape.　**4** Having slept for ten hours they were able to set out for Rome.　**5** She said she would invite her friends to see the jewels.　**6** If we obtain a favourable wind, we shall set sail immediately.

110

1 We asked him when he would complete the work.　**2** I will beg my father to allow me to go.　**3** Don't invite her. She says she won't come. **4** He is so rich that he has three carriages.　**5** Having sighted Rome they wished to arrive before night.　**6** When you complete the work, I will give you the money.

111

(Note: the last four sentences, where the gerundive is required, may be omitted at this stage at the teacher's discretion.)
1 By (their) love of fighting they won a great empire.　**2** The hour of meeting was announced to the citizens.　**3** By remaining in the camp he avoided death.　**4** By finding this out he was able to win a victory.　**5** He did this for the purpose of harming us.　**6** He said these things for the sake of persuading the citizens.　**7** This wind is not suitable for (= *ad*) sailing.　**8** For the sake of pleasing (his) mother he stayed at home. **9** They sent soldiers for the purpose of defending the walls.　**10** He fought well for the sake of winning glory.　**11** Caesar went to Britain for the sake of punishing the inhabitants.　**12** Workmen came for the purpose of repairing the ships.

112

(Note: these may be deferred at the teacher's discretion)
1 The prisoners must be led away.　**2** The mountain had to be captured. **3** This book will have to be read. **4** We have to change these laws. **5** Caesar had to do everything at the same time.　**6** They will have to announce the great disaster.　**7** Fathers must be obeyed.　**8** The general had to be persuaded.　**9** The children must not be harmed.　**10** I must sail to Greece.　**11** We must advance at once.　**12** You must not stay here.

113

(Note: exercises **113** to **120** revise gerund, gerundive and passive of intransitive verbs. Each group of sentences is in approximate order of difficulty.)
1 By fighting bravely he won great glory.　**2** They had no hope of escaping.　**3** For the sake of living for a long time he gave money to doctors.　**4** The eagle must not be betrayed to the enemy.　**5** I must urge on my horse.　**6** We must swim in this river.　**7** I know that I must not hesitate.　**8** Suddenly a shout was raised, 'Do not betray the eagle'. **9** They threw weapons for the purpose of frightening the enemy.　**10** He said that he had to set out at once.

1 There is no chance of advancing.   **2** We set out early for the sake of arriving early.   **3** These ships will have to be repaired.   **4** They must repair this ship.   **5** A fierce battle was fought here.   **6** He said he had come for the purpose of encouraging the soldiers.

1 We shall cross the river by swimming.   **2** No chance of fighting was given to us.   **3** Three legions must be drawn up in front of the camp.   **4** He said that we must resist the attack.   **5** He said that we must obey the laws.   **6** He came here for the sake of seeing his mother.

1 Cavalry must be sent ahead at once.   **2** I think that you must break through the line-of-battle.   **3** By fighting, not by fleeing will you win a victory.   **4** He sent ten cohorts to drive back the enemy (use *ad* with gerundive).   **5** I must go away at once: the city must be saved.   **6** Thus does one go to the stars.

1 He sent one legion for the sake of foraging.   **2** When will you make an end of speaking?   **3** We must withstand this attack.   **4** The weather is not suitable for (= *ad*) sailing.   **5** By reading books you can become learned.   **6** A rush was made (use *concurro*) towards the camp.

1 We must not abandon hope.   **2** Soldiers often gain money by plundering.   **3** The cavalry entered the city for the sake of plundering.   **4** Reinforcements must be sent at once.   **5** He said that the children must not stray.   **6** He went to the wood for the purpose of hiding the money.

1 A sortie must be made at once.   **2** We must find the cause of the defeat. **3** By working well we please the master.   **4** He said this for the purpose of pleasing the citizens.   **5** A shout is being raised in the city.   **6** He said that the laws must be obeyed.

1 I have no hope of paying.   **2** Two ships must be launched.   **3** Next day a fierce battle will be fought.   **4** He says he must draw up the legions. **5** Don't give them a chance of escaping.   **6** By launching more ships we shall avoid defeat.

English-Latin Vocabulary

I abandon (*hope*), **dēpōn-o, -ĕre, -posui, -positum**
about, **ferē**, *adv.*
about, **de**, *prep. with abl.*
I accept, **accip-io, -ĕre, -cēpi, -ceptum**
I accuse, **accūso** (1)
I adorn, **orno** (1)
I advance, **prōgred-ior, -i, -gressus sum**
advice, **consilium** (2)
Aeschylus, **Aeschylus** (2)
I afflict, **afflīg-o, -ĕre, -flixi, -flictum**
after, **post**, *prep. with acc.*
against, **contra**, *prep. with acc.*
ago, **abhinc**, *adv.*
Alexander, **Alexand-er, -ri** (2)
alive, **vīvus**, *adj.*
all, **omn-is, -e**, *adj.*
I allow, **sin-o, -ĕre, sīvi, situm**
although, **cum**, *with subj.*: **quamquam**, *with indic.*
always, **semper**, *adv.*
I am, **sum, esse, fui**
I am able, **possum, posse, potui**
I am afraid of, **timeo** (2), *with acc.*
I am amazed, **mīror** (1)
I am unwilling, **nōlo, nōlle, nōlui**
ancient, **antīquus**, *adj.*
Androcles, **Androcl-ēs, -is**, *m.*
angry, **īrātus**, *adj.*
animal, **anim-al, -ālis**, *n.*
I announce, **nuntio** (1)
any longer, **diutius**, *adv.*
I appeal to, **appello** (1), *with acc.*
I appease, **plāco** (1)
I approach, **apprŏpinquo** (1)
I arise, **orior, orīri, ortus sum**
arithmetic, **arithmētica** (1)
arms (=weapons), **arm-a, -ōrum** (2) *pl.*
army, **exercitus** (4)
I arrest, **comprehend-o, -ĕre, -i, -prehensum**
Arria, **Arria** (1), *f.*

I arrive, **perven-io, -īre, -vēni, -ventum**
I ask, **rŏgo** (1)
I ask for, **rŏgo** (1), *with acc.*
Asia, **Asia** (1)
I attack, **oppugno** (1); **aggred-ior, -i, aggressus sum**
at once, **statim**, *adv.*
at the same time, **simul**, *adv.*
Aurora, **Aurōra** (1)
I avoid, **vīto** (1)

bank (*of river*), **rīpa** (1)
baths, **balne-ae, -ārum** (1) *pl.*
battle, **proelium** (2)
beast, wild, **fera** (1)
I beat, whip, **verbero** (1)
beautiful, **pulch-er, -ra, -rum**, *adj.*
because, **quod**, *conj.*
I become, **fīo, fīeri, factus sum**
before, **ante**, *prep. with acc.*
I beg, **ōro** (1)
I begin, **incip-io, -ĕre, -cēpi, -ceptum**
I believe, **crēd-o, -ĕre, -ĭdi, -ĭtum**
I betray, **prōd-o, -ĕre, -idi, -itum**
I blame, **culpo** (1)
I blow, **adflo** (1)
I board (*a ship*), **conscend-o, -ĕre, -scendi, -scensum**
bold, **aud-ax** (*gen.* **-ācis**), *adj.*
book, **lĭb-er, -ri** (2)
boy, **puer, -i** (2)
brave, **fort-is, -e**, *adj.*
I breach **dīru-o, -ĕre, -i, -rutum**
bread, **pān-is, -is**, *m.*
I break through, **perrump-o, -ĕre, -rūpi, -ruptum**
bridge, **pons, pontis**, *m.*
I bring, **fero, ferre, tuli, lātum**
I bring back, **redūc-o, -ĕre, -duxi, -ductum**
I bring forward, **prōdūc-o, -ĕre, -duxi -ductum**
Britain, **Britannia** (1)
brother, **frāt-er, -ris**, *m.*

I build, **aedifico** (1)
building, **aedificium** (2)
I burn, **incend-o, -ĕre, -i, -censum**
business, **negōtium** (2)
but, **sed,** *conj.*
I buy, **emo, emĕre, ēmi, emptum**
by (*of person*), **a, ab,** *prep. with abl.*

Caesar, **Caes-ar, -aris,** *m.*
I call together, **convŏco** (1)
camp, **castr-a, -ōrum** (2) *pl.*
I can, am able, **possum, posse, potui**
Capitol, **Capitōlium** (2)
captain (*of ship*), **magist-er, -ri** (2)
I capture, **cap-io, -ĕre, cēpi, captum**
carriage, **raeda** (1)
I carry away, **dēfero, -ferre, -tuli, -lātum**
catapult, **catapulta** (1)
I cause, **effic-io, -ĕre, -fēci, -fectum**
cause, **causa** (1)
cavalry, **equit-es, -um,** *m. pl.*
cave, **spēlunca** (1)
I celebrate, **celebro** (1)
centurion, **centuri-o, -ōnis,** *m.*
chance, **facult-as, -ātis,** *f.*
I change, **mūto** (1) *trans.*
I chase, **fugo** (1)
children, **līber-i, -ōrum** (2) *pl.*
chorus, **chŏrus** (2)
Christian, **Christiānus** (2)
citadel, **arx, arcis,** *f.*
citizen, **cīv-is, -is,** *c.*
city, **urbs, urbis,** *f.*
I climb, **ascend-o, -ĕre, -i, ascensum**
I collect, **collĭg-o, -ĕre, -lēgi, -lectum**
I come, **vĕn-io, -īre, vēni, ventum**
I come down, **descend-o, -ĕre, -i, -scensum**
I come together, **concurr-o, -ĕre, -curri, -cursum**
companion, **com-es, -ĭtis,** *c.*
I compel, **cōg-o, -ĕre, coēgi, coactum**
I complete, **perfic-io, -ĕre, -fēci, -fectum**
I condemn, **damno** (1)
I conspire, **coniūro** (1)
consul, **cons-ul, -ŭlis,** *m.*
Cornelia, **Cornēlia** (1)
I corrupt, **corrump-o, -ĕre, -rūpi, -ruptum**
couch, **lectus** (2)

country(side), **rūs, rūris,** *n.*
country-house, **villa** (1)
I cover, **teg-o, -ĕre, texi, tectum**
cow, **vacca** (1)
cowardly, **ignāvus,** *adj.*
Crassus, **Crassus** (2)
I cross, **trans-ĕo, -īre, -ii** *or* **-īvi, -ĭtum**
cruel, **crūdēl-is, -e,** *adj.*
I cure, **sāno** (1)

daily, **cotĭdie,** *adv.*
I damage, **afflicto** (1)
dancer, **saltāt-or, -ōris,** *m.*
I dare, **aud-eo, ēre, ausus sum**
Darius, **Darius** (2)
day, **dies** (5) *m.*
dead, **mortuus,** *adj.*
death, **mors, mortis,** *f.*
I deceive, **fall-o, -ĕre, fefelli, falsum**
I decide, **constitu-o, -ĕre, -stitui, -stitutum**
I dedicate, **dēdico** (1)
deed, **factum** (2)
I defeat, **vinc-o, -ĕre, vīci, victum**
defeat, **clād-es, -is,** *f.*
I defend, **defend-o, -ĕre, -i, -fensum**
I delay, **moror** (1), *intrans.*
I depart, **discēd-o, -ĕre, -cessi, -cessum**
I despair, **dēspēro** (1)
I despise, **contemn-o, -ĕre, -tempsi, -temptum**
I destroy, **dēl-eo, -ēre, -ēvi, -ētum**
dew, **rōs, rōris,** *m.*
I die, **mor-ior, -i, mortuus sum**
difficult, **difficil-is, -e,** *adj.*
I dig (*a ditch*), **dūc-o, -ĕre, duxi, ductum**
I dig up, **effŏd-io, -ĕre, -fōdi, -fossum**
dinner, **cēna** (1)
disaster, **clād-es, -is,** *f.*
I disband, **dīmitt-o, -ĕre, -mīsi, -missum**
disease, **morbus** (2)
ditch, **fossa** (1)
I do, **fac-io, -ĕre, fēci, factum**
doctor, **medicus** (2)
dog, **can-is, -is,** *c.*
I draw up, **instru-o, -ĕre, -struxi, -structum**
dress, **vest-is, -is,** *f.*

I drive, **pell-o, -ĕre, pepuli, pulsum**
I drive back, **repell-o, -ĕre, reppŭli, repulsum**
I drive on, **impell-o, ĕre, -pŭli, -pulsum**

eagle, **aquila** (1)
early, **māne,** *adv.*
earth, **terra** (1)
easy, **facil-is, -e,** *adj.*
I eat, **ĕdo, ĕdĕre, ēdi, ēsum**
eight, **octo,** *indec.*
eloquence, **ēloquentia** (1)
emperor, **princ-eps, -ĭpis,** *m.*
empire, **imperium** (2)
I encourage, **hortor** (1)
end, **fīn-is, -is,** *m.*
enemy, **hostes, hostium,** *m. pl.*
I enter, **intro** (1)
equal, **pār** (*gen.* **păris**), *adj.*
I escape, **effug-io, -ĕre, -fūgi**
everyone, **omnes,** *m. pl.*
everything, **omnia,** *n. pl.*
I examine, **inspic-io, -ĕre, -spexi, -spectum**
example, **exemplum** (2)
exile, **exilium** (2)

to face, **spectāre ad**
faithful, **fidēl-is, -e,** *adj.*
I fall, **cad-o, -ĕre, cecĭdi, cāsum**
fame, **fāma** (1)
farm, **fundus** (2)
farmer, **agricola** (1) *m.*
father, **păt-er, -ris,** *m.*
favourable, **secundus,** *adj.*
I fear, **timeo** (2)
fear, **tim-or, -ōris,** *m.*
I feed, **alo, alĕre, aluī, altum,** *trans.*
I feel grateful, **grātiam habeo**
field, **ager, agri** (2)
fierce, **fer-ox** (*gen.* **-ōcis**), *adj.* **atr-ox** (*gen.* **-ōcis**), *adj.*
I fight, **pugno** (1)
I find, **invĕn-io, -īre, -vēni, -ventum**
I find out, learn, **cognosc-o, -ĕre, -nōvi, -nĭtum**
I finish, **fīnio** (4)
fire, **ign-is, -is,** *m.*
first, **prīmus,** *adj.*
five, **quinque,** *indec.*
I flee, **fug-io, -ĕre, fūgi**

I flow, **flu -o, -ĕre, fluxi, fluxum**
I follow, **sequ-or, -i, secūtus sum**
food, **cibus** (2)
foolish, **stultus,** *adj.*
foot, **pēs, pĕdis,** *m.*
I forage, **pābulor** (1)
I forbid, **vet-o, -āre, -ui, -itum**
forces, **cōpi-ae, -ārum** (1) *pl.*
I form (*a plan*), **cap-io, -ĕre, cēpi, captum**
I fortify, **mūnio** (4)
I found (*a city*), **cond-o, -ĕre, -didi, -ditum**
friend, **amīcus** (2)
I frighten, **terreo** (2)
from, **a, ab,** *prep. with abl.*
front of, in, **pro,** *prep. with abl.*

game, **lūdus** (2)
garden, **hortus** (2)
gate, **porta** (1)
Gaul, **Gallia** (1)
general, **dux, ducis,** *m.*
geometry, **geōmetria** (1)
I get possession of, **pot-ior, -īri, -ītus sum,** *with abl.*
gift, **dōnum** (2)
girl, **puella** (1)
I give, **do, dăre, dĕdi, dătum**
I give thanks, **grātias ago**
glad, **laetus,** *adj.*
gladiator, **gladiāt-or, -ōris,** *m.*
glory, **glōria** (1)
I go, **ĕo, īre, -ii** *or* **īvi, ĭtum**
I go away, **abĕo, -īre, -ii** *or* **-īvi, -ĭtum**
I go round, **circumeo** (*as* **eo**)
I go to meet, **obviam eo,** *with dat.*
god, **deus** (2)
goddess, **dea** (1)
gold, **aurum** (2)
good, **bonus,** *adj.*
grateful, I feel, **grātiam habeo**
great, **magnus,** *adj.*
Greece, **Graecia** (1)
Greek, **Graecus** (2)
Greek, **Graecus,** *adj.*
I greet, **salūto** (1)
I guard, **custōdio** (4)
guard, **cust-os, -ōdis,** *m.*

I halt, **consist-o, ĕre, -stiti**
I hand over, **trād-o, -ĕre, -didi, -ditum**

I happen, **fīo, fīeri, factus sum**
harbour, **portus** (4)
I have, **habeo** (2)
I hear, **audio** (4)
helmsman, **gubernāt-or, -ōris,** *m.*
I help, **adiūv-o, -āre, -iūvi, -iūtum**
help, **auxilium** (2)
here, **hīc,** *adv.*
to here, **hūc,** *adv.*
Herodotus, **Hērŏdŏtus** (2)
I hesitate, **cunctor** (1)
I hide, **cēlo** (1) *trans.*
high, **altus,** *adj.*
himself, herself, etc. **ipse, ipsa, ipsum,**
    adj.
I hold, contain, **contin-eo, -ēre, -ui,**
    -tentum
home, **domus** (2 & 4), *f.*
Homer, **Homērus** (2)
I hope, **spēro** (1)
hope, **spes** (5)
hour, **hōra** (1)
house, **domus** (2 & 4), *f.*
how? **quomodo?**
how big? **quantus?** *adj.*
how many? **quot?** *indec.*
huge, **ing-ens** (*gen.* **-entis**), *adj.*
hundred, one, **centum,** *indecl.*
I hurl (*stones*), **mitt-o, -ěre, mīsi,**
    missum
I hurt, **noceo** (2) *with dat.*
husband, **vir, viri,** *m.*

image, **simulācrum** (2)
I imitate, **imitor** (1)
immediately, **statim,** *adv.*
I import, **importo** (1)
in, **in,** *prep. with abl.*
inhabitant, **incŏla** (1) *c.*
innocent, **innoc-ens** (*gen.* **-entis**), *adj.*
I inscribe, **inscrīb-o, -ěre, -scripsi,**
    -scriptum
into, **in,** *prep. with acc.*
I invite, **invīto** (1)
Italy, **Ītalia** (1)

a Jew, **Iūdaeus** (2)
jewel, **gemma** (1)
judge, **iūd-ex, -ĭcis,** *m.*
I jump down, **dēsil-io, -īre, -ui,**
    -sultum
Jupiter, **Iuppiter, Iŏvis,** *m.*

jury, **iūdices,** *m. pl.*

I kill, **occīd-o, -ěre, -cīdi, -cīsum**
    interfic-io, -ěre, -fēci, -fectum
kind, **benignus,** *adj.*
king, **rex, rēgis,** *m.*
knot, **nōdus** (2)
I know, **scio** (4)
know, I do not, **nescio** (4)

land, **terra** (1)
language, **lingua** (1)
large, **magnus,** *adj.*
Latin (language), **lingua Latīna**
I launch, **dēdūc-o, -ěre, -duxi,**
    -ductum
law, **lex, lēgis,** *f.*
I lead, **dūc-o, -ěre, duxi, ductum**
I lead away, **abdūc-o, -ěre, -duxi,**
    -ductum
I learn, **disc-o, -ěre, dĭdĭci**
learned, **doctus,** *adj.*
I leave, **relinqu-o, -ěre, -līqui,**
    -lictum
legion, **legi-o, -ōnis,** *f.*
lest, **nē,** *conj.*
letter (*for post*), **epistola** (1)
letter (*of alphabet*), **littera** (1)
liberty, **lībert-as, -ātis,** *f.*
I lick, **mulc-eo, -ēre, mulsi, mulsum**
life, **vīta** (1)
lightning, **fulm-en, -ĭnis,** *n.*
I like, **amo** (1)
line, **ord-o, -ĭnis,** *m.*
line-of-battle, **acies** (5)
lion, **leo, leōnis,** *m.*
I listen to, **audio** (4) *with acc.*
I live (= am alive), **vīv-o, -ěre, vixi,**
    victum
I live (= dwell), **habito**(1)
Livy, **Livius** (2)
London, **Londinium** (2)
long, **longus,** *adj.*
longer, any, **diutius,** *adv.*
I look after, **curo** (1)
I look at, **specto** (1)
I loosen, **solv-o, -ěre, -i, solūtum**
I love, **amo** (1)
love, **am-or, -ōris,** *m.*
I lower, **dēmitt-o, -ěre, -mīsi,**
    -missum
Lucian, **Luciānus** (2)

Macedonians, **Macĕdŏn-es, -um,** *m. pl.*

magistrate, **magistrātus** (4)

I make, **fac-io, -ĕre, fēci, factum**

man, **vir, viri** (2)

many, **mult-i, -ae, -a,** *pl. adj.*

I march, **contend-o, -ĕre, -i**

market place, **fŏrum** (2)

master, **magist-er, -ri** (2)

medicine, **medicīna** (1)

I meet, **conven-io, -īre, -vēni, -ventum**

meet, I go to, **obviam eo,** *with dat.*

messenger, **nuntius** (2)

miles, **mīlia passuum** (*see page* 38)

mirror, **speculum** (2)

money, **pecūnia** (1)

month, **mens-is, -is,** *m.*

moon, **lūna** (1)

mother, **māt-er, -ris,** *f.*

mountain, **mons, montis,** *m.*

much (= by much), **multo,** *adv.*

my, **meus,** *adj.*

nature, **nātūra** (1)

near, **prope,** *prep. with acc.*

I neglect, **negleg-o, -ĕre, -lexi, -lectum**

neighbour, **fīnitimus** (2)

never, **nunquam,** *adv.*

next, **posterus,** *adj.*

night, **nox, noctis,** *f.*

no one, **nēmo** (*acc.* **nēminem,** *gen.* **nullius**)

not, **nōn,** *adv.*

I obey, **pāreo** (2) *with dat.*

I obtain, **nancisc-or, -i, nactus sum**

I open, **aper-io, īre, -ui, -tum**

I order, **iŭb-eo, -ēre, iussi, iussum**

other, **alius,** *adj.*

the other (of two), **alter, -a, -um,** *adj.*

our, **nost-er, -ra, -rum,** *adj.*

out of, **ex.** *prep. with abl.*

I overcome, **supero** (1)

pace, **passus** (4)

Paetus, **Paetus** (2)

part, **pars, partis,** *f.*

I pay, **pend-o, -ĕre, pependi, pensum**

peace, **pax, pācis,** *f.*

people (men & women), **homin-es, -um** *pl.*

people (= nation), **populus** (2)

I persecute, **persequ-or, -i, persecūtus sum**

a Persian, **Persa** (1) *m.*

I persuade, **persuād-eo, -ēre, -suāsi, -suāsum,** *with dat.*

philosopher, **philosophus** (2)

philosophy, **philosophia** (1)

I place, **pōn-o, -ĕre, posui, positum**

plan, **consilium** (2)

I plead a case, **causam dīc-o, -ĕre, dixi, dictum**

I please, **placeo** (2) *with dat.*

I plot, **coniūro** (1)

I plunder, **dīrip-io, -ĕre, -ui, -reptum** *trans.* **praedor** (1), *intrans.*

poet, **poēta** (1) *m.*

poison, **venēnum** (2)

poor (= wretched), **miser, -a, -um,** *adj.*

poor (in money), **paup-er** (*gen.* -**ĕris**), *adj.*

I praise, **laudo** (1)

I pray, **precor** (1)

I prefer, **mālo, malle, mālui**

I prepare, **paro** (1)

I prevent, **prohibeo** (2), *with inf.*

Priam, **Prĭămus** (2)

prison, **carc-er, -ĕris,** *m.*

prisoner, **captīvus** (2)

I promise, **prōmitt-o, -ĕre, -mīsi, -missum**

protection, **praesidium** (2)

province, **prōvincia** (1)

I punish, **punio** (4)

punishment, **supplicium** (2)

pupil, **discipulus** (2)

pure, **pūrus,** *adj.*

purpose of, for the, **ad,** *prep. with acc.*

I put on, **indu-o, -ĕre, -i, -dūtum**

I put out, **exstingu-o, -ĕre, -stinxi, -stinctum**

queen, **rēgīna** (1)

I raise, **toll-o, -ĕre, sustuli, sublātum**

rampart, **vallum** (2)

rather than, **potius quam**

I read, **leg-o, -ĕre, lēgi, lectum**

reader, **lect-or, -ōris,** *c.*

I realise, **sent-io, -īre, sensi, sensum**

I recover, **recupero** (1)
to refresh oneself, **sē reficĕre**
reinforcements, **cōpiae nŏvae** (1) *pl.*
I release, **lībero** (1)
I remain, **man-eo, -ēre, mansi, mansum**
Remus, **Remus** (2)
I repair, **refic-io, -ĕre, -fēci, -fectum**
I report, **nuntio** (1)
I resist (*a person*), **resist-o, -ĕre, restiti,** *with dat.*
I resist (*an attack*), **sustin-eo, -ēre, -ui, sustentum**
I return (*intrans.*), **red-ĕo, -īre, -ii** *or* **-īvi, -ĭtum**
rich, **dīves** (*gen.* **dīvĭtis**), *adj.*
I rise, get up, **surg-o, -ĕre, surrexi, surrectum: orior, orīri, ortus sum**
river, **fluvius** (2)
road, **via** (1)
rock, **saxum** (2)
I roll down (*trans.*), **dēvolv-o, -ĕre, -i, -volutum**
Roman, **Rōmānus** (2)
Roman, **Rōmānus,** *adj.*
Rome, **Rōma** (1)
Romulus, **Rōmulus** (2)
I run, **curr-o, -ĕre, cucurri, cursum**

I sacrifice, **sacrifico** (1)
safe, **tūtus,** *adj.*
safety, **sal-us, ūtis,** *f.*
I sail, **nāvigo** (1)
sail, **vēlum** (2)
sailor, **nauta** (1) *m.*
sake of, for the, **causa,** *prep. with gen.* (*follows its noun*)
same, **īdem, eadem, ĭdem**
same time, at the, **simul,** *adv.*
I save, **servo** (1)
I say, **dīc-o, -ĕre, dixi, dictum**
sea, **mare, maris,** *n.*
seat, **sēd-es, -is,** *f.*
I see, **vĭd-eo, -ēre, vīdi, vīsum**
I seem, **vĭd-eor, -ēri, vīsus sum**
senate, **senātus** (4)
I send, **mitt-o, -ĕre, mīsi, missum**
I send ahead, **praemitto** (*like* mitto)
serious, **grav-is, -e,** *adj.*
serpent, **serp-ens, -entis,** *f.*
I set free, **lībero** (1)

I set out, **proficisc-or, -i, profectus sum**
I set sail, **nāvem solvo**
seven, **septem,** *indec.*
seventy, **septuāginta,** *indec.*
several, **complures,** *adj. pl.*
I shine forth, **effulg-eo, -ēre, -fulsi**
ship, **nāv-is, -is,** *f.*
shore, **līt-us, -ŏris,** *n.*
I shout, **clāmo** (1)
shout, **clām-or, -ōris,** *m.*
I show, **ostend-o, -ĕre, -i, ostentum : monstro** (1)
sick, **aeg-er, -ra, -rum,** *adj.*
I sight, **conspic-io, -ĕre, -spexi, -spectum**
signal, **signum** (2)
I am silent, **taceo** (2)
since, **cum,** *conj.*
I sit, **sed-eo, -ēre, sēdi, sessum**
site, **sĭtus** (4)
six, **sex,** *indec.*
sixth, **sextus,** *adj.*
sixty, **sexāginta,** *indec.*
skilled (in), **perītus,** *adj. with gen.*
I slaughter, **caed-o, -ĕre, cecīdi, caesum**
slave, **servus** (2)
I sleep, **dormio** (4)
smoke, **fūmus** (2)
I snatch up, **corrip-io, -ĕre, -ripui, -reptum**
so, **tam,** *adv. with adjs. and advs.*
so great, **tantus,** *adj.*
so much, **adeo,** *adv.*
Socrates, **Sōcrat-ēs, -is,** *m.*
soldier, **mīl-es, -ĭtis,** *m.*
some. . .others, **alii. . . alii**
son, **fīlius** (2)
soon, **mox,** *adv.*
Sophocles, **Sŏphŏcl-ēs, -is,** *m.*
sortie, **ērupti-o, -ōnis,** *f.*
south, **merīdies** (5) *m.*
south wind, **nŏtus** (2)
I speak, **loqu-or, -i, locūtus sum**
spear, **hasta** (1)
speed, **celerit-as, -ātis,** *f.*
I spend the winter, **hiemo** (1)
I stand, **sto, stāre, stĕti, stătum**
star, **stella** (1)
I state, **affirmo** (1)
state, Roman, **rēs publica**

statue, **statua** (1)
I stay, **man-eo, -ēre, mansi, mansum**
step, **gradus** (4)
still, **etiam,** *adv.*
stone, **saxum** (2)
storm, **tempest-ās, -ātis,** *f.*
storm, I take by, **expugno** (1)
story, **fābula** (1): **historia** (1)
strange, **nǒvus,** *adj.*: **mīrus,** *adj.*
I stray, **vagor** (1)
street, **via** (1)
strong, **validus,** *adj.*
study, **studium** (2)
suddenly, **repente,** *adv.*
suitable, **idōneus,** *adj.*
sun, **sōl, sōlis,** *m.*
support, **subsidium** (2)
I surround, **circumven-io, -īre, -vēni, -ventum: circum-do, -dǎre, -dědi, -dǎtum**
I swim, **nato** (1)
sword, **gladius** (2)
Syracuse, **Syracūs-ae, -ārum,** *f. pl.*

Tacitus, **Tacitus** (2)
I take place, **fīo, fīeri, factus sum**
I take (*food, drink*), **sūm-o, -ěre, sumpsi, sumptum**
I take by storm, **expugno** (1)
I talk, **loqu-or, -i, locūtus sum**
I teach, **doc-eo, -ēre, -ui, doctum**
teacher, **magist-er, -ri,** (2)
I tell (*a story*), **narro** (1)
temple, **templum** (2)
ten, **decem,** *indec.*
tent, **tabernāculum** (2)
tenth, **decimus,** *adj.*
than, **quam,** *adv.*
thanks, I give, **grātias ago**
that, **ille, illa, illud**
that, in order, **ut,** *with subj.*
theatre, **theātrum** (2)
Thebes, **Thēb-ae, -ārum,** *f. pl.*
thing, **rēs** (5)
I think, **puto** (1)
third, **tertius,** *adj.*
thirty, **trīginta,** *indec.*
this, **hīc, haec, hōc**
thousand, **mille,** *indec.*
thousands, **mīl-ia, -ium,** *n. pl.*
I threaten, **minor** (1)

three, **tres** (*gen.* **trium**), *adj.*
I throw, **conic-io, -ěre, -iēci, -iectum**
I throw away, **abic-io, -ěre, -iēci, -iectum**
Thucydides, **Thūcўdid-ēs, -is,** *m.*
to (= towards), **ad,** *prep. with acc.*
tomb, **sepulcrum** (2)
I toss, **iacto** (1)
tower, **turr-is, -is,** *f.*
town, **oppidum** (2)
traitor, **prōdit-or, -ōris,** *c.*
I travel, **iter facio**
tree, **arb-or, -ǒris,** *f.*
triumph, **triumphus** (2)
Troy, **Troia** (1)
true, **vērus,** *adj.*
I try, **cōnor** (1)
twenty, **vīginti,** *indec.*
two, **duo, duae, duo,** *adj.*
two hundred **ducent-i, -ae, -a,** *adj.*

under, **sub,** *prep. with acc. and abl.*
I undertake, **suscip-io, -ěre, -cēpi, -ceptum**
unwilling, I am, **nōlo, nōlle, nōlui**
uproar, **tumultus** (4)
I urge, **admoneo** (2)
I urge on, **incǐto** (1)
I use, **ūtor, ūti, ūsus sum,** *with abl.*
use, **ūsus** (4)

I vanish, **ēvānesc-o, -ěre, -vānui**
Veii, **Vei-i, -ōrum** (2) *pl.*
Vergil, **Vergilius** (2)
vice, **vitium** (2)
victim, **hostia** (1) *c.*
victory, **victōria** (1)
I violate, **violo** (1)

waggon, **carrus** (2)
I wait, **moror** (1): **man-eo, -ēre mansi, mansum**
I walk, **ambulo** (1)
wall, **mūrus** (2)
I want, wish, **vǒlo, velle, vǒlui**
war, **bellum** (2)
I warn, **admoneo** (2)
water, **ǎqua** (1)
way, manner, **mǒdus** (2)
weapon, **tēlum** (2)
weather, **tempest-as, -ātis,** *f.*
I weep, **fleo, flēre, flēvi, flētum**

I welcome, **salūto** (1)

well, **bene,** *adv.*

what? which? **qui, quae, quod,**
interrog. adj.

what sort of? **quāl-is, -e,** *adj.*

when? **quando?**

when, **cum,** *conj.*

where? **ubi?**

to where? **quo?**

I whip, **verbero** (1)

who? what? **quis, quid,** *interrog. pron.*

whole, **tōtus** (*gen.* **tōtius**)**,** *adj.*

why? **cur?**

wicked, **improbus,** *adj.*

wide, **lātus,** *adj.*

wild beast, **fera** (1)

willingly, **libenter,** *adv.*

I win, gain, **comparo** (1)

I win (*a victory*), **reporto** (1)

wind, **ventus** (2)

winter, **hiems, hiĕmis,** *f.*

wise, **sapi-ens** (*gen.* **-entis**)**,** *adj.*

woman, **fēmina** (1)

wood, forest, **silva** (1)

wood, firewood, **lignum** (2)

I work, **labōro** (1)

work, **ŏp-us, -ĕris,** *n.*: **lab-or,-ōris,** *m.*

workman, **fab-er, -ri** (2)

I worship, **col-o, -ĕre, colui, cultum**

worthy, **dignus,** *adj. with abl.*

I wound, **vulnero** (1)

wound, **vuln-us, -ĕris,** *n.*

I write, **scrīb-o, -ĕre, scripsi,
scriptum**

year, **annus** (2)

young man, **iuven-is, -is,** *m.*

your, **tuus; vest-er, -ra, -rum,** *adj.*

Accidence

The alphabet
The Latin alphabet is the same as the English except that it has neither *j* nor *w*.

Latin *i* may be either a vowel or a consonant. As a consonant it is sometimes wrongly written as *j*.

Pronunciation

Latin	as English	Example
ae	high	**hast*ae***
au	how	**ca*u*sa**
c	k	**in*c*ola**
e (short)	pet	**f*e*ra**
e (long)	day	**terr*e*bam**
g	gun	**re*g*ina**
i (long)	deep	**v*i*ta**
i (short)	dip	**v*i*a**
i (conson.)	y	**ad*i*uvo**
o (short)	pot	**in*c*ola**
o (long)	mow	***o*ra**
oe	boy	**pr*oe*lium**
u (short)	us	**fund*u*s**
u (long)	fool	**d*u*co**
v	w	***v*ia**

Marking of vowel length
1 Short vowels are not marked except in vocabularies where they are needed to aid pronunciation.
2 A long vowel inside a word is marked ⁻ in declensions and vocabularies, but not in exercises.
3 If a word ends with a vowel, that vowel is not marked but note these rules:
   (a) *I* at the end of a word is nearly always long (agri, amici, etc.). But in *mihi, tibi, sibi* it is optional and in *ubi* and *ibi* it is short.
   (b) *O* at the end of a word is nearly always long (intro, amico, etc.). But in *ego* and *modo* (= *only*) it is short.
   (c) *U* at the end of a word is always long (tu, gradu, etc.).
   (d) *A* at the end of a word is usually long, as *hasta* (abl.), *porta* (imperative). But the nominative and vocative singular of 1st group nouns and neuter plural *a* endings are short: hasta (nom. or voc.), bella (neut. pl.).
   (e) *E* at the end of a word is usually short, as *nave* (abl.), *domine* (voc.),

rege (imperative). But the singular imperative of 2nd group verbs, adverbs from -*us* adjectives and ablative singular of 5th group nouns end with long *e*: timē (imperative), improbē (adverb), diē (ablative of *diēs*).

INDICATIVE ACTIVE OF THE FOUR CONJUGATIONS

Principal parts:

amo,	**amāre,**	**amāvi,**	**amātum**	I love
moneo,	**monēre,**	**monui,**	**monitum**	I advise
rego,	**regere,**	**rexi,**	**rectum**	I rule
audio,	**audīre**	**audīvi,**	**audītum**	I hear

Present	*Imperfect*	*Future*	*Perfect*	*Pluperf.*	*Fut.-perf.*
love, am	was	will	loved,	had	will have
loving,	loving	love	have loved,	loved	loved
do love			did love		

am-

			amāv-		
o	ābam	ābo	i	eram	ero
ās	ābas	ābis	isti	eras	eris
at	ābat	ābit	it	erat	erit
āmus	ābamus	ābimus	imus	erāmus	erimus
ātis	ābatis	ābitis	istis	eratis	eritis
ant	ābant	ābunt	ērunt	erant	erint

mon-

			monu-		
eo	ēbam	ēbo	i	eram	ero
ēs	ēbas	ēbis	isti	eras	eris
et	ēbat	ēbit	it	erat	erit
ēmus	ēbamus	ēbimus	etc.	etc.	etc.
ētis	ēbatis	ēbitis			
ent	ēbant	ēbunt			

reg-

			rex-		
o	ēbam	am	i	eram	ero
is	ēbas	ēs	isti	eras	eris
it	ēbat	et	it	erat	erit
imus	ēbamus	ēmus	etc.	etc.	etc.
itis	ēbatis	ētis			
unt	ēbant	ent			

aud-

			audīv-		
io	iēbam	iam	i	eram	ero
īs	iēbas	iēs	isti	eras	eris
it	iēbat	iet	it	erat	erit
īmus	iēbamus	iēmus	etc.	etc.	etc.
ītis	iēbatis	iētis			
iunt	iēbant	ient			

Hints:

1 Verbs with infinitive **-ēre** are conjugated like **moneo.**
2 Verbs with infinitive **-īre** are conjugated like **audio.**
3 Verbs ending in **-o** with infinitive **-āre** are conjugated like **amo.**
4 Verbs ending in **-o** with infinitive **-ĕre** are conjugated like **rego.**
5 The *present stem* comes from the *first* principal part; the *perfect stem* is obtained by removing the 'i' from the *third* principal part.
6 The *perfect tenses* have the same endings in all verbs.
7 The futures of **amo** and **moneo** are similar but are quite different from the futures of **rego** and **audio.**

INDICATIVE PASSIVE OF THE FOUR CONJUGATIONS

Present	*Imperf.*	*Future*	*Perfect*	*Pluperf.*	*Fut.-perf.*
am loved,	was	will	was loved,	had	will have
am being	being	be	have been	been	been
loved	loved	loved	loved	loved	loved
am-			**amātus**	**amātus**	**amātus**
or	ābar	ābor	sum	eram	ero
āris	ābāris	āberis	es	eras	eris
ātur	ābātur	ābitur	est	erat	erit
			amāti	**amāti**	**amāti**
āmur	ābāmur	ābimur	sumus	erāmus	erimus
āmini	ābāmini	ābimini	estis	eratis	eritis
antur	ābantur	ābuntur	sunt	erant	erunt
mon-			**monitus**	**monitus**	**monitus**
eor	ēbar	ēbor	sum	eram	ero
ēris	ēbāris	ēberis	etc.	etc.	etc.
ētur	ēbātur	ēbitur			
			moniti	**moniti**	**moniti**
ēmur	ēbāmur	ēbimur	sumus	erāmus	erimus
ēmini	ēbāmini	ēbimini	etc.	etc.	etc.
entur	ēbantur	ēbuntur			
reg-			**rectus**	**rectus**	**rectus**
or	ēbar	ar	sum	eram	ero
eris	ēbāris	ēris	etc.	etc.	etc.
itur	ēbātur	ētur			
			recti	**recti**	**recti**
imur	ēbāmur	ēmur	sumus	erāmus	erimus
imini	ēbāmini	ēmini	etc.	etc.	etc.
untur	ēbantur	entur			

Present	Imperf.	Future	Perfect	Pluperf.	Fut.-perf.
aud-			**audītus**	**audītus**	**audītus**
ior	iēbar	iar	sum	eram	ero
īris	iēbāris	iēris	etc.	etc.	etc.
ītur	iēbātur	iētur			
			audītī	**audītī**	**audītī**
īmur	iēbāmur	iēmur	sumus	erāmus	erimus
īminī	iēbāminī	iēminī	etc.	etc.	etc.
iuntur	iēbantur	ientur			

INDICATIVE OF THE VERB *TO BE*

Principal parts: **sum esse fui**

Present	Imperf.	Future	Perfect	Pluperf.	Fut.-perf.
I am	I was	I will/ shall be	I have been, was	I had been	I will have been
			fu-		
sum	eram	ero	i	eram	ero
es	eras	eris	isti	eras	eris
est	erat	erit	it	erat	erit
sumus	erāmus	erimus	etc.	etc.	etc.
estis	eratis	eritis			
sunt	erant	erunt			

INDICATIVE OF IRREGULAR VERBS

1 eo īre īvi itum to go

Present	Imperf.	Future	Perfect	Pluperf.	Fut.-perf.
go, am going	was going	will go	went, have gone	had gone	will have gone
			īv-		
eo	ībam	ībo	i	eram	ero
īs	ības	ībis	isti	eras	eris
it	ībat	ībit	it	erat	erit
īmus	ībāmus	ībimus	imus	erāmus	erimus
ītis	ībatis	ībitis	istis	eratis	eritis
eunt	ībant	ībunt	ērunt	erant	erint

The compounds of *eo*, **pereo** (perish), **abeo** (go away), **ineo** (go in), **transeo** (cross), **obeo** (go to meet), **redeo** (return), **adeo** (go towards), etc., are done like the simple verb *but* they prefer -ii to -īvi in the Perfect. **Perii, abii**, etc., rather than **perīvi, abīvi**, etc.

2 possum posse potui to be able

Present	Imperf.	Future	Perfect	Pluperf.	Fut.-perf.
am able, can	was able	will be able	was able, could	had been able	will have been able

	pot-		**potu-**		
possum	eram	ero	i	eram	ero
potes	eras	eris	isti	eras	eris
potest	erat	erit	it	erat	erit
possumus	erāmus	erimus	imus	erāmus	erimus
potestis	eratis	eritis	istis	eratis	eritis
possunt	erant	erunt	ērunt	erant	erint

Note:

(*a*) In the first three tenses the forms are the same as for the verb *to be* with **pos-** as prefix if the verb *to be* begins with an *s*; with **pot-** as prefix if the verb *to be* begins with an *e*.

(*b*) **Possum** = I am able, I can. **Non possum** = I cannot. **Non poteram** or **non potui** = I was not able, I could not.

3 volo	**velle**	**volui**	to wish, be willing
4 nōlo	**nōlle**	**nōlui**	to be unwilling
5 mālo	**mālle**	**mālui**	to prefer

Present	Imperf.	Future	Perfect	Pluperf.	Fut.-perf.
		(meanings given are for *volo*)			
wish, am wishing	was wishing	will wish	wished, have wished	had wished	will have wished

	vol-		**volu-**		
volo	ēbam	am	i	eram	ero
vīs	ēbas	ēs	isti	eras	eris
vult	ēbat	et	it	erat	erit
volumus	ēbamus	ēmus	imus	erāmus	erimus
vultis	ēbatis	ētis	istis	eratis	eritis
volunt	ēbant	ent	ērunt	erant	erint

	nōl-		**nōlu-**		
nōlo	ēbam	am	i	eram	ero
nōnvīs	ēbas	ēs	etc.	etc.	etc.
nōnvult	ēbat	et			
nōlumus	ēbamus	ēmus			
nōnvultis	ēbatis	ētis			
nōlunt	ēbant	ent			

188

| Present | Imperf. | Future | Perfect | Pluperf. | Fut.-perf. |
	māl-		**mālu-**		
mālo	ēbam	am	i	eram	ero
māvīs	ēbas	ēs	etc.	etc.	etc.
māvult	ēbat	et			
mālumus	ēbamus	ēmus			
māvultis	ēbatis	ētis			
mālunt	ēbant	ent			

Note:

(a) **nōlo** is the abbreviated form of **nōn volo**: **mālo** is the short form of **magis volo** (I wish more).

(b) Always use **nōlo,** etc., for 'I do not wish', 'I am unwilling', never use **nōn volo,** etc.

6 fero ferre tuli lātum   to bear; bring

Active Voice

Present	Imperf.	Future	Perfect	Pluperf.	Fut.-perf.
bear, am	was	will	bore, have	had	will have
bearing	bearing	bear	borne	borne	borne
	fer-		**tul-**		
fero	ēbam	am	i	eram	ero
fers	ēbas	ēs	etc.	etc.	etc.
fert	ēbat	et			
ferimus	ēbamus	ēmus			
fertis	ēbatis	ētis			
ferunt	ēbant	ent			

Passive Voice

Present	Imperf.	Future	Perfect	Pluperf.	Fut.-perf.
am borne,	was	will	was borne,	had	will have
am being	being	be	have been	been	been
borne	borne	borne	borne	borne	borne
	fer-		**lātus**	**lātus**	**lātus**
feror	ēbar	ar	sum	eram	ero
ferris	ēbāris	ēris	es	eras	eris
fertur	ēbātur	ētur	est	erat	erit
			lāti	**lāti**	**lāti**
ferimur	ēbāmur	ēmur	sumus	erāmus	erimus
ferimini	ēbāmini	ēmini	estis	eratis	eritis
feruntur	ēbantur	entur	sunt	erant	erunt

7 capio   capere   cēpi   captum   to take, capture

Active Voice

Present	Imperf.	Future	Perfect	Pluperf.	Fut.-perf.
take, am taking	was taking	will take	took, have taken	had taken	will have taken
capi-			**cēp-**		
capio	ēbam	am	i	eram	ero
capis	ēbas	ēs	isti	eras	eris
capit	ēbat	et	it	erat	erit
capimus	ēbamus	ēmus	etc.	etc.	etc.
capitis	ēbatis	ētis			
capiunt	ēbant	ent			

Passive Voice

Present	Imperf.	Future	Perfect	Pluperf.	Fut.-perf.
am taken, am being taken	was being taken	will be taken	was taken, have been taken	had been taken	will have been taken
capi-			**captus**	**captus**	**captus**
capior	ēbar	ar	sum	eram	ero
caperis	ēbāris	ēris	es	eras	eris
capitur	ēbātur	etur	est	erat	erit
capimur	ēbāmur	ēmur	etc.	etc.	etc.
capimini	ēbāmini	ēmini			
capiuntur	ēbantur	entur			

Note:

(a) The *i* of **capio** is retained except before *i*, short *er* and final *e*. So **capis** (not **capiis**), **caperis** (present passive) (not **capieris**).

(b) Among other verbs like **capio** are:

facio	**facere**	**fēci**	**factum**	to make; to do
iacio	**iacere**	**iēci**	**iactum**	to throw
fugio	**fugere**	**fūgi**	**fugitum**	to flee
interficio	**interficere**	**interfēci**	**interfectum**	to kill

8 facio facere fēci factum to make; to do

The active endings are the same as for **capio**

In the passive the perfect, pluperfect and future-perfect tenses are normal; in present, imperfect and future tenses **facio** is replaced by **fio**.

fīo fieri factus sum to be made, to become, etc.

Present	Imperf.	Future	Perfect	Pluperf.	Fut.-perf.
am made,	was	will	was made,	had	will have
am being	being	be	have been	been	been
made	made	made	made	made	made

	fī-		factus	factus	factus
fīo	ēbam	am	sum	eram	ero
fīs	ēbas	ēs	es	eras	eris
fit	ēbat	et	est	erat	erit
fīmus	ēbamus	ēmus	etc.	etc.	etc.
fītis	ēbatis	ētis			
fīunt	ēbant	ent			

Note: **fio** (like verb *to be*) cannot govern an accusative.
He was made king = **Factus est rex** (nominative).

IMPERATIVE MOOD

Active Voice

am-ā	**mon-ē**	**reg-ĕ**	**aud-ī**
-āte	-ēte	-ĭte	-īte

Passive Voice

am-āre	**mon-ēre**	**reg-ĕre**	**aud-īre**
-āmini	-ēmini	-ĭmini	-īmini

Irregular Imperatives

sum (I am)	**es, este**
eo (I go)	**ī, īte**
nōlo (I am unwilling)	**nōlī, nōlīte**
fero (I bear)	**fer, ferte**
facio (I make)	**fac, facite**

capio (I capture) and other verbs of the same type

cap-ĕ, cap-ĭte

Singular of **dico, duco, facio, fero** is **dīc, dūc, fac, fer.**
Singular of **scio** (I know) is **scito.**
patior (I suffer) and other deponents like it **pat-ĕre, pat-ĭmini.**
possum, volo, malo have no imperative mood.

SUBJUNCTIVE ACTIVE OF THE FOUR CONJUGATIONS

Present may love	*Imperfect* might love	*Perfect* may have loved	*Pluperfect* might have loved
am-	**am-**	**amāv-**	**amāv-**
em	ārem	erim	issem
es	ares	eris	isses
et	aret	erit	isset
ēmus	arēmus	erimus	issēmus
etis	aretis	eritis	issetis
ent	arent	erint	issent
mon-	**mon-**	**monu-**	**monu-**
eam	ērem	erim	issem
eas	eres	eris	isses
eat	eret	erit	isset
eāmus	erēmus	etc.	etc.
eatis	eretis		
eant	erent		
reg-	**reg-**	**rex-**	**rex-**
am	erem	erim	issem
as	eres	eris	isses
at	eret	erit	isset
āmus	erēmus	etc.	etc.
atis	eretis		
ant	erent		
aud-	**aud-**	**audīv-**	**audīv-**
iam	īrem	erim	issem
ias	irēs	eris	isses
iat	iret	erit	isset
iāmus	irēmus	etc.	etc.
iatis	iretis		
iant	irent		

SUBJUNCTIVE PASSIVE OF THE FOUR CONJUGATIONS

Present may be loved	*Imperfect* might be loved	*Perfect* may have been loved	*Pluperfect* might have been loved
am-	**am-**	**amātus**	**amātus**
er	ārer	sim	essem
ēris	arēris	sis	esses
etur	aretur	sit	esset

Present	Imperfect	Perfect	Pluperfect
am-	**am-**	**amāti**	**amāti**
emur	aremur	sīmus	essēmus
emini	aremini	sitis	essetis
entur	arentur	sint	essent
mon-	**mon-**	**monitus**	**monitus**
ear	ērer	sim	essem
eāris	erēris	sis	esses
eatur	eretur	sit	esset
		moniti	**moniti**
eamur	erēmur	sīmus	essēmus
eamini	eremini	etc.	etc.
eantur	erentur		
reg-	**reg-**	**rectus**	**rectus**
ar	erer	sim	essem
āris	erēris		
atur	eretur		
		recti	**recti**
amur	eremur	sīmus	essēmus
amini	eremini		
antur	erentur		
aud-	**aud-**	**audītus**	**audītus**
iar	īrer	sim	essem
iāris	irēris		
iatur	iretur		
		audīti	**audīti**
iamur	iremur	sīmus	essēmus
iamini	iremini		
iantur	irentur		

SUBJUNCTIVES OF THE VERB *TO BE*

may be	might be	may have been	might have been
sim	essem	**fu-**erim	**fu-**issem
sis	esses	eris	isses
sit	esset	erit	isset
sīmus	essēmus	erimus	issēmus
sitis	essētis	eritis	issētis
sint	essent	erint	issent

SUBJUNCTIVES OF IRREGULAR VERBS

Present	Imperfect	Perfect	Pluperfect
īre			
eam	īrem	īverim	īvissem
eas	ires	iveris	ivisses
eat	iret	iverit	ivisset
eāmus	irēmus	iverimus	ivissēmus
eatis	iretis	iveritis	ivissetis
eant	irent	iverint	ivissent
posse			
possim	possem	potuerim	potuissem
possis	posses	potueris	potuisses
possit	posset	potuerit	potuisset
possīmus	possēmus	potuerimus	potuissēmus
possitis	possetis	potueritis	potuissetis
possint	possent	potuerint	potuissent
velle			
velim	vellem	voluerim	voluissem
velis	velles	etc.	etc.
velit	vellet		
velīmus	vellēmus		
velitis	velletis		
velint	vellent		
ferre			
feram	ferrem	tulerim	tulissem
feras	ferres	etc.	etc.
ferat	ferret		
ferāmus	ferrēmus		
feratis	ferretis		
ferant	ferrent		
capere			
capiam	caperem	cēperim	cēpissem
capias	caperes	etc.	etc.
capiat	caperet		
capiāmus	caperēmus		
capiatis	caperetis		
capiant	caperent		
fieri			
fiam	fierem	factus sim	factus essem
fias	fieres	factus sis	factus esses
fiat	fieret	factus sit	factus esset
fiāmus	fierēmus	facti sīmus	facti essēmus
fiatis	fieretis	facti sitis	facti essetis
fiant	fierent	facti sint	facti essent

PARTICIPLES ACTIVE AND PASSIVE
OF THE FOUR CONJUGATIONS

Present Active	*Future Active*	*Perfect Passive*
amans (while) loving	**amātūrus** about to love	**amātus** having been loved
monens (while) advising	**monitūrus** about to advise	**monitus** having been advised
regens (while) ruling	**rectūrus** about to rule	**rectus** having been ruled
audiens (while) hearing	**audītūrus** about to hear	**audītus** having been heard

Note: Latin verbs do not have a Present or Future Participle Passive. Only Deponent Verbs have a Perfect Participle with Active meaning (**progressus** = having advanced).

PARTICIPLES OF IRREGULAR VERBS

futūrus—about to be. This verb has no present participle.
iens (*gen.* **euntis**)—(while) going, **itūrus**—about to go.
The verb **possum** has no participles.
volens—(while) wishing), **nōlens**—(while) being unwilling.
ferens—(while) bearing, **lātūrus**—about to bear, **lātus**—having been borne.
faciens—(while) making, **factūrus**—about to make, **factus**—having been made

INFINITIVES ACTIVE AND PASSIVE
OF THE FOUR CONJUGATIONS

First Conjugation

Present	**am-āre**	to love	**am-āri**	to be loved
Perfect	**amāv-isse**	to have loved	**amātus esse**	to have been loved
Future	**amātūrus esse**	to be about to love	**amātum īri**	to be about to be loved

Second Conjugation

Present	**mon-ēre**	to advise	**mon-ēri**	to be advised
Perfect	**monu-isse**	to have advised	**monitus esse**	to have been advised
Future	**monitūrus esse**	to be about to advise	**monitum īri**	to be about to be advised

	Third Conjugation			
Present	**reg-ĕre**	to rule	**reg-i**	to be ruled
Perfect	**rex-isse**	to have ruled	**rectus esse**	to have been ruled
Future	**rectūrus esse**	to be about to rule	**rectum īri**	to be about to be ruled

	Fourth Conjugation			
Present	**aud-īre**	to hear	**aud-īri**	to be heard
Perfect	**audīv-isse**	to have heard	**audītus esse**	to have been heard
Future	**audītūrus esse**	to be about to hear	**audītum īri**	to be about to be heard

INFINITIVES OF IRREGULAR VERBS

esse—to be. **fuisse**—to have been. **fore** or **futūrus esse**—to be about to be

īre—to go. **īvisse**—to have gone. **itūrus esse**—to be about to go

posse—to be able. **potuisse**—to have been able. No Future.

velle—to wish. **voluisse**—to have wished. No Future.

nōlle—to be unwilling. **nōluisse**—to have been unwilling. No future.

mālle—to prefer. **māluisse**—to have preferred. No Future.

ferre—to bear. **tulisse**—to have borne. **lātūrus esse**—to be about to bear.

ferri—to be borne. **lātus esse**—to have been borne. **lātum īri**—to be about to be borne.

facĕre—to make. **fēcisse**—to have made. **factūrus esse**—to be about to make.

fiĕri—to be made. **factus esse**—to have been made. **factum īri**—to be about to be made.

Declension	Singular						Plural					
	N.	V.	A.	G.	D.	Ab.	N.	V.	A.	G.	D.	Ab.
1												
hasta	a	a	am	ae	ae	ā	ae	ae	as	ārum	īs	īs
2												
fundus	us	e	um	i	o	o	i	i	os	ōrum	īs	īs
ager/puer	er	er	um	i	o	o	i	i	os	ōrum	īs	īs
bellum	um	um	um	i	o	o	a	a	a	ōrum	īs	īs
3												
miles	—	—	em	is	i	e	es	es	es	um	ibus	ibus
navis	—	—	em	is	i	e	es	es	es	ium	ibus	ibus
nomen	—	—	—	is	i	e	a	a	a	um	ibus	ibus
4												
manus	us	us	um	ūs	ui	u	ūs	ūs	ūs	uum	ibus	ibus
genu	u	u	u	ūs	u	u	ua	ua	ua	uum	ibus	ibus
5												
spes	es	es	em	ei	ei	ē	es	es	es	ērum	ēbus	ēbus

Some Exceptions

Fīlia (daughter) is like **hasta** but dat. and abl. pl. **fīliābus**

		Sing.	Plur.
Deus (god)	N.	deus	di (or) dei
	V.	deus	di (or) dei
	A.	deum	deos
	G.	dei	deōrum (or) deum
	D., Ab.	deo	dis, diis (or) deis

Fīlius (son) and all proper names in **-ius** omit the **-e** of the Voc. Sing.
  Fīli, Claudi (from **Claudius**)
Vir (man) N. vir   V. vir   A. virum   G. viri   D. viro   Ab. viro

Some 3rd declension nouns whose Abl. Sing. ends in **-i**:
        vīs (force), **sitis** (thirst), **secūris** (axe),
        cubīle (bed), **mare** (sea), **animal** (animal).

3rd declension nouns ending in **-e, -al, -ar** usually have **-ia** in N. V.
  Acc. plural **maria** (seas), **animālia** (animals), **calcāria** (spurs).

Domus (house, home) is a mixture of 2nd and 4th declensions:

	Sing.	Plur.
N.	domus	domūs
V.	domus	domūs
A.	domum	domos, domūs
G.	domi, domūs	domōrum, domuum
D.	domo, domui	domibus
Ab.	domo	domibus

PRONOUNS

1 Personal Pronouns: **ego,** I; **tu,** you; **is, ea, id,** he, she, it (Part One, pages 47–8)

	Singular		*Plural*	
N.	ego	I	nōs	we
A.	mē	me	nōs	us
G.	mei	of me	nostrum *or* nostri	of us
D.	mihi	to me	nōbīs	to us
Ab.	mē	by, with me	nōbīs	by, with us
N.	tū	you	vōs	you (pl.)
A.	tē	you	vōs	you
G.	tui	of you	vestrum *or* vestri	of you
D.	tibi	to you	vōbīs	to you
Ab.	tē	by, with you	vōbīs	by, with you

Singular

N.	is	he	ea	she	id	it
A.	eum	him	eam	her	id	it
G.	ēius	of him	ēius	of her	ēius	of it
D.	ei	to him	ei	to her	ei	to it
Ab.	eo	by, with him	eā	by, with her	eo	by, with it

Plural

N.	ii *or* ei	they	eae	ea
A.	eos	them	eas	ea
G.	eōrum	of them	eārum	eōrum
D.	iīs *or* eīs	to them	iīs, eīs	iīs, eīs
Ab.	iīs *or* eīs	by, with them	iīs, eīs	iīs, eīs

2 Reflexive pronouns (Part One, pages 63–4)

A.	sē	himself, herself, itself, themselves
G.	sui	of himself, herself, itself, themselves
D.	sibi	to himself, herself, itself, themselves
Ab.	sē	by, with himself, herself, itself, themselves

3 Demonstrative Pronouns: **hic,** this; **ille,** that

	Singular			*Plural*		
	M.	*F.*	*N.*	*M.*	*F.*	*N.*
N.	hīc	haec	hōc	hi	hae	haec
A.	hunc	hanc	hōc	hos	has	haec
G.	huius	huius	huius	hōrum	hārum	hōrum
D.	huīc	huīc	huīc	hīs	hīs	hīs
Ab.	hōc	hāc	hōc	hīs	hīs	hīs

	Singular			Plural		
N.	ille	illa	illud	illi	illae	illa
A.	illum	illam	illud	illos	illas	illa
G.	illius	illius	illius	illōrum	illārum	illōrum
D.	illi	illi	illi	illīs	illīs	illīs
Ab.	illo	illā	illo	illīs	illīs	illīs

Note: the meanings of **is, ea, id** and **ille, illa, illud** are interchangeable. **is, ea, id** can mean *that* and **ille, illa, illud** can mean *he, she, it.*

4 Definitive pronouns: **idem,** same; **ipse,** self

	Singular			Plural		
	M.	F.	N.	M.	F.	N.
N.	īdem	eadem	idem	iidem	eaedem	eadem
A.	eundem	eandem	idem	eosdem	easdem	eadem
G.	eiusdem	eiusdem	eiusdem	eōrundem	eārundem	eōrundem
D.	eidem	eidem	eidem	eīsdem *or* iisdem		(all genders)
Ab.	eodem	eādem	eodem	eīsdem *or* iisdem		(all genders)

ipse is declined like **ille,** except that it has **ipsum** in the Neuter singular nom. and acc.

5 Relative Pronoun: **qui, quae, quod** (Part One, pages 54–5)

	Singular			Plural		
	M.	F.	N.	M.	F.	N.
N.	qui	quae	quod	qui	quae	quae
A.	quem	quam	quod	quos	quas	quae
G.	cuius	cuius	cuius	quōrum	quārum	quōrum
D.	cui	cui	cui	quibus	quibus	quibus
Ab.	quo	quā	quo	quibus	quibus	quibus

ADJECTIVES OF THE 1ST AND 2ND DECLENSIONS

Class One: adjectives ending in **-us**

	Singular			Plural		
	M.	F.	N.	M.	F.	N.
N.	bon-us	bon-a	bon-um	bon-i	bon-ae	bon-a
V.	-e	-a	-um	-i	-ae	-a
A.	-um	-am	-um	-os	-as	-a
G.	-i	-ae	-i	-ōrum	-ārum	-ōrum
D.	-o	-ae	-o	-īs	-īs	-īs
Ab.	-o	-ā	-o	-īs	-īs	-īs

Class Two: adjectives in **-er** (dropping **e** to form stem)

	M.	*F.*	*N.*	*M.*	*F.*	*N.*
	nigr-	nigr-	nigr-	nigr-	nigr-	nigr-
N.	**niger**	a	um	i	ae	a
V.	**niger**	a	um	i	ae	a
	nigr-					
A.	um	am	um	os	as	a
G.	i	ae	i	ōrum	ārum	ōrum
D.	o	ae	o	īs	īs	īs
Ab.	o	ā	o	īs	īs	īs

Class Three: adjectives in **-er** (retaining **e** to form stem)

	M.	*F.*	*N.*	*M.*	*F.*	*N.*
	miser-	miser-	miser-	miser-	miser-	miser-
N.	**miser**	a	um	i	ae	a
V.	**miser**	a	um	i	ae	a
	miser-					
A.	um	am	um	os	as	a
G.	i	ae	i	ōrum	ārum	ōrum
D.	o	ae	o	īs	īs	īs
Ab.	o	ā	o	īs	īs	īs

Irregularities: The vocative singular masculine of **meus** (my) is **mi; tuus** and **suus** have no vocative case.

ADJECTIVES OF THE 3RD DECLENSION
Class One: adjectives in **-is,** neuter singular in **-e**

	Singular		*Plural*	
	M. & F.	*N.*	**M. & F.**	*N.*
N.	**omn-**is	**omn-**e	**omn-**es	**omn-**ia
V.	-is	-e	-es	-ia
A.	-em	-e	-es	-ia
G.	-is	-is	-ium	-ium
D.	-i	-i	-ibus	-ibus
Ab.	-i	-i	-ibus	-ibus

Class Two: adjectives with neuter singular as nominative masculine

	M. & F.	*N.*	**M. & F.**	*N.*
N.	**ingens**	**ingens**	**ingent-**es	**ingent-**ia
V.	**ingens**	**ingens**	-es	-ia
A.	**ingent-**em	**ingens**	-es	-ia
G.	-is	**ingent-**is	-ium	-ium
D.	-i	-i	-ibus	-ibus
Ab.	-i	-i	-ibus	-ibus

Class Three: adjectives in **-er** with one feminine form

	M. & F.	N.	M. & F.	N.
N.	ācer ācr-is	ācr-e	ācr-es	ācr-ia
V.	ācer ācr-is	-e	-es	-ia
A.	ācr-em	-e	-es	-ia
G.	-is	-is	-ium	-ium
D.	-i	-i	-ibus	-ibus
Ab.	-i	-i	-ibus	-ibus

Note:

(*a*) **Celer** is like **ācer** but keeps **e** throughout: **celer, celeris, celere.**

(*b*) **Pauper** (poor), **dīves** (rich), **superstes** (surviving), **quadrupes** (four-footed) and a few others have **-e** in the ablative singular and **-um** in genitive plural. They are rarely used in the neuter gender.

(*c*) **Memor** (mindful), **immemor** (unmindful), **vigil** (wakeful) and a few others have **-i** in ablative singular but **-um** in the genitive plural.

Class Four: all comparative adjectives in **-ior**

	Singular		*Plural*	
	M. & F.	N.	M. & F.	N.
N.	melior	melius	meliōr-es	meliōr-a
V.	melior	melius	-es	-a
A.	meliōr-em	melius	-es	-a
G.	-is	meliōr-is	-um	-um
D.	-i	-i	-ibus	-ibus
Ab.	-e	-e	-ibus	-ibus

Note:

(*a*) These adjectives have abl. sing. **-e**, gen. pl. **-um**, and neut, plur. **-a**.

(*b*) **Vetus** (old) has endings like **melior**.

(*c*) **Plūres** (more) has genitive **plūrium**.

COMPARISON OF ADJECTIVES

The degrees of comparison are *positive* (e.g. brave), *comparative* (e.g. braver), *superlative* (e.g. bravest).

1 *Regular comparison*: add **-ior** to the stem for the comparative and **-issimus** to the stem for the superlative.

longus (long) **long-ior** (longer) **long-issimus** (longest)
fortis (brave) **fort-ior** (braver) **fort-issimus** (bravest)
audax (bold) **audāc-ior** (bolder) **audāc-issimus** (boldest)

2 Adjectives in **-er** form the comparative as in 1 above, but add **-rimus** to *Nominative* Masculine Singular to form the superlative.

pulcher **pulchr-ior** **pulcher-rimus**
miser **miser-ior** **miser-rimus**

3 Six adjectives in **-ilis** add **-limus** to the stem to form their superlative.

facilis (easy)	**facil-ior**	**facil-limus**
humilis (humble)	**humil-ior**	**humil-limus**

also **difficilis** (difficult), **similis** (like), **dissimilis** (unlike), **gracilis** (slender).

4 Adjectives in **-us** preceded by a vowel form the comparative by using the adverb **magis** (more) and the superlative by using **maxime** (most).

idōneus	suitable
magis idōneus	more suitable
maxime idōneus	most suitable

5 Among irregular comparisons are the following:

bonus (good)	**melior**	**optimus**
malus (bad)	**pēior**	**pessimus**
magnus (great)	**māior**	**maximus**
parvus (small)	**minor**	**minimus**
multus (much)	**plūs**	**plūrimus**
multi (many)	**plūres**	**plūrimi**
senex (old)	**senior** (or) **nātu māior**	**nātu maximus**
iuvenis (young)	**iunior**	**nātu minimus**

Note:
All comparatives are declined like **melior,** p. 201. **Minor** (smaller) merely omits the **i** of the stem. All superlatives are declined like **bonus.**

FORMATION OF ADVERBS

1 *Positive*

(**a**) Add **-ē** to stem of 1st and 2nd declension adjectives

dignus—dign-ē (worthily)
pulcher—pulchr-ē (beautifully)
miser—miser-ē (wretchedly)

(**b**) Add **-iter** to stem of 3rd declension adjectives

fortis—fort-iter (bravely)
fēlix—fēlīc-iter (happily, successfully)
ācer—ācr-iter (keenly)
celer—celer-iter (quickly)

(**c**) Add **-er** only if the 3rd declension stem ends in **-nt**

sapiens—sapient-er (wisely)

2 *Comparative*

Take the *neuter singular* of the comparative adjective

dignius, pulchrius, miserius, fortius, fēlīcius, ācrius, celerius, sapientius

3 *Superlative*

Change the **-us** of the superlative adjective to **-e**

dignissime, pulcherrime, maxime, fortissime, sapientissime, facillime

4 *Some Exceptions*

tūtus—tūto (safely)	**bonus—bene** (well)
facilis—facile (easily)	**magnus—magnopere** (greatly)
tristis—triste (sadly)	**multus—multum** (much)
audax—audācter (boldly)	**prīmus—prīmum** (first)

5 *A List of other Common Adverbs*

hīc	here	**ibi**	there
hūc	to here	**eo**	to there
hinc	from here	**inde**	from there
heri	yesterday	**hodie**	today
cras	tomorrow	**cotidie**	daily
saepe	often	**saepius**	more often
saepissime	very often		
diu	for a long time	**diutius**	for a longer time
diutissime	for a very long time		
ante, antea	previously	**post, postea**	later; afterwards
clam	secretly	**prīmo**	at first
etiam	even; also	**repente**	suddenly
fere	about, almost	**rursus**	again
forte	by chance	**satis**	enough
frustra	in vain	**semper**	always
iam	by now, already	**sīc**	thus, in this way
interea	meanwhile	**simul**	at the same time
itaque	and so, therefore	**sōlum**	only
iterum	a second time, again	**statim**	at once
magis	more	**subito**	suddenly
mox	soon; later	**tam** (*with adjs. & advs.*)	so
nunc	now	**tamen**	however, yet
nunquam	never	**tandem**	at last
paene	almost	**tum**	then
paulisper	for a short time	**unquam**	ever

NOTES ON THE NUMERALS

1 Ūnus is declined as follows:

	Masc.	*Fem.*	*Neut.*
N.	unus	una	unum
A.	unum	unam	unum
G.	unius	unius	unius
D.	uni	uni	uni
Ab.	uno	unā	uno

2 Duo is declined as follows:

	Masc.	*Fem.*	*Neut.*
N.	duo	duae	duo
A.	duos (or) duo	duas	duo
G.	duōrum	duārum	duōrum
D.	duōbus	duābus	duōbus
Ab.	duōbus	duābus	duōbus

3 Tres is declined as follows:

	Masc. & Fem.	*Neut.*
N.	tres	tria
A.	tres	tria
G.	trium	trium
D.	tribus	tribus
Ab.	tribus	tribus

4 The cardinal numbers from **quattuor** (4) to **centum** (100) are indeclinable

5 The hundreds from **ducenti** (200) to **nōngenti** (900) are declined like the plural of **bonus.**

6 All the ordinal numbers are declined like **bonus.**

7 **Mīlia** is a neuter plural noun meaning 'thousands (of)' and is followed by a noun in the genitive case. See page 93, Part One.
The declension of **mīlia** is:
(*N. V. Ac.*) **mīlia,** (*G.*) **mīlium,** (*D. Ab.*) **mīlibus**

NUMERALS

	Symbol	Cardinal	Ordinal
1	I	ūnus, ūna, ūnum	prīmus, -a, -um
2	II	duo, duae, duo	secundus (or) alter
3	III	tres, tria	tertius
4	IV	quattuor	quartus
5	V	quīnque	quintus
6	VI	sex	sextus
7	VII	septem	septimus
8	VIII	octo	octāvus
9	IX	novem	nōnus
10	X	decem	decimus
11	XI	ūndecim	ūndecimus
12	XII	duodecim	duodecimus
13	XIII	tredecim	tertius decimus
14	XIV	quattuordecim	quartus decimus
15	XV	quindecim	quintus decimus
16	XVI	sēdecim	sextus decimus
17	XVII	septemdecim	septimus decimus
18	XVIII	duodēvīginti	duodēvīcēsimus
19	XIX	ūndēvīginti	ūndēvīcēsimus
20	XX	vīginti	vīcēsimus
21	XXI	vīginti ūnus (or) ūnus et vīginti	vīcēsimus prīmus (or) ūnus et vīcēsimus
22	XXII	vīginti duo (or) duo et vīginti	vīcēsimus secundus (or) alter et vīcēsimus
29	XXIX	ūndētrīginta	ūndētrīcēsimus
30	XXX	trīginta	trīcēsimus
40	XL	quadrāginta	quadrāgēsimus
50	L	quīnquāginta	quīnquāgēsimus
60	LX	sexāginta	sexāgēsimus
70	LXX	septuāginta	septuāgēsimus
80	LXXX	octōginta	octōgēsimus
90	XC	nōnāginta	nōnāgēsimus
100	C	centum	centēsimus
200	CC	ducenti, -ae, -a	ducentēsimus
300	CCC	trecenti, -ae, -a	trecentēsimus
400	CCCC	quadringenti, -ae, -a	quadringentēsimus
500	D	quīngenti, -ae, -a	quīngentēsimus
600	DC	sēscenti, -ae, -a	sēscentēsimus
700	DCC	septingenti, -ae, -a	septingentēsimus
800	DCCC	octingenti, -ae, -a	octingentēsimus
900	DCCCC	nōngenti, -ae, -a	nōngentēsimus
1,000	M	mīlle	mīllēsimus
10,000	XM	decies mīlle (or) decem mīlia	decies mīllēsimus

Maps

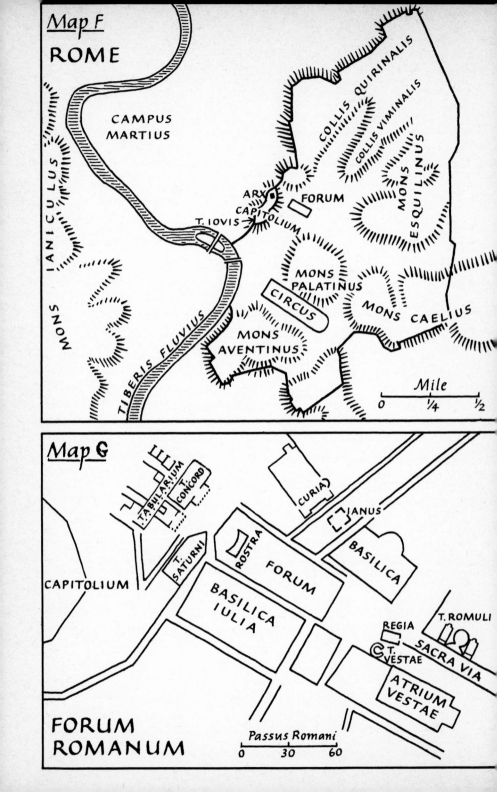

Map F
ROME

IANICULUS

CAMPUS
MARTIUS

COLLIS QUIRINALIS

COLLIS VIMINALIS

MONS
ESQUILINUS

ARX
CAPITOLIUM

FORUM

T. IOVIS

MONS

MONS
PALATINUS

CIRCUS

MONS CAELIUS

MONS
AVENTINUS

TIBERIS FLUVIUS

Mile

0   ¼   ½

Map G

TABULARIUM

CONCORD

CURIA

IANUS

BASILICA

T.
SATURNI

ROSTRA

FORUM

CAPITOLIUM

BASILICA
IULIA

REGIA

T. ROMULI

T.
VESTAE

SACRA VIA

ATRIUM
VESTAE

FORUM
ROMANUM

Passus Romani

0   30   60

o H
HIBERNIA
EBORACUM
BRITANNIA
Tamesis F.
CANTIUM
MORINI
Rhenus F.
GERMANIA
Hister F.
OCEANUS
GALLIA
Rhodanus F.
ITALIA
HISPANIA
CORSICA
ROMA
CAMPANIA
VESUVIUS M.
POMPEII
SARDINIA
BALEARES
MARE INTERNUM
SICILIA
CARTHAGO
AFRICA
Miles
0 100 200 300
ESTERN EUROPE

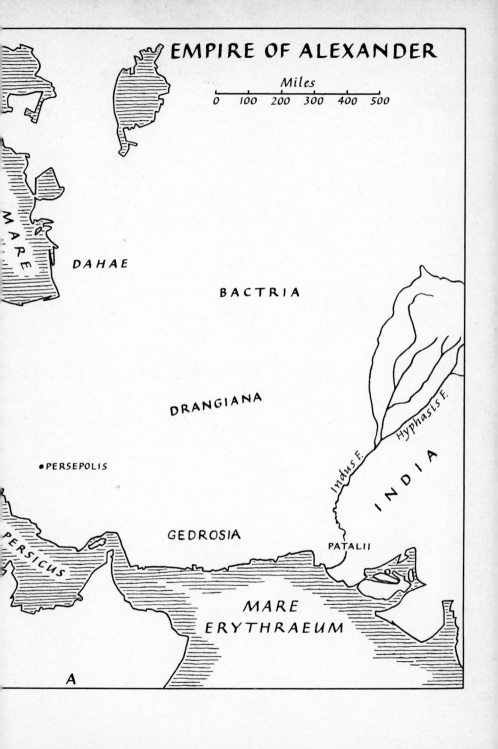

EMPIRE OF ALEXANDER

Miles

0   100   200   300   400   500

MARE

DAHAE

BACTRIA

DRANGIANA

Indus F.

Hyphasis F.

INDIA

•PERSEPOLIS

PERSICUS

GEDROSIA

PATALII

MARE
ERYTHRAEUM

A

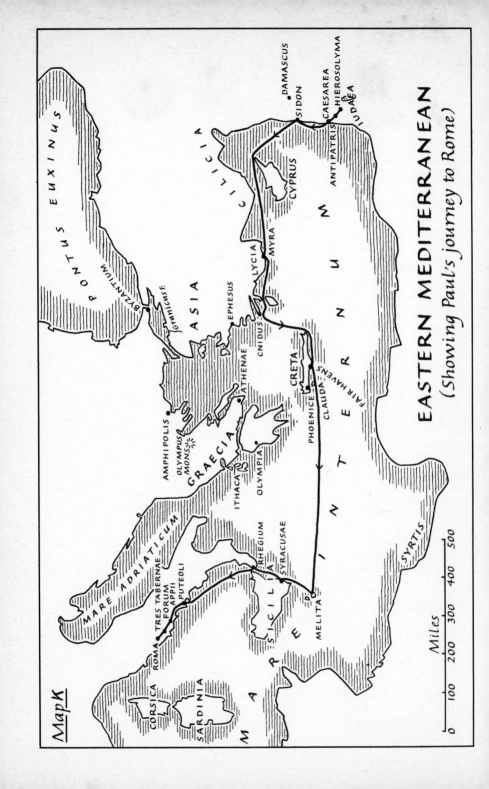

Map K

EASTERN MEDITERRANEAN
(Showing Paul's journey to Rome)